COMPUTER CONCEPTS

ILLUSTRATED STANDARD EDITION

2ND EDITION

June Jamrich Parsons

Dan Oja

COURSE
TECHNOLOGY

ONE MAIN STREET, CAMBRIDGE, MA 02142

an International Thomson Publishing company I(T)P®

Cambridge • Albany • Bonn • Boston • Cincinnati • London • Madrid • Melbourne • Mexico City
New York • Paris • San Francisco • Singapore • Tokyo • Toronto • Washington

Computer Concepts—Illustrated Standard Edition, 2nd Edition is published by Course Technology.

MANAGING EDITOR:	**Nicole Jones Pinard**
PRODUCT MANAGER:	**Jeanne Herring**
PRODUCTION EDITOR:	**Debbie Masi**
CONTRIBUTING AUTHOR:	**Rachel Biheller Bunin**
DEVELOPMENT EDITOR:	**Pam Conrad**
CONSULTING EDITOR:	**Susan Solomon**
INTERIOR DESIGNER:	**Joseph Lee Design**
COVER DESIGNER:	**Joseph Lee Design**
PHOTO AND VIDEO RESEARCHER:	**Abby Reip**
VIDEO EDITOR:	**Jeanne Busemeyer, Hyde Park Publishing Services**
ANIMATIONS:	**Planet Interactive**
COMPOSITION:	**GEX, Inc.**

© 1998 by Course Technology—I(T)P®

For more information contact:

Course Technology
One Main Street
Cambridge, MA 02142

ITP Europe
Berkshire House 168-173
High Holborn
London WCIV 7AA
England

Nelson ITP, Australia
102 Dodds Street
South Melbourne, 3205
Victoria, Australia

ITP Nelson Canada
1120 Birchmount Road
Scarborough, Ontario
Canada M1K 5G4

International Thomson Editores
Seneca, 53
Colonia Polanco
11560 Mexico D.F. Mexico

ITP GmbH
Königswinterer Strasse 418
53227 Bonn
Germany

ITP Asia
60 Albert Street, #15-01
Albert Complex
Singapore 189969

ITP Japan
Hirakawacho Kyowa Building, 3F
2-2-1 Hirakawacho
Chiyoda-ku, Tokyo 102
Japan

Trademarks

Course Technology and the Open Book logo are registered trademarks of Course Technology. The Ilustrated Series and Illustrated Projects are trademarks of Course Technology.

I(T)P® The ITP logo is a registered trademark of International Thomson Publishing Inc.

Some of the product names and company names used in this book have been used for identification purposes only and may be trademarks or registered trademarks of their respective manufacturers and sellers.

Disclaimer

Course Technology reserves the right to revise this publication and make changes from time to time in its content without notice.

0-7600-5491-6—text and CD

0-7600-5972-1—text only

Printed in the United States of America

1 2 3 4 5 6 7 8 9 10 BM 02 01 00 99 98

Exciting New Illustrated Products

The Illustrated Projects™ Series: The Quick, Visual Way to Apply Computer Skills

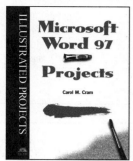

Looking for an inexpensive, easy way to supplement almost any application text and give your students the practice and tools they'll need to compete in today's competitive marketplace? Each text includes more than 50 real-world, useful projects—like creating a resume and setting up a loan worksheet—that let students hone their computer skills. These two-color texts have the same great two-page layout as the Illustrated Series.

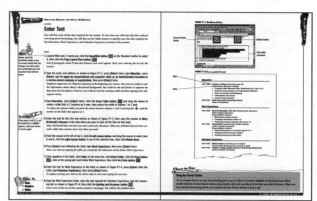

Illustrated Projects titles are available for the following:

- ▶ Microsoft Access
- ▶ Microsoft Excel
- ▶ Microsoft Office Professional
- ▶ Microsoft Publisher
- ▶ Microsoft Word

- ▶ Creating Web Sites
- ▶ World Wide Web
- ▶ Adobe PageMaker
- ▶ Corel WordPerfect

Illustrated Interactive™ Series: The Safe, Simulated Way to Learn Computer Skills

The Illustrated Interactive Series uses multimedia technology to teach computer concepts and application skills. Students learn via a CD-ROM that simulates the actual software and provides a controlled learning environment in which every keystroke is monitored. Plus, all products in this series feature the same step-by-step instructions as the Illustrated Series. An accompanying workbook reinforces the skills that students learn on the CD.

Illustrated Interactive titles are available for the following applications:*

- ▶ Microsoft Office 97
- ▶ Microsoft Word 97
- ▶ Microsoft Excel 97

- ▶ Microsoft Access 97
- ▶ Microsoft PowerPoint 97
- ▶ Computer Concepts

Standalone & networked versions available. Runs on Windows 3.1, 95, and NT. CD-only version available for Computer Concepts and Office 97.

CourseKits : Offering You the Freedom to Choose

Balance your course curriculum with Course Technology's mix-and-match approach to selecting texts. CourseKits provide you with the freedom to make choices from more than one series. When you choose any two or more Course Technology products for one course, we'll discount the price and package them together so your students pick up one convenient bundle at the bookstore.

Contact your sales representative to find out more about these Illustrated products.

Preface

WELCOME TO *COMPUTER CONCEPTS—Illustrated Standard Edition, 2nd Edition*, the text that provides a fast-paced and engaging introduction to today's most cutting-edge computer concepts. This book's content and technology components are drawn from Course Technology's bestselling *New Perspectives on Computer Concepts, Introductory, 3rd Edition*. We've taken that impeccable content and adapted it to fit the highly visual and fast-paced approach of the Illustrated series. No other book gets your students up to speed faster! In addition, this book provides numerous opportunities to use technology to enhance learning—CD Connections, Course Labs, and InfoWeb links all provide students with added help, information, and practice with the concepts they encounter in the book. Icons throughout the book indicate when a corresponding CD Connection, Course Lab, or InfoWeb is available.

About this Book

What makes the information in this book so easy to access and digest? It's quite simple. Each concept is presented on two facing pages, with the main points discussed on the left page and large, dramatic illustrations presented on the right. Students can learn all they need to know about a particular topic without having to turn the page! This unique design makes information extremely accessible and easy to absorb, and provides a great reference for after the course is over. The modular structure of the book also allows for great flexibility; you can cover the units in any order you choose, and skip lessons if you like.

The sample lesson shown here highlights the standard elements and features that appear in every two-page lesson.

A single concept is presented in a two-page "information display" to help students absorb information quickly and easily.

Easy-to-follow introductions to every lesson focus on a single concept to help students get the point quickly.

In More Detail discussions provide additional key information on the main concept.

Exploring computer functions

A BASIC COMPUTER SYSTEM WAS previously defined as a device that accepts input, processes data, stores data, and produces output. To understand a basic computer system, it is important to look more closely at these basic computer functions. Refer to Figure A-3 which illustrates the fundamental computer functions and components that help the computer accomplish each function.

Using a Mouse

von Neumann

IN MORE DETAIL

- A computer accepts input: Computer **input** is whatever is put into a computer system. Input can be supplied by a person, by the environment, or by another computer. Some examples of the kinds of input a computer can process are the words and symbols in a document, numbers for a calculation, instructions for completing a process, pictures, audio signals from a microphone, and temperatures from a thermostat.

- A computer processes data: **Data** refers to the symbols that describe people, events, things, and ideas. Computers manipulate data in many ways, and we call this manipulation "processing." In the context of computers, then, we can define a **process** as a systematic series of actions a computer uses to manipulate data. Some of the ways a computer can process data include performing calculations, sorting lists of words or numbers, modifying documents and pictures according to user instructions, and drawing graphs. A computer processes data in a device called the **central processing unit** or **CPU**.

- A computer stores data: A computer must store data so it is available for processing. The places a computer puts data are referred to as **storage**. Most computers have more than one location for storing data. The place where the computer stores data depends on how the data is being used. The computer puts data in one place while it is waiting to be processed and another place when it is not needed for immediate processing. **Memory** is an area that holds data waiting to be processed. Storage is the area where data can be left on a permanent basis while it is not needed for processing.

- A computer produces output: Computer **output** is the result produced by a computer. Some examples of computer output include reports, documents, music, graphs, and pictures.

| John von Neumann | When the photo in Figure A-2 was published in 1947, the caption read, "Dr. John von Neumann stands in front of a new Electronic 'Brain,' the fastest computing machine for its degree of precision yet made. The machine which can do 2,000 multiplications in one second and add or subtract 100,000 times in the same period was displayed today for | the first time at the Institute for Advanced Study. Its fabulous memory can store 1,024 numbers of 12 decimal places each. Dr. von Neumann was one of the designers of the wonder machine." | FIGURE A-2  |

A-4 ▶ COMPUTER CONCEPTS

Icons in the margins indicate that an interactive lab or InfoWeb is featured for that lesson.

News to Use boxes relate the course material to real-world situations to arm students with practical information.

Oversized illustrations in every lesson bring important concepts to life.

Icons to the right of the figure captions indicate that a CD Connection is available that further illustrates the concept covered in this figure.

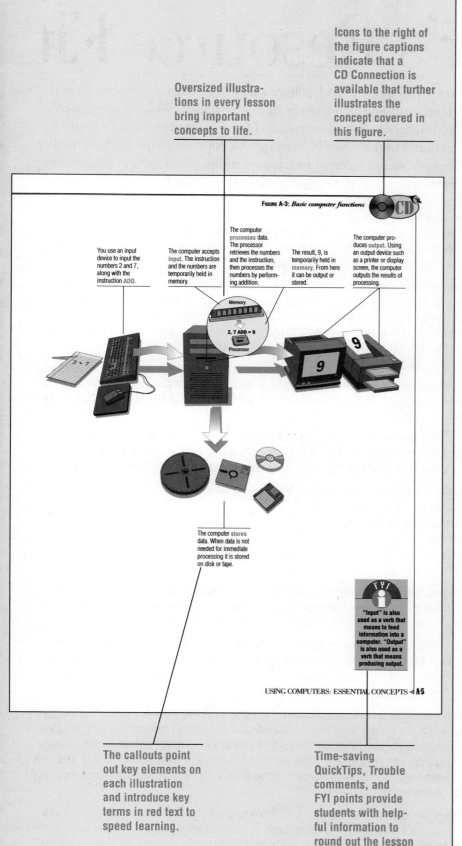

FIGURE A-3: *Basic computer functions*

You use an input device to input the numbers 2 and 7, along with the instruction ADD.

The computer accepts input. The instruction and the numbers are temporarily held in memory.

The computer processes data. The processor retrieves the numbers and the instruction, then processes the numbers by performing addition.

The result, 9, is temporarily held in memory. From here it can be output or stored.

The computer produces output. Using an output device such as a printer or display screen, the computer outputs the results of processing.

Memory

2, 7 ADD = 9

Processor

The computer stores data. When data is not needed for immediate processing it is stored on disk or tape.

FYI

"Input" is also used as a verb that means to feed information into a computer. "Output" is also used as a verb that means producing output.

USING COMPUTERS: ESSENTIAL CONCEPTS A-5

The callouts point out key elements on each illustration and introduce key terms in red text to speed learning.

Time-saving QuickTips, Trouble comments, and FYI points provide students with helpful information to round out the lesson information.

Other Features

The two-page lesson format featured in this book provides students with a powerful learning experience. Additionally, this book contains the following features:

- **Outstanding Assessment and Reinforcement**— Every unit concludes with a wide variety of assessment exercises to test students' understanding and reinforce the material covered. Concepts Review questions check students' knowledge of the key points in the unit. Independent Challenges provide assignments that enable students to explore on their own to develop critical thinking skills. Lab Assignments let students work further with the interactive Course Labs featured with this text.

- **Practical tips for today's computer user**—This book arms students with useful information they can apply at home or on the job.

- A **Buyer's Guide Appendix** provides real-world advice to help students purchase their own computers, software, and Internet services.

- **World Wide Web exposure**—To embrace the power of the information superhighway, this book provides opportunities for exploring the World Wide Web. InfoWebs on the student CD and Student Online and Offline Companions offer students the chance to explore the Internet for further information on topics covered in the book. Web Work Independent Challenge assignments at the end of each unit also encourage students to use the Web as a resource to get information. These exercises are labeled with a Web Work icon.

Instructor's Resource Kit

The Instructor's Resource Kit is Course Technology's way of putting the resources and information needed to teach and learn effectively into your hands. With an integrated array of teaching and learning tools that offer you and your students a broad range of technology-based instructional options, we believe this kit represents the highest quality and most cutting-edge resources available to instructors today. Many of these resources are available at **www.course.com**. The resources available with this book are:

▶ **Optional Student CD-ROM**—Available with this text is an optional student CD-ROM that contains all of the technology components needed to enhance students' learning of concepts discussed in the book. Included on the CD are the CD Connections, InfoWebs, and Course Labs that are referenced throughout the book. When students see an icon for one of the technology components, they will find a corresponding element on the CD.

  • **Student Offline Companion**—Also on the student CD-ROM is a Student Offline Companion that enables students to explore InfoWeb topics without having to go online. Using just a browser and the Student Offline Companion, which contains Web pages that have been cached from the Internet and included in browsable form on the CD, students can follow InfoWeb links without having an Internet connection. To use the Student Offline Companion on the CD, choose **Offline InfoWebs** from the list of CD components for the unit in which you are working.

The CD Connections, InfoWebs, Course Labs, and Student Offline Companion are also provided on the Instructor's Resource Kit CD. Adopters of this text are granted the right to post these technology components on any stand-alone computer or network. See pages vii through ix for a complete description of CD Connections, InfoWebs, and Course Labs, and for a list of the Course Labs that are available with this text.

▶ **Course Test Manager**—Designed by Course Technology, this cutting-edge Windows-based testing software helps instructors design, administer, and print tests and pre-tests. A full-featured program, Course Test Manager also has an online testing component that allows students to take tests at the computer and have their exams automatically graded.

▶ **Instructor's Manual**—The quality-assurance tested Instructor's Manual includes:
  • Solutions to all lessons and end-of-unit material
  • Detailed lecture topics for each unit with teaching tips
  • Extra Independent Challenges
  • Task References
  • Transparency Masters

▶ **Course Presenter**—Course Presenter is a lecture presentation tool that combines the many technology resources available to you and puts them together in an easy-to-use, flexible format. It includes a predesigned presentation for each unit of the textbook, including the video clips, animations, and Course Labs. You can also customize this presentation to your own preferences.

▶ **WWW.COURSE.COM**—We encourage students and instructors to visit our web site at **www.course.com** to find articles about current teaching and software trends, featured texts, interviews with authors, demos of Course Technology's software, Frequently Asked Questions about our products, and much more. This site is also where you can gain access to the Faculty Online Companion or Student Online Companion for this text—see below for more information.

▶ **Faculty Online Companion**—Available at **www.course.com**, this World Wide Web site offers Course Technology customers a password-protected Faculty Lounge where you can find everything you need to prepare for class, including the Instructor's Manual in an electronic Portable Document Format (PDF) file as well as Adobe Acrobat Reader software. Periodically updated items include any updates and revisions to the text and Instructor's Manual, links to other Web sites, and access to student and solution files. This site will continue to evolve throughout the semester. Contact your customer service representative for the site address and password.

▶ **Student Online Companion**—The Student Online Companion for this book is a Web site where students can go to gain access to the online InfoWeb links, which are updated on a regular basis. You can connect to the Student Online Companion from the CD by choosing **Online InfoWebs** from the list of CD components for the unit in which you are working. You can also access the Student Online Companion via **www.course.com** or by going directly to the following URL: **http://www.course.com/Illustrated/concepts/**

About The Technology

CD Connections

CD Connections reveal videos, animations, screen tours, and other treasures to enhance learning and retention of key concepts. CD Connection icons appear to the right of figure captions and within News to Use boxes to indicate when a corresponding CD Connection is available.

InfoWebs

InfoWebs connect you to Web links, film, video, TV, print, and electronic resources. InfoWebs stay up-to-date and solve the problem of constantly changing URLs. If you have Internet access, you can click on an InfoWeb and be linked directly to resources on the Internet using your browser of choice. If you do not have Internet access, you can use the Student Offline Companion to link to the main page of each InfoWeb as well as to explore InfoWeb topics as though you were online. An InfoWeb icon on the left page of a lesson indicates that an InfoWeb is featured for that particular concept.

Course Labs

Concepts come to life with the Labs—22 highly-interactive tutorials that combine illustrations, animations, digital images, and simulations. Course Labs guide you step-by-step through a topic, present you with Quick Checks, let you explore on your own, test comprehension, and provide printed feedback. Lab assignments are included at the end of each relevant unit. A Course Lab icon on the left page of a lesson indicates that a Course Lab is featured for that particular concept.

All the Course Labs available with this text are listed below.

Peripheral Devices
This Lab uses descriptions, drawings, and animations to explain the functions of many popular peripheral devices.

Using a Mouse
This Lab guides students through basic mouse functions and operations. Interactive exercises using dialog boxes enable students to practice mouse skills.

Using a Keyboard
Students learn the parts of the keyboard and basic keyboard operations. They practice basic keyboarding with interactive typing exercises, including a self-paced typing tutor that helps improve speed and accuracy.

DOS Command-Line Interface
This Lab presents students with concepts and basic skills associated with the DOS command-line, and provides hands-on practice typing commands at a live DOS prompt.

User Interface
Students are presented with user interfaces on a general/conceptual level, and then have the opportunity to interact with menu-driven, prompted dialog, command-line, graphical, and combination interfaces.

UNIT F

E-Mail
Students use a simple e-mail program to learn essential e-mail skills including creating, sending, forwarding, replying, printing, and saving mail.

The Internet: World Wide Web
Students interact with a simulated Web browser to explore home pages, URL's, linking, and hypertext. You can assign this Lab even if an Internet connection is not available.

Web Pages & HTML
This Lab is a primer on HTML basics and shows how HTML is used to create pages. Students then see how they can modify these pages and view them in a browser.

UNIT G

Data Backup
Using a simulated business environment, this Lab teaches basic backup procedures. Students experience data loss, attempt to restore lost data, and learn first-hand the value of regular backup procedures.

APPENDIX

A BUYER'S GUIDE

Buying a Computer
Students interpret advertisements and compare features to make buying decisions, using an online glossary.

Credits

CyberClass

COURSE TECHNOLOGY IS PLEASED TO BRING YOU CYBERCLASS FROM HYPERGRAPHICS Corporation. CyberClass is a totally new Web-based tool for distance and on-campus settings. It is available in three levels:

Level 1

■ CyberClass Stories: Stories about real corporations and their use of computers, with links to their sites

■ Practice Tests: 20 randomly generated test questions covering the key concepts of each unit that can be taken repeatedly to test understanding of each unit's content

■ Link to InfoWebs

■ Electronic FlashCards: A self-study aid for students to test their understanding of key concepts and terminology

Level 2

■ All of Level 1 features plus a customizable and secure Web site for instructors to use for their class(es)

■ Syllabus Posting

■ Assignments Posting

■ Submit Assignments: A template designed to have students submit assignments to the instructor via e-mail efficiently

■ Hot Links: Links that the instructor can post for students

■ Student Bulletin Board

■ Send and View Messages: Messaging among class members and instructor

■ Class Roster: Can be secured by the instructor. Students can enter their personal data into the roster (including name, phone number, email address, and so on)

■ CyberChallenge: An online real-time game testing knowledge of computer concepts

■ Instructor-supervised Text Chat: For such things as online real-time office hours, mini-lectures, group work, discussion groups, and so on

■ Administration Utilities: Accessible by instructors only, includes capabilities such as editing the roster and editing user information

Level 3

■ All of Level 1 and Level 2 features

■ Audio Class Conferencing: Servers can run off of instructor's Windows 95 Pentium computer (up to 30 students), the school's network (up to 200 students), or HyperGraphics's servers (upon sign-up with HyperGraphics). Instructor controlled and monitored.

■ Synchronous Assessment over the Web: Using Course Technology's Course Test Manager as the backbone

At the CyberClass site—**www.cyber-class.com**—we will be continually updating and improving the site based on student and instructor feedback.

Brief Contents

Contents

UNIT D Computer Files and Data Storage — D-1

UNIT E Computer Architecture — E-1

UNIT F   Computer Networks and the Internet   F-1

UNIT G   Data Security and Control   G-1

APPENDIX   A Buyer's Guide   1

Using Computers: Essential Concepts

IN THIS UNIT YOU WILL LEARN WHICH COMPUTER components are necessary for communication between people and computers. You will also learn about user interfaces typically found on today's computer systems and ways to respond to what you see on the computer screen. The unit concludes with a discussion about manuals, reference guides, and tutorials—all of which can help you learn how to interact with a specific computer system or software package.

OBJECTIVES

Define computers

Explore computer functions

Introduce microcomputers

Categorize computers

Review peripheral devices

Understand pointing devices

Examine keyboards

Examine output devices

Communicate with computers: prompts, wizards, and command-line interfaces

Communicate with computers: menus and dialog boxes

Use graphical user interfaces

Use resources

Defining computers

COMPUTERS HAVE BEEN CALLED "mind tools" because they enhance our ability to perform tasks that require mental activity. Computers are adept at performing activities such as making calculations quickly, sorting large lists, and searching through vast information libraries. Humans can do all these activities, but a computer can often accomplish them much faster and more accurately. Our ability to use a computer complements our mental capabilities and makes us more productive. The key to making effective use of the computer as a tool is to know what a computer does, how it works, and how you can use it.

This book defines a **computer** as a device that accepts input, processes data, stores data, and produces output. A computer is actually part of a computer system. This lesson identifies the basic elements of a computer system.

IN MORE DETAIL

- ☞ A **computer system** includes hardware, peripheral devices, and software. Refer to Figure A-1 for a picture of a basic computer system.

- ☞ **Hardware** includes the electric, electronic, and mechanical devices used for processing data. The computer itself is part of the computer system hardware. In addition to the computer, the term "hardware" refers to components called peripheral devices.

- ☞ **Peripheral devices** expand the computer's input, output, and storage capabilities.

- ☞ An **input device** is a peripheral device used to gather and translate input into a form that the computer can process. As a computer user you will probably use the keyboard as your main input device.

- ☞ An **output device** is a peripheral device that displays, prints, or transfers the results of processing from the computer memory. As a computer user you will probably use the monitor as your main output device.

- ☞ A computer requires a set of instructions, called **software** or a **computer program**, which tells the computer how to perform a particular task. Software sets up a computer to do a particular task by telling the computer how to interact with the user and how to process the user's data.

Why does a computer need software?

A computer without software is like a tape player without tapes or a CD player without any CDs. Without software, a computer is just a useles gadget that does not let you do much more than turn it on and off. Fortunately, software is plentiful and available for an astonishing number of tasks, including producing resumes, managing a small business, helping you study for the Graduate Record Examination, teaching you Spanish, helping you plan your diet, composing music, and taking you on an adventure through a dangerous labyrinth.

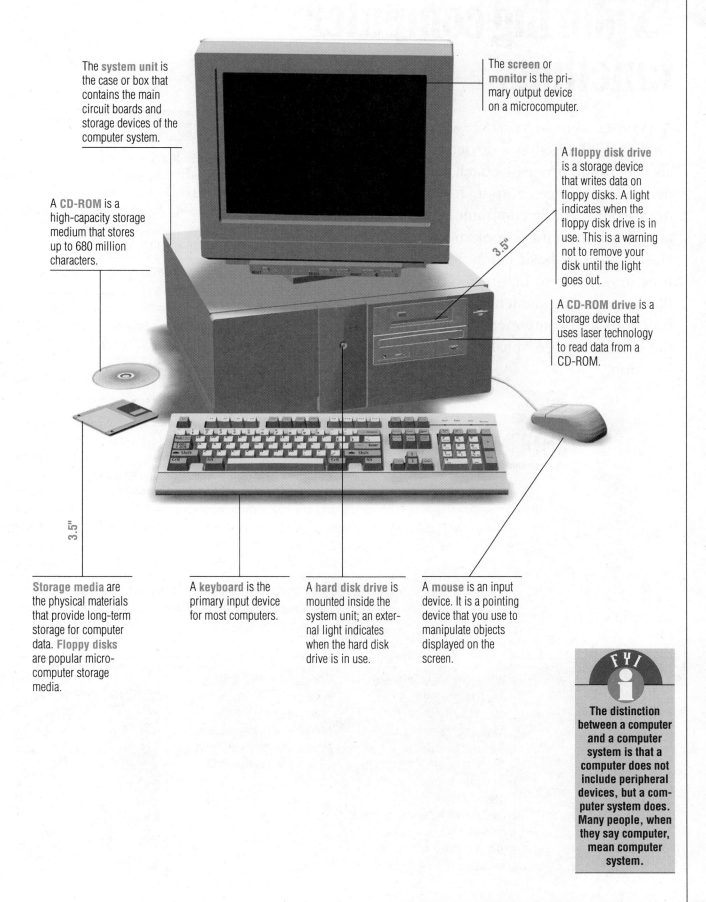

The **system unit** is the case or box that contains the main circuit boards and storage devices of the computer system.

A **CD-ROM** is a high-capacity storage medium that stores up to 680 million characters.

The **screen** or **monitor** is the primary output device on a microcomputer.

A **floppy disk drive** is a storage device that writes data on floppy disks. A light indicates when the floppy disk drive is in use. This is a warning not to remove your disk until the light goes out.

A **CD-ROM drive** is a storage device that uses laser technology to read data from a CD-ROM.

Storage media are the physical materials that provide long-term storage for computer data. **Floppy disks** are popular micro-computer storage media.

A **keyboard** is the primary input device for most computers.

A **hard disk drive** is mounted inside the system unit; an external light indicates when the hard disk drive is in use.

A **mouse** is an input device. It is a pointing device that you use to manipulate objects displayed on the screen.

FYI

The distinction between a computer and a computer system is that a computer does not include peripheral devices, but a computer system does. Many people, when they say computer, mean computer system.

Exploring computer functions

A BASIC COMPUTER SYSTEM WAS previously defined as a device that accepts input, processes data, stores data, and produces output. To understand a basic computer system, it is important to look more closely at these basic computer functions. Refer to Figure A-3 which illustrates the fundamental computer functions and components that help the computer accomplish each function.

von Neumann

IN MORE DETAIL

☞ A computer accepts input: Computer **input** is whatever is put into a computer system. Input can be supplied by a person, by the environment, or by another computer. Some examples of the kinds of input a computer can process are the words and symbols in a document, numbers for a calculation, instructions for completing a process, pictures, audio signals from a microphone, and temperatures from a thermostat.

☞ A computer processes data: **Data** refers to the symbols that describe people, events, things, and ideas. Computers manipulate data in many ways, and we call this manipulation "processing." In the context of computers, then, we can define a **process** as a systematic series of actions a computer uses to manipulate data. Some of the ways a computer can process data include performing calculations, sorting lists of words or numbers, modifying documents and pictures according to user instructions, and drawing graphs. A computer processes data in a device called the **central processing unit** or **CPU**.

☞ A computer stores data: A computer must store data so it is available for processing. The places a computer puts data are referred to as **storage**. Most computers have more than one location for storing data. The place where the computer stores data depends on how the data is being used. The computer puts data in one place while it is waiting to be processed and another place when it is not needed for immediate processing. **Memory** is an area that holds data waiting to be processed. Storage is the area where data can be left on a permanent basis while it is not needed for processing.

☞ A computer produces output: Computer **output** is the result produced by a computer. Some examples of computer output include reports, documents, music, graphs, and pictures.

John von Neumann

When the photo in Figure A-2 was published in 1947, the caption read, "Dr. John von Neumann stands in front of a new Electronic 'Brain,' the fastest computing machine for its degree of precision yet made. The machine which can do 2,000 multiplications in one second and add or subtract 100,000 times in the same period was displayed today for *the first time at the Institute for Advanced Study. Its fabulous memory can store 1,024 numbers of 12 decimal places each. Dr. von Neumann was one of the designers of the wonder machine."*

FIGURE A-2

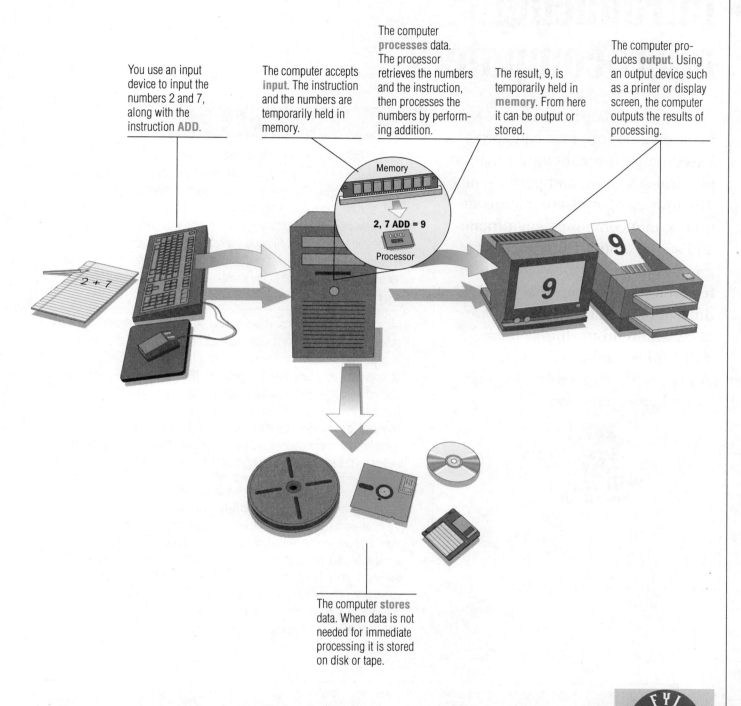

You use an input device to input the numbers 2 and 7, along with the instruction **ADD**.

The computer accepts **input**. The instruction and the numbers are temporarily held in memory.

The computer **processes** data. The processor retrieves the numbers and the instruction, then processes the numbers by performing addition.

The result, 9, is temporarily held in **memory**. From here it can be output or stored.

The computer produces **output**. Using an output device such as a printer or display screen, the computer outputs the results of processing.

The computer **stores** data. When data is not needed for immediate processing it is stored on disk or tape.

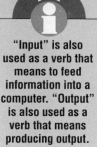

"Input" is also used as a verb that means to feed information into a computer. **"Output"** is also used as a verb that means producing output.

Introducing microcomputers

COMPUTERS TRADITIONALLY HAVE been divided into four categories based on their technology, function, physical size, cost, and performance. The four categories are microcomputers, minicomputers, mainframes, and supercomputers. These categories, however, evolve with the technology. The lines that divide the different computer categories are fuzzy and tend to shift as more powerful computers become available. This discussion begins with microcomputers.

Microcomputers

IN MORE DETAIL

☛ The typical microcomputer: **Microcomputers**, also known as personal computers or PCs, are the computers you typically find in homes and small businesses. The microcomputer you use might be a stand-alone unit, or it might be connected to other computers so you can share data and software with other users. However, even when your computer is connected to others, it will generally carry out only your processing tasks. A microcomputer processor performs about 200 million operations per second. Microcomputers come in many shapes and sizes, as you can see in Figure A-4.

☛ Microcomputer platforms: Hundreds of companies manufacture microcomputers, but there are only a small number of microcomputer designs or **platforms**. Today there are two major microcomputer platforms: IBM-compatibles and Macintosh-compatibles. **IBM-compatible computers**, also referred to as **PC-compatibles**, are based on the architecture of the first IBM microcomputer. IBM still manufactures a full line of PCs. IBM-compatible computers are manufactured by Compaq, Dell, Gateway, and hundreds of other companies. The second major microcomputer platform is based on the Macintosh computer, manufactured by Apple Computer, Inc.

☛ Microcomputer compatibility: Computers that operate in essentially the same way are said to be **compatible**. Two computers are compatible if they can communicate with each other, share the same software, share data, and use the same peripheral devices. Not all microcomputers are compatible with each other. The IBM platform and the Macintosh platform are not regarded as compatible. Both IBM and Apple have been trying to overcome compatibility problems with platforms that use a built-in translation process to run both IBM and Macintosh software. Now, sharing data between these two platforms is inconvenient, but not impossible.

Hardware product life cycle

Microcomputers and related products are changing rapidly. Ideas for new products are everywhere; users express their needs for improved features, engineers produce more efficient designs, scholars publish new theories, and competitors announce new products. As a consumer, you should be wary of making purchasing decisions based on product announcements. A product announcement can precede the actual product by several years. Products that are announced but never made or marketed are referred to as **vaporware**.

New microcomputers and their products offer the latest features and often sell for a premium price. When a product is first introduced, the hardware manufacturer usually establishes a list price slightly higher than its previous generation of products.

▼ A **standard desktop microcomputer** fits on a desk and runs on power from a standard electrical outlet. The display screen is usually placed on top of the horizontal "desktop" case.

▼ A **microcomputer** with a **tower case** contains the same basic components as a standard desktop microcomputer, but the vertically oriented case is larger and allows more room for expansion. The tower unit can be placed on the floor to save desk space.

▲ A **notebook computer** is small and light, giving it the advantage of portability that a standard desktop computer does not have. A notebook computer can run on power from an electrical outlet or on batteries.

▲ A **personal digital assistant (PDA)**, or **palm-top computer** achieves even more portability than a notebook computer by shrinking or eliminating some standard components, such as the keyboard. On a keyboardless PDA, a touch-sensitive screen accepts characters drawn with your finger. PDAs easily connect to desktop computers to exchange and update information.

Categorizing computers

MICROCOMPUTERS ARE FAMILIAR TO us in our daily lives. This lesson will help you to become familiar with computers in the three other categories of computers as well: minicomputers, mainframes, and supercomputers. However, because the characteristics of each computer category shift and change as technolgy advances, it is difficult to categorize a particular computer unless you have up-to-date technical expertise. So, if you want to categorize a particular computer, look at the sales literature to find out how the manufacturer classifies it.

Minicomputers

Mainframes

Supercomputers

IN MORE DETAIL

Minicomputers are somewhat larger than microcomputers and are generally used in business and industry for specific tasks, such as processing payroll. One minicomputer can carry out the processing tasks for many users. If you are using a minicomputer system, you use a terminal to input your processing requests and view the results. A **terminal** is a device used for input and output, but not for processing. Your terminal transmits your processing request to the minicomputer. The minicomputer sends back results to your terminal when the processing is complete. The minicomputer system with several terminals in Figure A-5 is fairly typical.

Mainframes are large, fast, and fairly expensive computers, generally used by business or government to provide centralized storage, processing, and management for large amounts of data and to provide that data on demand to many users. Mainframes remain the computer of choice in situations where reliability, data security, and centralized control are necessary. As with a minicomputer, one mainframe computer carries out processing tasks for multiple users who input processing requests using a terminal. To process large amounts of data, mainframes often include more than one processing unit. One processing unit directs overall operations. A second processing unit handles communication with all the users requesting data. A third processing unit finds the data requested by users. A typical mainframe computer is shown in Figure A-6.

Supercomputers are the largest, fastest, and most expensive type of computer. Unlike minicomputers and mainframes, supercomputers are not designed to optimize processing for multiple users. Instead, supercomputers use their significant processing power to solve a few very difficult problems such as predicting the weather and modeling nuclear reactions. The speed of a supercomputer can reach one trillion instructions per second. A picture of a supercomputer is shown in Figure A-7.

Computer networks

*A **computer network** is a collection of computers and other devices connected to share data, hardware, and software. A network can connect microcomputers, minicomputers, and mainframes. A network has advantages for an organization and its users. For example, if a group of users shares a printer on a network, the organization* *saves money because it does not have to purchase a printer for every user. Network users can send messages to others on the network and retrieve data from a centralized storage device. The world's largest computer network, the Internet, provides connections for millions of computers all over the globe. The Internet provides many* *information services, but the most popular is the World Wide Web, often referred to as the Web. Computer sites all over the world store data of various sorts, such as weather maps, census data, product information, course syllabi, music, and images. Connect your computer to the Web to access this information.*

▶ The **minicomputer** handles processing tasks for multiple users. This minicomputer can handle up to 20 users.

▶ The **minicomputer's printer** provides printed output for all the users.

The **minicomputer's storage device** contains data for all the users in one centralized location.

Terminals act as each user's main input and output device. The terminal has a keyboard for input and a display screen for output, but it does not process the user's data. Instead, processing requests must be transmitted from the terminal to the minicomputer.

FIGURE A-6: *A mainframe computer*

The closet-sized system unit for the IBM S/390 G-4 mainframe computer contains the processing unit, memory, and circuitry to support multiple terminals.

FIGURE A-7: *A supercomputer*

The Cray T3E supercomputer, configurable with six to 2,048 processors provides the computing power to tackle the world's most challenging computing problems.

Reviewing peripheral devices

Microcomputer, minicomputer, mainframe, and supercomputer systems all include peripheral devices which are used to input, output, and store data. This lesson discusses the hardware components you are likely to use on a typical microcomputer system.

Peripheral Devices

☞ What are peripheral devices? **Peripheral devices** are equipment used with a computer to enhance its functionality. They are devices that are "outside" of, or in addition to, the computer. For example, a printer is a popular peripheral device used with microcomputers, minicomputers, and mainframe computers, but the computer can function without one. The keyboard, monitor, mouse, and disk drive for your microcomputer are also peripheral devices, even though they were included with your basic computer system. Figure A-8 shows some of the more popular peripheral devices used with microcomputers.

☞ Why use peripheral devices? Peripheral devices allow you to expand and modify your basic computer system. For example, you might purchase a computer that includes a mouse, but you might want to modify your system by purchasing a track ball to use instead of the mouse. You might want to expand your computer's capabilities by adding a scanner so you can input photographs. If you're an artist, you might want to add a graphics tablet, so you can sketch pictures using a pencil-like stylus. A peripheral device called a modem connects your computer to the telephone system so you can access information stored on other computers.

Installing peripheral devices

Most microcomputer peripheral devices are designed for installation by users who don't have technical expertise. When you buy a peripheral device it usually comes with installation instructions and specially designed software. You should carefully follow the instructions to install the device. The instructions will also give you directions on how to install any software that might be necessary to use the peripheral device. The Plug and Play feature in Windows 95 lets the system do all the installing and configuring of additional peripheral devices. Plug and Play identifies the new device and sets it up to work with your computer system.

INPUT DEVICES

▲ A **keyboard** is the main input device for most computer systems

◄ A **computer video camera** records an image of the person sitting at a computer or of a small group. Special digitizing hardware and software convert the image into a signal a computer can store and transmit.

▲ A **bar code reader** gathers input data by reading bar codes, such as the universal product codes on supermarket products. Bar code readers are also used at library circulation desks to track books.

▲ A **track ball** is a pointing device that you might use as an alternative to a mouse. You roll the ball to position the pointer on the screen. Unlike a mouse, a track ball doesn't move on the desk and therefore requires less space.

◄ A **mouse** is a pointing device you use to manipulate on-screen objects.

▲ A **sheet scanner** converts text or images on paper documents into an electronic format that the computer can display, print, and store.

▲ A **hand scanner** converts a 4-6" section of text or graphics into electronic format. To use the scanner, you pull it over the text you want to convert.

OUTPUT PROJECTION DEVICES

▲ A **monitor** is an output device the computer uses to display the results of processing. A touch-sensitive screen displays options you can select by touching them on the screen.

◄ A **computer projector** generates a large image of what's on the computer screen. Suitable for conference and lecture presentations.

OUTPUT PRINTING DEVICES

▲ A **laser printer** uses the same technology as a photocopier to print professional-quality text and graphics. Heat fuses a fine dark powder, called toner, onto paper to create text and images.

◄ An **LCD projection display panel** is placed on an overhead projector to produce a large display of the information shown on the computer screen.

▲ A **color ink-jet printer** creates characters and graphics by spraying ink onto paper.

► A **plotter** uses pens to draw an image on paper. Plotters are often used by architects and engineers to produce multicolor line drawings.

OTHER PERIPHERALS

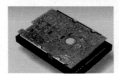

▲ A **disk drive** stores data.

► A **sound card** can be installed inside the system unit to give a computer the capability to accept audio input from a microphone, play sound files stored on disks or CD-ROMs, and produce audio output through speakers or earphones.

► A **modem** transfers data from one computer to another over telephone lines. An external modem has its own case. An internal modem is installed inside the computer system unit.

QUICK TIP

Always make sure the computer is turned off before you attempt to connect a peripheral device so you don't damage your computer system.

Understanding pointing devices

POINTING DEVICES SUCH AS A MOUSE, a track ball, or a lightpen help you manipulate objects and select menu options. The most popular pointing device is the mouse. Virtually every computer is equipped with a mouse. Figure A-9 shows you how to hold and use a mouse.

Using a Mouse

IN MORE DETAIL

- The **mouse** is a pointing device used to input data. This input device is used to manipulate objects displayed on the screen. A pointer on the screen shows the movement of the mouse.

- A **pointer**—usually shaped like an arrow—moves on the screen in a way that corresponds to how you move the mouse on a hard surface like your desk.

- You "**click** the mouse" by pressing the left mouse button a single time to select an object on the monitor.

- You "**double-click**" by clicking the mouse twice in rapid succession. Some operations require you to double-click.

- You can use the mouse to **drag** objects from one screen location to another by clicking the object, holding down the mouse button, and moving the mouse to the new location for the object. When the object is in its new location, you release the mouse button.

- Other pointing devices: Although a mouse is the standard pointing device used with desktop computers, alternative pointing devices are more convenient to use with notebook computers. The three most popular options— track point, touch pad, and built-in track ball—are described in Figure A-10.

Why some mice have three buttons and others have one or two

The mouse you use with a Macintosh computer only has one button. IBM-compatible computers use either a two- or three-button mouse. A two-button mouse allows you to right-click an object, which provides another way of manipulating the object. For example, if clicking the left button selects an object, clicking the right button might bring up a menu of actions you can do with the object. On a three-button mouse, you rarely use the third button. Some three-button mice, however, allow you to click the middle button once instead of double-clicking the left mouse button. This feature is useful for people who have trouble double-clicking. It also helps prevent some muscular stress injuries that result from excessive clicking.

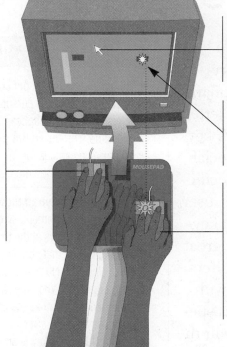

A pointer on the screen, usually shaped like an arrow, moves as you move the mouse on a hard surface.

To hold the mouse, rest the palm of your right hand on the mouse so your index finger is positioned over the left mouse button. Lightly grasp the mouse using your thumb and ring finger.

To select an object, use the mouse to position the pointer on the object, then click the left mouse button.

If you move the mouse to the right on your desk, the pointer moves to the right on your screen. When you pull the mouse toward the front of the desk, the pointer moves to the bottom of the screen.

QUICK TIP

If you are left handed, you can hold the mouse in your left hand and click the right mouse button. Most software has a left handed mouse option to switch the functions of the mouse buttons.

FIGURE A-10: *Notebook pointing devices*

Track point

Touch pad

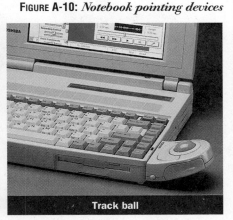

Track ball

▲ A track point is a small eraser-like device embedded among the typing keys. To control the on-screen pointer, you push the track point up, left, right, or down. Buttons for clicking and double-clicking are located in front of the spacebar.

▲ A touch pad is a touch-sensitive device. By dragging your finger over the surface, you control the on-screen pointer. Two buttons equivalent to mouse buttons are located in front of the touch pad.

▲ A track ball is like an upside-down mouse. By rolling the ball with your fingers, you control the on-screen pointer. Buttons for clicking are often located above or to the side of the track ball.

TROUBLE

Suppose you are dragging an object, but your mouse runs into an obstacle on your desk. You can just pick up the mouse, move it to a clear space, and continue dragging.

Examining keyboards

MOST COMPUTERS ARE EQUIPPED with a **keyboard** as the primary input device. A computer keyboard includes keys or buttons with letters and numbers as well as several keys with special characters and special words to control computer-specific tasks. Virtually every computer user interface requires you to use a keyboard. You don't have to be a great typist, but to use a computer effectively, you should be familiar with the computer keyboard and its special keys. Figure A-11 shows you the location of the keys on a standard computer keyboard.

Using a Keyboard

IN MORE DETAIL

○━ You use the keys to input commands, respond to prompts, and type the text of documents. A cursor or an insertion point indicates where the characters you type will appear. The **cursor** appears on the screen as a flashing underline. The **insertion point** appears on the screen as a flashing vertical bar. You can change the location of the cursor or insertion point using the arrow keys or the mouse.

○━ The **numeric keypad** provides you with a calculator-style input device for numbers and arithmetic symbols. You can type numbers using either the set of number keys at the top of the keyboard or the keys on the numeric keypad. Notice that some keys on the numeric keypad contain two symbols. When the Num Lock key is activated, the numeric keypad will produce numbers. When the Num Lock key is not activated, the keys on the numeric keypad move the cursor in the direction indicated by the arrows on the keys.

The Num Lock key is an example of a toggle key. A **toggle key** switches back and forth between two modes. The Caps Lock key is also a toggle key. When you press the Caps Lock key you switch or "toggle" into uppercase mode. When you press the Caps Lock key again you toggle back into lowercase mode.

○━ **Function keys**, those keys numbered F1 through F12, are located either at the top or along the side of your keyboard. They were added to computer keyboards to initiate commands. For example, with many software packages [F1] is the key you press to get help. The problem with function keys is that they are not standardized. In one program, you might press [F7] to save a document; but in another program, you might press [F5].

○━ **Modifier keys** ([Ctrl] (Control), [Alt], and [Shift] keys): There are 12 function keys, but you usually need more than 12 commands to control software. Therefore, you can use the [Ctrl], [Alt], and [Shift] keys in conjunction with the function keys to expand the repertory of available commands. The [Alt] and [Ctrl] modifier keys also work in conjunction with the letter keys. Instead of using the mouse, you might use the [Alt] or [Ctrl] keys in combination with letter keys to access menu options. These are called **keyboard shortcuts**. If you see Alt+F1, [Alt F1], Alt-F1, or Alt F1 on the screen or in an instruction manual, it means to hold down the [Alt] key and press [F1]. You might see similar notations for using the [Ctrl] or [Shift] keys.

The **Esc** or "escape" key cancels an operation.

The **function keys** execute commands, such as centering a line of text or boldfacing text. The command associated with each function key depends on the software you are using.

Each time you press the **Backspace key**, one character to the left of the cursor is deleted. If you hold down the Backspace key, multiple characters to the left are deleted one by one until you release it.

The **Print Screen key** prints the contents of the screen when you use some software. With other software, the Print Screen key stores a copy of your screen in memory that you can manipulate or print with draw or paint software.

The function of the **Scroll Lock key** depends on the software you are using. This key is rarely used with today's software.

The **Num Lock key** is a toggle key that switches between number keys and cursor keys on the numeric keypad.

The **Pause key** stops the current task your computer is performing. You might need to hold down both the Ctrl key and the Pause key to stop the task.

Indicator lights show you the status of each toggle key: Num Lock, Caps Lock, and Scroll Lock. The Power light indicates whether the computer is on or off.

The **Caps Lock key** capitalizes all the letters you type when it is engaged, but does not produce the top symbol on keys that contain two symbols. This key is a toggle key, which means that each time you press it, you switch between uppercase and lowercase modes. There is usually an indicator light on the keyboard to show which mode you are in.

Hold down the **Ctrl key** while you press another key. The result of Ctrl key combinations depends on the software you are using.

Hold down the **Alt key** while you press another key. The result of Alt key combinations depends on the software you are using.

Press **Enter** when you finish typing a command.

Hold down the **Shift key** while you press another key. The Shift key capitalizes letters and produces the top symbol on keys that contain two symbols.

End takes you to the end of the line or the end of a document, depending on the software you are using.

The **cursor keys** move your position on the screen up, down, right, or left.

Home takes you to the beginning of a line or the beginning of a document, depending on the software you are using.

Page Up displays the previous screen of information. **Page Down** displays the next screen of information.

If you are having wrist problems and you are using a mouse and a keyboard, you may want to try using a touch pad as your input device.

[Ctrl]+[C] was used in the early days of computing to tell the computer to stop what it was doing. [Ctrl]+[C] works as a keyboard shortcut for the Copy command in today's graphical user interfaces.

Examining output devices

THE PRIMARY OUTPUT DEVICE ON A microcomputer is the monitor. A **monitor** is a display device that converts the electrical signals from the computer into points of light on a screen to form an image. A monitor is a required output device for just about every computer-user interface. A computer display system consists of a monitor and a **graphics card**, also called a **video display adapter** or **video card**. A graphics card is an expansion card that controls the signals that the computer sends to the monitor. Whereas you manipulate the keyboard and mouse to communicate with the computer, the monitor is what the computer manipulates to communicate with you by displaying results, prompts, menus, and graphical objects. Monitors are manufactured with different features that determine whether they can display color and graphics.

After monitors, printers are the second most common peripheral output device for many computer systems. This is because if you want to have a hard copy (paper copy) of your output, you need a printer.

Display System

Printers

IN MORE DETAIL

☞ Monochrome monitors: The first microcomputer monitors and the displays on many terminals still in use today are character-based. A **character-based display** divides the screen into a grid of rectangles. The set of characters that the screen can display is not modifiable; therefore, it is not possible to display different sizes or styles of characters. Character-based displays are technically classified as monochrome displays because they use only one color to display text on a black background.

☞ Color monitors: Factors that influence the quality of the monitor include screen size, maximum resolution, and dot pitch. A **graphics display** or **bit-map display** divides the screen into a matrix of small dots called **pixels**. Any characters or graphics the computer displays on the screen must be constructed of dot patterns within the screen matrix. **Dot pitch** is a measure of image clarity: a smaller dot pitch means a crisper image. Technically, dot pitch is the distance in millimeters between like-colored pixels. The more dots your screen displays in the matrix, the higher the **resolution**. The specifications for a monitor include its **maximum resolution**—the maximum number of pixels it can display. Standard resolutions include 640 x 480, 800 x 600, 1024 x 768, 1280 x 1024, and 1600 x 1200.

Screen size is the measurement in inches from one corner of the screen diagonally across to the opposite corner. Most computer systems are packaged with a 14-inch or 15-inch screen. With a 17-inch monitor you can switch to a high resolution to fit more windows on the screen, and the text will still be reasonably large.

On most monitors, the viewable image does not stretch to the edge of the screen, instead a black border makes the image smaller than, for example, the 15-inch size specified. Many computer vendors now include a measurement for the **viewable image size (vis)**, as shown in Figure A-12.

☞ Printers: **Dot matrix printers** create letters and graphics by striking an inked ribbon with a column of small wires called *pins*. By activating some wires in the column, but not activating others, the printer creates patterns for letters and numbers. The more pins in the column, the better the print quality. Therefore, a 24-pin dot matrix printer is capable of better quality output than a 9-pin printer.

Ink-jet printers produce characters and graphics by spraying ink onto paper. The print head is a matrix of fine spray nozzles. Patterns are formed by activating selected nozzles. An ink-jet printer typically forms a character in a 20 x 20 matrix, producing a high-quality printout. Color ink-jet printers cost a little more, but produce much higher-quality output than color dot matrix printers. Ink-jet and personal laser printers (see Figure A-13) provide high-quality print on plain paper.

► A **monitor** is an output device the computer uses to display the results of processing.

As with a TV, the monitor's viewable image size is less than the screen size. A 15-inch monitor has approximately a 13.9-inch vis.

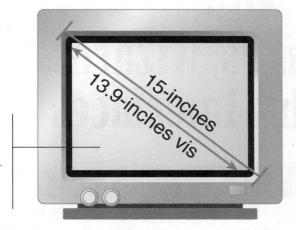

15-inches

13.9-inches vis

Video display adapters can use special graphics chips called accelerated video adapters to increase the speed at which images are displayed.

► Laser printers use the same technology as duplicating machines. A laser charges a pattern of particles on a drum which picks up a powdery black substance called toner. The toner is transferred onto paper that rolls past the drum. In the past, the price of laser printers limited their use to businesses and large organizations. Laser printer prices have decreased, however, making them affordable for individuals.

► Color laser printers work by reprinting each page for each primary color. For each reprint, the paper must be precisely positioned so each color is printed in exactly the right spot. This dramatically increases the complexity of the print mechanism and the amount of time required to print each page.

► Operating costs of laser printers include replacement toner cartridges and print drums. The estimated cost of a laser printing is about $.05 per page.

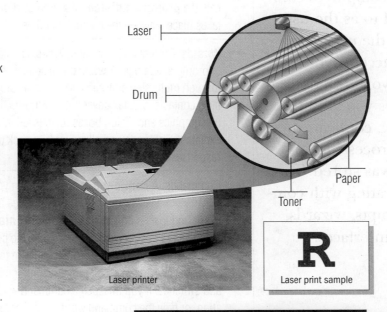

Laser

Drum

Paper

Toner

Laser printer

Laser print sample

Characteristics	
✓	Moderate to high price
✓	High-quality output
✓	More expensive to operate
✓	Cannot print multipart forms
✓	Fast
✓	Quiet
✓	Expensive, high-quality color
✓	Durable

It is important to realize that the maximum resolution you can use is determined by both the graphics card and the monitor. If your graphics card supports 1600 × 1200 resolution, but your monitor supports only 1280 × 1024, the maximum resolution you can use will be 1280 × 1024.

Communicating with computers: prompts, wizards, and command-line interfaces

To effectively use the computer, you must communicate with it; you must tell the computer what tasks to perform, and you must accurately interpret the information the computer provides to you. The means by which humans and computers communicate is referred to as the **user interface**. Through the user interface, the computer accepts your input and presents you with output. This output provides you with the results of processing, confirms the completion of the processing, or indicates that data was stored. Three means of communicating with computers are with prompts, wizards, and command-line interfaces.

DOS Command-Line Interface

IN MORE DETAIL

▢— Prompts: A **prompt** is a message displayed by the computer that asks for input from the user. Some prompts, such as "Enter your name:," are helpful and easy to understand, even for beginners. Other prompts, like A:\>, are less helpful. In response to a computer prompt, you enter the requested information or follow the instruction.

A sequence of prompts is sometimes used to develop a user interface called a **prompted dialog**. In a prompted dialog, a sort of conversation takes place between the computer and user.

▢— Wizards: Current commercial software tends to use "wizards" instead of prompted dialogs. A **wizard** is a sequence of screens that direct you through multi-step software tasks such as creating a graph, a list of business contacts, or a fax cover sheet. Wizards, like the one in Figure A-14, use graphics and dialog boxes (discussed in the next lesson) to help explain the prompts and allow users to back up and change their responses.

▢— Commands: A **command** is an instruction you input to tell the computer to carry out a task. An interface that requires the user to type in commands is referred to as a **command-line user interface**. Each word in a command results in a specific action by the computer.

The commands you input must conform to a specific syntax. **Syntax** specifies the sequence and punctuation for command words, parameters, and switches. If you misspell a command word, leave out required punctuation, or type the command words out of order, you will get an **error message** or **syntax error**. When you get an error message or syntax error, you must figure out what is wrong with the command and retype it correctly.

Is the user interface hardware or software?

The user interface is a combination of software and hardware. The software that controls the user interface defines its characteristics. For example, software controls whether you accomplish tasks by manipulating graphical objects or typing commands. The hardware controls the way you physically manipulate the computer to establish communication, for example, whether you use a keyboard, mouse, or your voice to input commands. After you have a general understanding of user interfaces, you will be able to quickly figure out how to make the computer do what you want it to do.

The Business Card Wizard helps you create business cards that you can print on a laser printer.

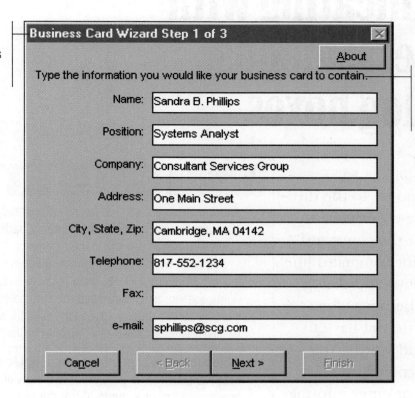

The wizard prompts you at each step. First, you enter the information you want printed on the card.

Business Card Wizard Step 1 of 3

About

Type the information you would like your business card to contain.

Name:	Sandra B. Phillips
Position:	Systems Analyst
Company:	Consultant Services Group
Address:	One Main Street
City, State, Zip:	Cambridge, MA 04142
Telephone:	817-552-1234
Fax:	
e-mail:	sphillips@scg.com

Cancel | < Back | Next > | Finish

FYI

A classic example of a poorly designed computer prompt is the screen message, "Press any key to continue." Apparently, some users have become frustrated when they can't find a key on the keyboard labeled "Any Key!"

QUICK TIP

If you forget the correct command word or punctuation, or if you find yourself using an unfamiliar command-line user interface, you may be able to find help right on the computer. Type **Help** and press Enter to access help built into the software.

Next you decide what style you'd like for your business card. The wizard lets you move forward, or backward to change your responses until the business card is set up to your satisfaction.

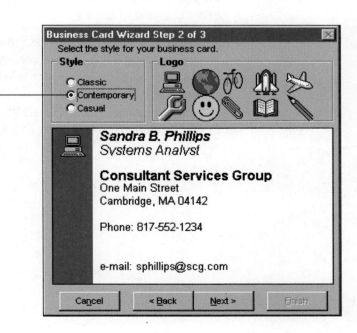

Business Card Wizard Step 2 of 3

Select the style for your business card.

Style
- ○ Classic
- ● Contemporary
- ○ Casual

Logo

Sandra B. Phillips
Systems Analyst

Consultant Services Group
One Main Street
Cambridge, MA 04142

Phone: 817-552-1234

e-mail: sphillips@scg.com

Cancel | < Back | Next > | Finish

Communicating with computers: menus and dialog boxes

MENUS AND DIALOG BOXES WERE developed as a response to the difficulties many people experienced trying to remember the command words and syntax for command-line user interfaces. Menus and dialog boxes are popular because when you use them, you do not have to remember command words. You simply choose the command you want from a menu or enter information in a dialog box specific to the task you want the computer to complete.

User Interfaces

IN MORE DETAIL

☞ A **menu** displays a list of commands or options. Each line of the menu is a command and is referred to as a **menu option** or a **menu item**. Figure A-15 shows you how to use a menu.

You might wonder how a menu can present all the commands you want to input. Obviously, there are many possibilities for combining command words, so there could be hundreds of menu options. Two methods are generally used to present a reasonably sized list of menu options. One method uses a menu hierarchy. The other method uses a dialog box.

☞ A **hierarchy** is an organization of things ranked one above the other. For example, a business might show the hierarchy of its employees on an organizational chart. A **menu hierarchy**, as the name implies, arranges menus in a hierarchical structure. After you make a selection from one menu, a submenu appears, and you can make additional choices by selecting an option from the submenu. Some software has a fairly complex menu hierarchy, making it difficult to remember how to find a particular menu option.

☞ A **dialog box** displays the options associated with a command. Instead of leading to a submenu, some menu options lead to a dialog box. You fill in the dialog box to indicate specifically how you want the command carried out, as shown in Figure A-16.

Dialog box controls let you specify settings and other command parameters. Figure A-17 explains how to use some common dialog box controls.

The **menu bar** is usually at the top of the screen. The menu bar for this software package includes File, Edit, View, Image, Options, and Help menus. To use this pull-down menu, you first select which menu you want to use from a menu bar.

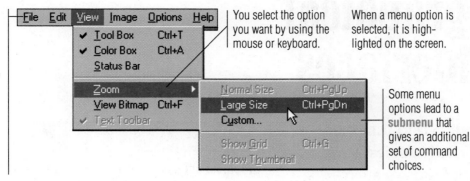

You select the option you want by using the mouse or keyboard.

When a menu option is selected, it is highlighted on the screen.

Some menu options lead to a **submenu** that gives an additional set of command choices.

The Print option on the File menu displays three dots to indicate that this menu option leads to a dialog box.

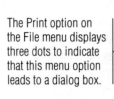

When you select Print, the Print dialog box opens. The dialog box prompts you to enter specifications about how the computer should carry out the Print task.

Click this button to display a list of printers you can use.

Although a dialog box appears in conjunction with a menu, it is really a different type of user interface element. It combines the characteristics of both menus and prompts.

Indicate how much of your document you want to print by clicking one of these buttons.

When you are satisfied with the print specifications, click OK.

Change the number of copies by clicking either of these buttons.

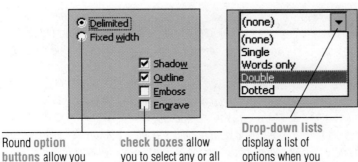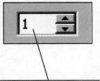

Round **option buttons** allow you to select one of the options. Square

check boxes allow you to select any or all of the options.

Drop-down lists display a list of options when you click the arrow button.

Spin boxes let you increase or decrease a number by clicking the arrow buttons. You can also type a number in the box.

Using graphical user interfaces

GRAPHICAL USER INTERFACES OR
GUIs (pronounced "gooies") are
found on most of today's microcomputers. GUIs are based on the
philosophy that people can use
computers intuitively—that is, with
minimal training—if they can manipulate on-screen objects that represent tasks or commands.

IN MORE DETAIL

☞ **Graphical objects** are key elements of GUIs. A graphical object is a small picture on the screen that you can manipulate using a mouse or other input device. Each graphical object represents a computer task, command, or a real-world object. You show the computer what you want it to do by manipulating an object instead of entering commands or selecting menu options. Graphical objects are explained in Figure A-18.

An example of manipulating on-screen objects is the way you delete a document using Windows. The documents you create are represented by icons that look like sheets of paper. A Recycle Bin represents the place where you put documents you no longer want. Suppose you used your computer to write a report named "Sport Statistics," but you no longer need the report stored on your computer system. You use the mouse to drag the Sport Statistics icon to the Recycle Bin and erase the report from your computer system, as explained in Figure A-19.

☞ Most graphical user interfaces are based on a metaphor in which computer components are represented by real-world objects. For example, a user interface using a **desktop metaphor** might represent documents as file folders and storage as a filing cabinet.

☞ Graphical user interfaces often contain menus and prompts in addition to graphical objects because graphical user interface designers found it diffi-cult to design icons and tools for every possible task, command, and option you might want to perform. Figure A-20 shows some of these elements in the Windows interface.

Starting a program

One of the most frequent computer activities you will perform is starting a program. You can start a program using commands, graphical objects, or a menu.
To start Microsoft Works using the DOS command-line user interface, you need to know the name of the program. For example, the computer calls

Microsoft Works "works." At the DOS prompt C:\>, type **works**, then press Enter.
To start Microsoft Works using the Windows 3.1 user interface, you move the pointer to the Microsoft Works graphical object and double-click the left mouse button.
To start Microsoft Works using the Windows 95 interface, use

the mouse to move the pointer to the Start button and click to view a menu of categories. Click Programs to display a list of program folders. Click Microsoft Works for the Windows folder to display the Microsoft Works folder. Click Microsoft Works to start the program.

▶ A **window** usually contains a specific piece of work. For example, a window might contain a document you are typing or a picture you are drawing. You can think of windows as work areas, analogous to different documents and books that you might have open on your desk. Just as you switch between the documents and books you have on your desk, you can switch between windows on the computer screen to work on different tasks.

A **button** helps you make a selection. Some buttons are labeled with pictures. These buttons are sometimes referred to as **tools**. When you click a button, sometimes its appearance changes to indicate that it has been activated.

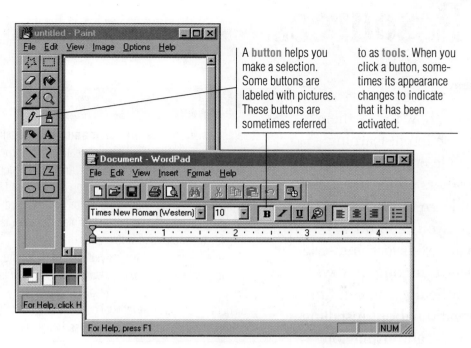

FIGURE A-19: *Manipulating on-screen objects*

FIGURE A-20: *The Windows 95 GUI*

An **icon** is a small picture that represents an object. When you select an icon, you indicate to the computer that you want to manipulate the object.

A selected icon is highlighted. The Sports Statistics icon on the left is selected, so it is highlighted with dark blue.

The **menu bar** displays menu titles. Selecting a menu title displays its pull-down menu.

The **tool bars** display buttons or tools that provide shortcuts to the commands on the menus.

This **wizard** appears when you click the Chart Wizard button. The Chart Wizard escorts you through the steps to create a chart or graph.

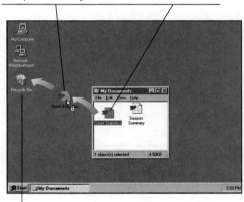

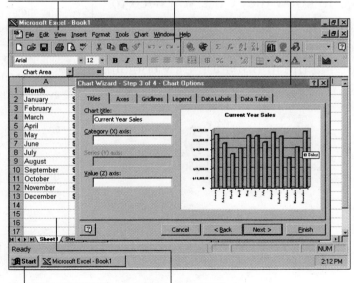

The Sport Statistics document is no longer needed. Use the mouse to drag the Sport Statistics document icon to the

Recycle Bin. Once it is placed in the Recycle Bin, the document will no longer appear in the document window.

The **taskbar** contains buttons that show you which software programs you are using.

A **window** in the background contains the data for the chart.

Using Resources

PART OF LEARNING ABOUT COMPUTER systems is learning how to use them. Individuals have different learning styles. Some people enjoy discovery learning while others prefer structured lectures. As you learn to use your computer system, you can find resources to match your learning style. If, when you use your computer system, you have difficulty, you can find "how to" information about installing computer hardware and using computer software in a variety of resources. These resources might be printed materials such as books or manuals, they might be courses that you take, they might even be available directly on your computer screen. To use these resources effectively, you need to know they exist, you need to know where to find them, and you need to develop some strategies for applying the information they contain.

Computer Terms   **Learning Styles**

IN MORE DETAIL

▯▬ Reference manuals: **Reference manuals** are usually printed books or online resources that describe each feature of a hardware device or software package. Reference manuals are usually included with the hardware or software that you buy. You can also find independent publishers who produce reference manuals for popular hardware and software. Most often, reference manuals are printed documents, but a recent trend is to provide computer-based reference manuals.

A reference manual is typically organized by features, rather than in the lesson format used by tutorials. Use a reference manual to find out if a feature exists or to find out how to use a feature. When you use a reference manual, you should first check the table of contents or index to locate the information you need, then turn to the appropriate section and read it carefully.

▯▬ Courses: Another approach to learning how to use computers is to take a course. Courses are available from schools, manufacturers, and private training firms and might last from several hours to several months. Courses about software packages tend to be laboratory-based with an instructor leading you through steps.

▯▬ Support line of a software or hardware company: A **support line** is a service offered over the phone by a hardware manufacturer or software publisher to customers who have questions about how to use a software or hardware product. Sometimes these support line calls are toll-free; sometimes they are not. You might also pay a fee for the time it takes the support person to answer your question.

▯▬ Online help: The term "online" refers to resources that are immediately available on your computer screen. Reference information is frequently available as **online help**, accessible from a Help menu, a button on the toolbar, or by typing **Help** at a command-line prompt. Figure A-21 shows you how to access online help for the Microsoft Office 97 software.

▯▬ Tutorials: A **tutorial** is a guided, step-by-step learning experience. Usually this learning experience teaches you the generic skills you need to use specific hardware or software.

Tutorials might be produced by the publisher of the software you want to use or by independent publishers. Tutorials come in a variety of forms, as listed in Table A-1, to match your learning style.

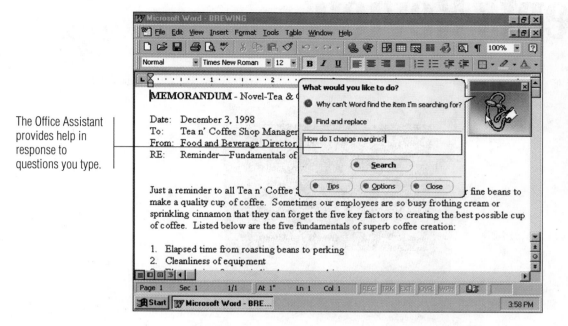

The Office Assistant provides help in response to questions you type.

TABLE **A-1**: *Reference resources*

RESOURCE		DESCRIPTION
Printed tutorial		Provides printed step-by-step instructions. To use a printed tutorial, you read how to do a step, then you try to do it on the computer. In the last few years, computer-based tutorials have become much more widespread.
Computer-based tutorial		Provides a simulation of the hardware or software and displays tutorial instructions in boxes or windows on the screen. Computer-based tutorials have an advantage over their printed counterparts because they can demonstrate procedures using computer animation.
Audio tutorial		Verbally walks you through the steps of the tutorial. An advantage to this type of tutorial is that you do not have to read instructions. You do have to stop the tutorial and rewind, however, if you do not hear or understand the instructions. You might like audio tutorials if you easily retain information presented in lectures.
Video tutorial		Visually illustrates how the software or hardware works. Some video tutorials are designed so that you watch them, take notes, then try the steps on the computer later. Other video tutorials are designed to be used while you are sitting at the computer. As with audio tutorials, you can stop and rewind video tutorials if you miss something.

Concepts Review

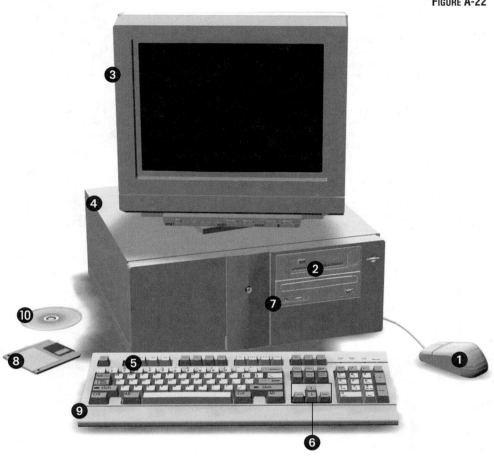

Label each element shown in Figure A-22.

1. _____

2. _____

3. _____

4. _____

5. _____

6. _____

7. _____

8. _____

9. _____

10. _____

Match each statement with the term it describes:

11. ____ Input
12. ____ Processing
13. ____ Terminal
14. ____ Mouse
15. ____ Mainframe

a. Systematic actions a computer uses to manipulate data

b. A pointing device used to input data

c. The symbols processed by a computer

d. Category of computer

e. Resembles a microcomputer but does not have any processing capability

Fill in the best answer:

16. The four functions performed by a computer are _____, _____, _____, and _____.

17. The computer puts data temporarily in _____ while the data is waiting to be processed.

18. When data is not needed for processing, the computer puts it in _____.

19. An IBM computer is _____ with a Compaq computer because it operates in essentially the same way.

20. If your organization wants to provide processing for more than 200 users and reliability, security, and centralized control are necessary, a(n) _____ computer would best meet your needs.

21. Most microcomputers are equipped with a(n) _____ as the primary input device and a(n) _____ as the primary output device.

22. You can use the _____ key and the _____ key in conjunction with letter keys instead of using the mouse to control menus.

23. A(n) _____, such as "Enter your name:," is one way a computer can tell the user what to do.

24. Instead of prompted dialogs, today's software tends to use _____ to direct a user through multi-step software tasks, such as creating a graph or creating a fax cover sheet.

25. Most _____ are based on a metaphor in which computer components are represented by real-world objects, such as a desktop metaphor in which documents are represented by folder icons.

INDEPENDENT CHALLENGE 1

To complete this independent challenge:

Draw a sketch of a computer system in your computer lab, home, or office and do the following:

1. Title the sketch appropriately, for example, "My Computer at Home."

2. List its brand name and model number, for example, "Dell Pentium."

3. Label the following parts, if applicable:

   monitor
   screen
   hard drive light
   3.5" disk drive
   power switch
   power light
   CD-ROM drive
   mouse printer
   printer (type)
   system unit
   keyboard

INDEPENDENT CHALLENGE 2

Computer magazines contain advertisements for a variety of microcomputers. The advertisements provide a wealth of information about the products.

To complete this independent challenge:

1. Find and photocopy an advertisement from a computer magazine for each of the following:

   Desktop computer
   Tower computer
   Notebook computer
   PDA

2. Label each component for each of the computers pictured in the advertisements.

3. Indicate if each component is an input device, an output device, processing device, or a storage device.

4. Compare the computers based on the advertisements. Answer questions such as the following:

   How are the units similar?

   How are they different?

5. In what situations would you be more likely to use one computer over another computer?

INDEPENDENT CHALLENGE 3

Do this project only if your school has a computer network for student use. If the network requires a user ID and password, get them. Learn how to log in. Your school might have a short tutorial that teaches you how to use the network, or your instructor might provide a demonstration.

To complete this independent challenge:

Write a one- to two-page step-by-step tutorial on how to log into the network. Your tutorial should include the following:

1. A title

2. An introductory paragraph explaining where the network is located, who can access it, and how students can get a user ID and password

3. Numbered steps to log into the network (if your lab policy requires that you turn on the computer each time you log in, you should include instructions for doing this in your tutorial)

4. Numbered steps for logging out of the network

INDEPENDENT CHALLENGE 4

Do this project only if your school provides you with access to the Internet. The Internet is a worldwide computer network that provides access to an astonishing variety of information. The Internet can be useful right from the start of this course. Several of the end-of-chapter projects refer you to information resources on the Internet. If you would like to use the Internet for these projects, this is a good time to get started.

There are several software tools to help you use the Internet, such as Internet Explorer or Netscape Navigator. This is an exploratory project that you can accomplish with the help of your instructor or with a tutorial prepared by your school.

To complete this independent challenge:

Find out how to use the Internet at your school and then answer the following questions:

1. What is the name of the software tool you use to access the Internet?

2. How do you access the "home page" for your school?

3. What other locations or "sites" are available from your home page? List at least five. How do you get to these other sites?

4. How can you keep track of where you have been on the Internet? (In other words, is there a way to bookmark sites?)

5. When you are finished browsing on the Internet, how do you quit?

LAB ASSIGNMENTS

The Course Labs are designed to help you master some of the key computer concepts and skills presented in each unit of the text. If you are using your school's lab computers, your instructor or technical support person should have installed the Labs software for you. If you want to use the Labs on your home computer, see the information in the Preface of this book.

Each Lab has two parts: Steps and Explore. Use Steps first to learn and review concepts. Read the information on each page and do the numbered steps. As you work through the Lab, you will be asked to answer Quick Check questions about what you have learned. At the end of the Lab, you will see a Summary Report of your answers to the Quick Checks. If your instructor wants you to turn in this Summary Report, click the Print button on the Summary Report screen.

When you have completed the Steps, you can click the Explore button to complete the Lab Assignments. You can also use Explore to practice the skills you learned and to explore concepts on your own.

The instructions for starting the Labs depend on whether your computer has Windows 3.1 or Windows 95. Use the appropriate set of steps for your computer system. Your instructor or technical support person might help you get started.

To begin the Lab from Windows 3.1 Program Manager:

1. Double-click the Course Labs group icon to open the Course Labs window.

2. Double-click the Illustrated Concepts icon to open a window containing icons for all the Labs.

3. Click the icon for the Lab you want to use.

4. Follow the instructions on the screen to enter your name and class section.

5. Read the instructions for using the Lab by clicking the Instructions button.

6. When you are ready to begin the Lab, click the Steps button.

To begin the Lab from Windows 95:

1. Click the Start button.

2. Point to Programs.

3. Point to Course Labs.

4. Click Illustrated Concepts to open a window containing icons for all the Labs.

5. Click the name of the Lab you want to use.

6. Read the instructions for using the Lab by clicking the Instruction button.

7. When you are ready to begin the Lab, click the Steps button.

PERIPHERAL DEVICES LAB

A wide variety of peripheral devices provide expandability for computer systems and provide users with the equipment necessary to accomplish tasks efficiently. In the Peripheral Devices Lab you will use an online product catalog of peripheral devices.

1. Complete the Steps to find out how to use the online product catalog. Click the Steps button and begin the Steps. As you work through the Steps, answer all of the Quick Check questions that appear. When you complete the Steps, you will see a Summary Report that summarizes your performance on the Quick Checks. Follow the directions on the screen to print the Summary Report.

2. After you know how to use the product catalog to look up products, features, and prices, use Explore to create an outline that shows the way peripheral devices are categorized in the catalog.

   a. List the characteristics that differentiate printers.

   b. List the factors that differentiate monitors.

   c. Describe the factors that determine the appropriate type of scanner for a task.

   d. List the peripheral devices in the catalog that are specially designed for notebook computers.

3. Suppose that the company that produces the peripheral devices catalog selected your name from its list of customers for a free scanner. You can select any one of the scanners in the catalog. Assume that you own a notebook computer to which you could attach any one of the scanners. Click the Explore button and use the catalog to help you write a one-page paper explaining which scanner you would select, why you would select it, and how you would use it.

4. Suppose you are in charge of information systems in a metropolitan hospital. Twenty nursing stations need printers. The printers will be used for a variety of reports. High print quality is not essential; but, of course, the reports must be readable. Some reports require more than one copy. Because they will be situated near patients, the printers must be quiet. Use the catalog in the Explore portion of the Lab to write a one-page paper in which you recommend a printer from the catalog for the nursing stations. Support your recommendation by explaining the advantages of the printer you selected and the disadvantages of the other printers available.

5. Suppose you own a basic computer system and want some of the devices as shown in Figure A-8 of this textbook. You have an idea that you can earn the money for your college tuition by using your computer to help other students produce spiffy reports with color graphs and scanned images. Your parents have agreed to "loan" you $1,000 to get started. Click the Explore button and look through the online peripheral devices catalog. List any of the devices that might help you with this business venture. Write a one-page paper explaining how you would spend your $1,000 to get the equipment you need to start the business.

USING A MOUSE LAB

A mouse is a standard input device on most of today's computers. You need to know how to use a mouse to manipulate graphical user interfaces and to use the rest of the Labs.

1. The Steps for the Using a Mouse Lab show you how to click, double-click, and drag objects using the mouse. Click the Steps button and begin the Steps. As you work through the Steps, answer all of the Quick Check questions that appear. When you complete the Steps, you will see a Summary Report that summarizes your performance on the Quick Checks. Follow the directions on the screen to print the Summary Report.

2. In Explore, demonstrate your ability to use a mouse and to control a Windows program by creating a poster. To create a poster, select a graphic, type the caption for the poster, then select a font, font styles, and a border. Print your completed poster.

USING A KEYBOARD LAB

To become an effective computer user, you must be familiar with your primary input device—the keyboard.

1. The Steps for the Using a Keyboard Lab provide you with a structured introduction to the keyboard layout and the function of special computer keys. Click the Steps button and begin the Steps. As you work through the Steps, answer all of the Quick Check questions that appear. When you complete the Steps, you will see a Summary Report that summarizes your performance on the Quick Checks. Follow the directions on the screen to print the Summary Report.

2. Click the Explore button to start the typing tutor. You can develop your typing skills using the typing tutor. Take the typing test and print out your results.

3. In Explore, try to improve your typing speed by 10 words per minute. For example, if you currently type 20 words per minute, your goal would be 30 words per minute. Practice each typing lesson until you see a message that indicates you can proceed to the next lesson. Create a Practice Record as shown here to keep track of how much you practice. When you have reached your goal, print out the results of a typing test to verify your results.

Practice Record

Name:_____

Section:_____

Start Date:_____

Start Typing Speed:_____wpm

End Date:_____

End Typing Speed:_____wpm

Lesson #:_____

Date Practiced/Time Practiced_____

DOS COMMAND-LINE INTERFACES LAB

The DOS command-line user interface provides a typical example of the advantages and disadvantages of command-line user interfaces. DOS was included with the original IBM PC computers to provide users with a way to accomplish system tasks such as listing, moving, and deleting files on disk. Although todays typical computer user prefers to use a graphical user interface such as Windows, DOS commands still function on most IBM-compatible computers.

1. Begin with Steps to learn how to use the DOS command-line interface. Click the Steps button and begin the Steps. As you work through the Steps, answer all of the Quick Check questions that appear. When you complete the Steps, you will see a Summary Report that summarizes your performance on the Quick Checks. Follow the directions on the screen to print the Summary Report.

2. In Explore, write out your answers to a through d.

   a. Explain the different results you get when you use the commands DIR, DIR /p, and DIR /w.

   b. What happens if you make a typing error and enter the command DUR instead of DIR? What procedure must you follow to correct your error?

   c. Enter the command DIR /? and explain what happens. Enter the command VER /? and explain what happens. What generalization can you make about the /? command parameter?

   d. Enter the command VER /p. Why do you think /p does not work with the VER command word, but it works with DIR?

3. Write a one-page paper summarizing what you know about command-line user interfaces and answer the following questions:

   a. Which DOS commands do you now know how to use?

   b. How do you know which commands to use to accomplish a task?

   c. How do you know what parameters work with each command?

   d. What kinds of mistakes can you make that will produce an error message?

   e. Can you enter valid commands that don't produce the results you want?

USER INTERFACES LAB

You have learned that the hardware and software for a user interface determine how you interact and communicate with the computer. In the User Interfaces Lab, you will try five different user interfaces to accomplish the same task—creating a graph.

1. Begin with the Steps to find out how each interface works. Click the Steps button and begin the Steps. As you work through the Steps, answer all of the Quick Check questions that appear. When you complete the Steps, you will see a Summary Report that summarizes your performance on the Quick Checks. Follow the directions on the screen to print the Summary Report.

2. In Explore, use each interface to make a 3-D pie graph using data set 1. Title your graphs "Cycle City Sales." Use the percent style to show the percent of each slice of the pie. Print each of the five graphs (one for each interface).

3. In Explore, select one of the user interfaces. Write a step-by-step set of instructions for how to produce a line graph using data set 2. This line graph should show lines and symbols, and have the title "Widget Production."

4. Using the user interface terminology you learned in this Lab and unit of the textbook, write a description of each of the interfaces you used in the Lab. Then, suppose you worked for a software publisher and you were going to create a software package for producing line, bar, column, and pie graphs. Which user interface would you use for the software? Why?

Software and Multimedia Applications

The quest for multipurpose machines has always challenged inventors. The computer is the most successful and versatile machine in history. The same computer can produce professionally typeset documents, translate French into English, produce music, diagnose diseases, and much more. A computer's versatility is possible because of software. In this unit you will learn how a computer uses software. You will learn the difference between system software and application software, you will find out about trends in multimedia computing, and you will learn about software licenses and copyright agreements.

OBJECTIVES

Understand computer software basics

Define operating systems

Examine operating systems

Review utilities and device drivers

Introduce application software

Introduce productivity software

Explore connectivity, graphics, and presentation software

Explore additional application software

Examine business software

Understand multimedia computing

Learn about purchasing and installing software

Review legal restrictions on software

Understanding computer software basics

COMPUTER SOFTWARE DETERMINES what a computer can do; and in a sense, it transforms a computer from one kind of machine to another—from a drafting station to a typesetting machine, from a flight simulator to a calculator, from a filing system to a music studio, and so on. The distinction between software, programs, and data is important. This lesson defines the terms *computer program, data,* and *software.*

IN MORE DETAIL

A **computer program** is a set of detailed, step-by-step instructions that tell a computer how to solve a problem or carry out a task. The steps in a computer program are written in a language that the computer can interpret or "understand." As you read through the simple computer program in Figure B-1, notice the number of steps required to perform a relatively simple calculation. At one time, computer users had to invest the time and expense of writing many of their own programs. Today, people rarely write computer programs for their personal computers, preferring to select from thousands of commercially written programs.

Data is the words, numbers, and graphics that describe people, events, things, and ideas. Data can be included in the software, like the data for a dictionary in a word-processing program, and you can create data, such as numbers you provide for a graph.

Software is a basic part of a computer system, but the term has more than one definition. In the early days of the computer industry, it became popular to use the term "software" for all the non-hardware components of a computer. In this context, software referred to computer programs and to the data used by the programs. In practice, the term "software" is usually used to describe a commercial product as shown in Figure B-2, which might include more than a single program and might also include data.

In this textbook, **software** is defined as instructions and associated data, stored in electronic format, that direct the computer to accomplish a task. Under this definition, computer software may include more than one computer program, if those programs work together to carry out a task. Also under this definition, software can include data, but data alone is not software. For example, word-processing software might include the data for a dictionary, but the data *you create* using a word processor is not referred to as software.

QUICK TIP

"Software" is a plural noun, so there is no such thing as "softwares." Use the term "software package" when referring to a particular example of software.

Software categories

Because there are so many software titles, categorizing software as either system software or application software is useful. System software helps the computer carry out its basic operating tasks. Application software helps the computer user carry out a task. System software and application software are further divided into subcategories. Use Figure B-3 to help you understand the differences between system and application software.

FIGURES: B-1: *A computer program that converts feet and inches to centimeters*

The first section of the program states that there are 12 inches in a foot and 2.54 centimeters in an inch.

The **var**, or variable, section lists the factors in the problem that might change each time you use the program.

When you use the program, it asks you to enter the length you want to convert.

The program converts the feet and inches you entered into inches.

```
program Conversion(input, output);

const
{
    inchesPerFoot = 12;
    centimetersPerInch = 2.54;

var
{
    feet, inches, lengthInInches: integer;
    centimeters: real;

begin
    write('What is the length in feet and inches?');
    readln(feet, inches);
    lengthInInches :=inchesPerFoot * feet + inches;
    centimeters :=centimetersPerInch * lengthInInches;
    writeln('The length in centimeters is ', centimeters:1:2)
end.
```

Next the program converts the inches into centimeters.

The program then displays the answer.

FIGURE B-2: *Software products*

A **software package** contains disks and a reference manual.

CD-ROMS or disks contain **programs**. For example, some of the programs that might be included in a word processor are a text editor, printing routines, and grammar checker.

The disks or CD might also contain **data**, such as a dictionary of words for the spell checker or a collection of pictures for adding visual interest to documents.

FIGURE B-3: *Software categories*

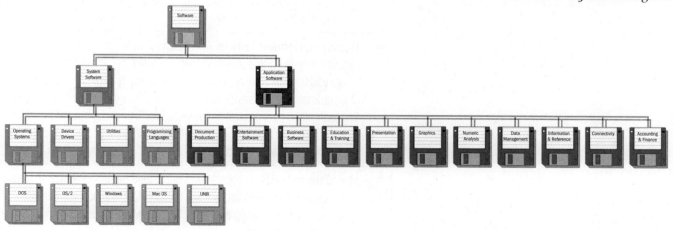

Defining operating systems

AN **OPERATING SYSTEM** IS THE software that controls the computer's use of its hardware resources such as memory and disk storage space. An operating system works like an air traffic controller to coordinate the activities within the computer. Just as an airport cannot function without air traffic controllers, a computer cannot function without an operating system. Figure B-4 helps you envision the relationship between your computer hardware, the operating system, and application software.

IN MORE DETAIL

○—᠇ The operating system provides **external services** that help users start programs, manage stored data, and maintain security. You, as the computer user, control these external functions. The operating system also provides **internal services**. It works behind the scenes while the application software is running to perform tasks essential to the efficient functioning of the computer system. These internal services are not generally under your control, but instead are controlled by the operating system itself. Refer to Figure B-5 to discover more details about what an operating system does.

○—᠇ **Control basic input and output**: An operating system controls the flow of data into and out of the computer, as well as to and from peripheral devices. It routes input to areas of the computer for processing and routes output to the screen, a printer, or any other output device you request.

○—᠇ **Ensure adequate space**: An operating system ensures that adequate space is available for each program that is running and makes sure that each processor quickly performs each program instruction. If you want to run two or more programs at a time—a process called **multi-tasking**—the operating system ensures that each program has adequate space and run time.

○—᠇ **Allocate system resources**: An operating system allocates system resources so programs run smoothly. A system resource is part of a computer system, such as a disk drive, memory, printer, or processor time, that can be used by a computer program.

○—᠇ **Manage storage space**: An operating system keeps track of the data stored on disks and CD-ROMs. Think of your disks as filing cabinets, your data as papers stored in file folders, and the operating system as the filing clerk. The filing clerk takes care of filing a folder when you finish using it. When you need something from your filing cabinet, you ask the filing clerk to get it. The filing clerk knows where to find the folder.

○—᠇ **Detect equipment failure**: An operating system monitors the status of critical computer components to detect failures that affect processing. When you turn on your computer, the operating system checks each of the electronic components and takes a quick inventory of the storage devices. For example, if an electrical component inside your computer fails, the operating system displays a message identifying the problem and does not let you continue with the computing session until the problem is fixed.

○—᠇ **Maintain security**: An operating system also helps maintain the security of the data on the computer system. For example, the operating system might not allow you to access the computer system unless you have a user ID and a password.

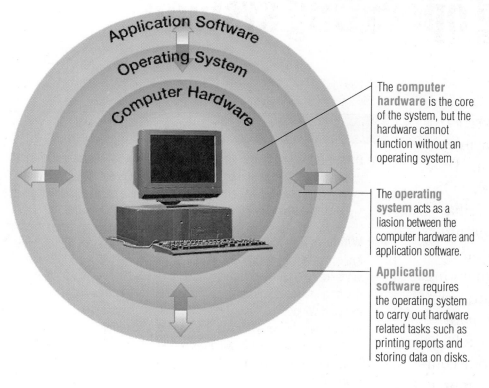

Application Software

Operating System

Computer Hardware

The **computer hardware** is the core of the system, but the hardware cannot function without an operating system.

The **operating system** acts as a liasion between the computer hardware and application software.

Application software requires the operating system to carry out hardware related tasks such as printing reports and storing data on disks.

FIGURE B-5: *Operating system functions*

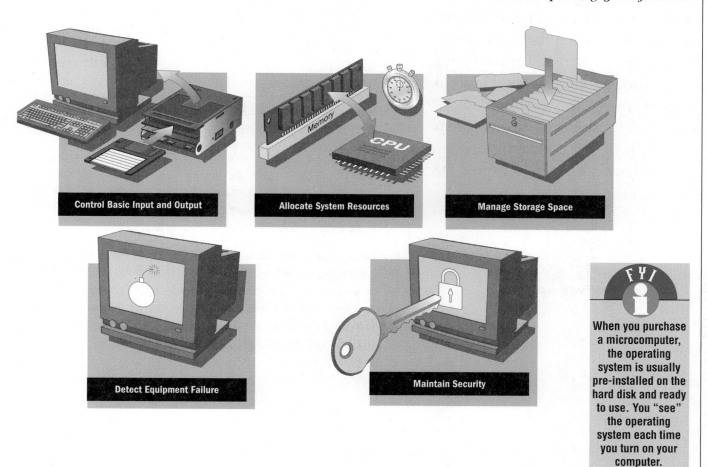

Control Basic Input and Output

Allocate System Resources

Manage Storage Space

Detect Equipment Failure

Maintain Security

When you purchase a microcomputer, the operating system is usually pre-installed on the hard disk and ready to use. You "see" the operating system each time you turn on your computer.

Examining operating systems

YOU MIGHT BE FAMILIAR WITH THE names of the most popular microcomputer operating systems: DOS, Microsoft Windows, and Mac OS. You are less likely to be familiar with the names of minicomputer and mainframe operating systems such as UNIX, VMS, and MVS. Operating systems for micro, mini, and mainframe computers perform many similar tasks. How can you tell which operating system your computer uses? Many microcomputer users can recognize an operating system by looking at the first screen that appears when they turn the computer on or by recognizing the operating system prompt. Figure B-6 shows screens for commonly used operating systems; reviewing them will help you recognize these operating systems when you encounter them in the future.

Operating Systems

The DOS prompt is a distinguishing feature of MS-DOS and PC-DOS.

The cursor shows your place on the screen.

DOS has been replaced by the Windows operating system on most of today's computers.

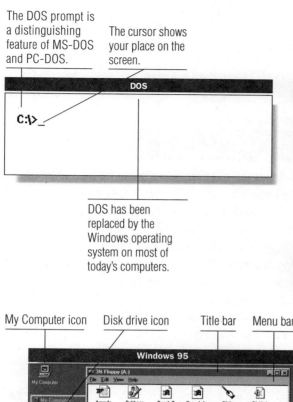

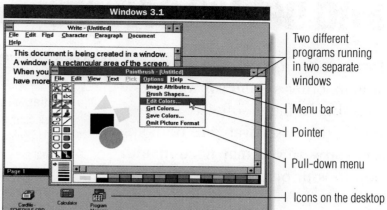

Two different programs running in two separate windows

Menu bar

Pointer

Pull-down menu

Icons on the desktop

My Computer icon   Disk drive icon   Title bar   Menu bar

Pull down menu   Menu bar   Icons

Document icon

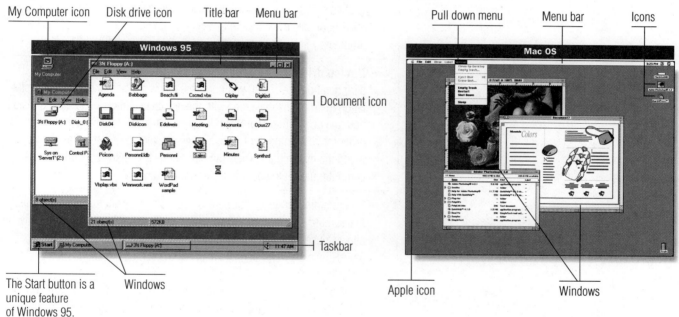

Taskbar

The Start button is a unique feature of Windows 95.

Windows

Apple icon   Windows

UNIX prompt

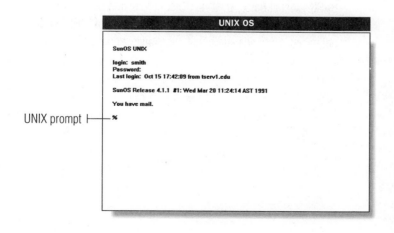

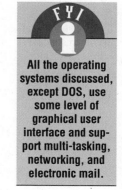

All the operating systems discussed, except DOS, use some level of graphical user interface and support multi-tasking, networking, and electronic mail.

Reviewing utilities and device drivers

IN ADDITION TO THE OPERATING system, other system software is available. Utilities software and device driver software are both system software you may need in addition to your operating system software.

If you have followed the instructions for installing a new device and its device driver but the device does not work, check with the manufacturer. You might need an updated version of the device driver.

IN MORE DETAIL

☞ **Utilities** are system software designed to augment the basic capabilities of your computer's operating system. Utilities provide a computer user with a way to control the allocation and use of hardware resources. Some utilities that are included with the operating system perform tasks such as preparing disks to hold data, providing information about the files on a disk, and copying data from one disk to another. Additional utilities can be purchased separately from software publishers and vendors. For example, Norton Utilities, published by Symantec, is a very popular collection of utilities software. Norton Utilities can retrieve data from damaged disks, make your data more secure by encrypting it, and help you troubleshoot problems with your computer's disk drives.

☞ **Device drivers** are system software that helps the computer control a peripheral device. When you purchase a new peripheral device, the installation instructions that come with the device usually tell you how to install both the device (hardware) and the necessary device drivers (software). In order for your computer to use a device driver, you must install it according to the instructions. Once the device driver is installed correctly, the computer uses it to communicate with the device.

☞ Programming language software is needed if you want to write programs that run on your computer. **Computer programming language** software allows a user to write programs using English-like instructions. These instructions are translated into a format the computer can interpret and directly process.

Most computer users do not need to write programs; therefore, most computers do not include computer programming language software. If you want to write programs, you must purchase programming language software. Today some of the most popular programming languages are BASIC, Visual Basic, C, C++, COBOL, Ada, and FORTRAN. Programming languages such as Java, JavaScript, J++, VBscript, CGI, and Perl are optimized to provide additional interactivity and animations on Web pages.

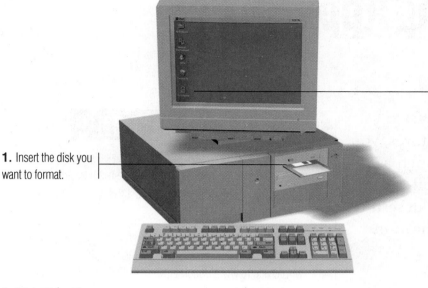

2. Click the **My Computer** icon to select it, then press **Enter**.

1. Insert the disk you want to format.

3. Click the **3½ Floppy (A:) icon** in the My Computer window.

4. Click **File** on the menu bar, then click **Format** to open the Format window.

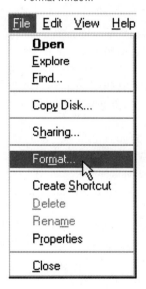

5. Make sure the Capacity box matches the size of the disk you want to format, then click the **Start** button.

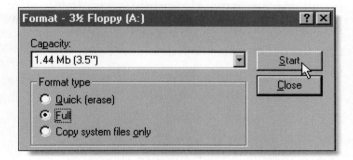

Formatting disks

One of the important tasks performed by an operating system utility is formatting a disk. Each disk must be formatted before you can store data on it. Think of formatting as creating the electronic equivalent of storage shelves. Before you can put things on the shelves, you must assemble the shelves. In a sim- *ilar way, before you can store data on a disk, you must make sure the disk is formatted. Your computer's operating system will provide basic utilities for formatting disks. Although you can buy preformatted disks, you still might need a disk format utility if you are going to use a disk that has not been prefor-* *matted or was formatted for a different type of computer. Figure B-7 shows how to use the format utility for Windows 95.*

Introducing application software

WHEN YOU SHOP FOR COMPUTER software in catalogs or stores, you might encounter terms such as productivity software, suites, and groupware. These terms describe broad categories of application software.

Software categorized as **application software** helps you accomplish a specific task using the computer. Application software helps you produce documents, perform calculations, manage financial resources, create graphics, compose music, play games, maintain files of information, and so on. Application software packages are sometimes referred to simply as **applications**. There is such a vast amount of application software, it is helpful to classify it. Figure B-8 shows an expanded view of the application software branch of the software hierarchy chart.

Application Software

IN MORE DETAIL

⊙━ **Productivity software** helps you work more effectively. Used by individuals, businesses, or organizations, the most popular types of productivity software include word-processing, spreadsheet, data management, and scheduling.

⊙━ The term **suite**, or **office suite**, refers to a number of applications that are packaged together and sold as a unit. A typical suite includes software you would use to write documents, work with numbers, create graphics, and keep track of data.

⊙━ **Groupware** provides a way for more than one person to collaborate on a project. It facilitates group document production, scheduling, and communication. Often it maintains a pool of data that can be shared by members of the workgroup.

⊙━ Software is also categorized by how it is used. One way to classify application software is to use these categories: document production, graphics, presentation, numeric analysis, data management, information and reference, connectivity, education and training, entertainment, accounting and finance, and business.

Document production software helps you create, edit, and publish documents. Connectivity software connects your computer to the Internet, to other computers, and to networks. The names of these functional categories are not consistent. For example, browsing through different software catalogs and perusing the shelves of computer stores, you might notice that connectivity software is sometimes referred to as communications software. As with much of the terminology used daily by nontechnical people, software categories might seem somewhat imprecise.

How much you use a computer, how much time it helps you save, and how much it improves the quality of your work depends on the software you select and use. The array of software applications is extensive, as you can see from the photograph in Figure B-9.

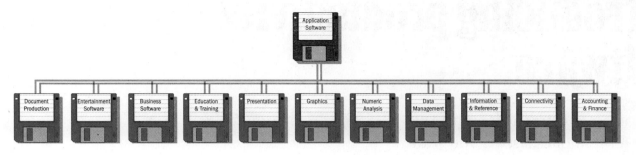

FIGURE B-9: *Extensive array of application software*

When a new software product first becomes available, one type of introductory offer called competitive upgrade is sometimes made to customers. The way this works is that the customers can switch to a new software product for a special price if they own the competitor's product.

Software lifecycle: the difference between versions and revisions

A new software product can be an entirely new product, a revision designed to add minor enhancements and eliminate bugs found in the current version, or a new version with significant enhancements. Before you buy software you should be familiar with the difference between a version and a revision. Revisions are often made available to current owners of the software at little or no cost. However, revisions are often released with little publicity because software companies can't afford to have every owner of the product request the new revision. New software products are usually released with a major advertising campaign. New versions of an existing product are also often released with much fanfare and are often offered at discounted prices to owners of the older versions to encourage them to switch to the new version rather than to a competing product. When a publisher offers a new version of the software you are using, it is usually a good idea to upgrade.

Introducing productivity software

DOCUMENT PRODUCTION SOFTWARE, as the term implies, assists you with composing, editing, designing, and printing documents. The three most popular types of document production software are word-processing, desktop publishing, and Web authoring software. **Numeric analysis software** simplifies tasks such as constructing numeric models of physical and social systems, and then analyzing those models to predict trends and understand patterns. Numeric analysis software includes spreadsheet, statistical, and graphing packages. **Data management software** stores, finds, updates, organizes, and reports information. Table B-1 lists some of the popular packages in each software category.

Desktop Publishing

3-D Graphics

IN MORE DETAIL

○━ **Word-processing software** gives you the ability to create, spell check, edit, and format a document on the screen before you commit it to paper. Because documents are in an electronic format, it is easy to reuse them, share them, and even collaborate on them.

○━ **Desktop publishing software** takes word-processing software one step further by helping you use graphic design techniques to enhance the format and appearance of a document. Although many page layout and design features are available in today's word-processing software, desktop publishing software provides more sophisticated features to help you produce professional quality output for newspapers, newsletters, brochures, magazines, and books.

○━ **Web authoring software** helps you design and develop customized Web pages that you can publish electronically on the Internet. Today's Web page design software helps authors avoid the technical task of authoring pages using hypertext markup language (HTML) by providing tools to compose the text for a Web page, assemble graphical elements, and automatically generate HTML tags.

○━ **Spreadsheet software** performs calculations based on numbers and formulas that you enter. A handy tool for quick calculations or more complex computational projects, spreadsheet software also allows you to create graphical views of your data. Spreadsheet software is frequently used by financial analysts to examine investment opportunities, by managers to create budgets, by educators to keep track of student grades, and by individuals to track personal finances.

○━ **Graphing software** transforms complex data into meaningful graphs that allow you to visualize and explore data. Graphing software performs basic calculations and statistical procedures and gives you added formatting flexibility to create more visually attractive graphs.

○━ **Statistical software** helps you analyze large sets of data to discover patterns and relationships. It is a helpful tool for summarizing survey results, test scores, experiment results, or population data. Most statistical software includes graphing capability so you can display and explore your data visually. See Figure B-10.

○━ A **database** is a collection of related files. **Database management software** provides a flexible way to join and summarize the information in more than one file. A **search engine** is capable of finding any record in a file management or database program that you specify in a fraction of a second. Search engine software that runs on your computer is sometimes called a **personal search engine**.

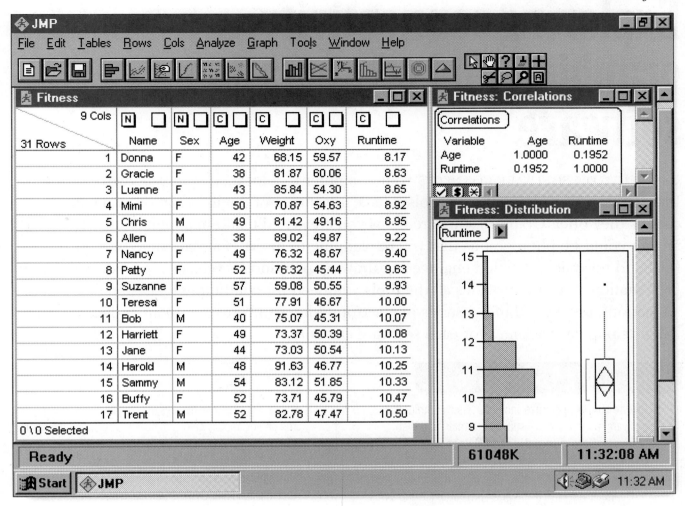

TABLE B-1: *Popular productivity software packages*

SOFTWARE CATEGORY	POPULAR PACKAGES
Word-processing software	Microsoft Word, Claris WordPerfect, Lotus Word Pro
Desktop publishing software	Quark XPress, Adobe PageMaker, Corel VENTURA, Microsoft Publisher
Web page authoring software	Claris Home Page, Microsoft Front Page
Spreadsheet software	Microsoft Excel, Lotus 1-2-3
Statistical software	SPSS, JMP, Data Desk
Database management software	Microsoft Access, Lotus Approach, Claris FileMaker Pro
Personal search engine software	ForeFront WebSeeker, Symantec FastFind

Exploring connectivity, graphics, and presentation software

CONNECTIVITY SOFTWARE CONNECTS your computer to a local computer network or the Internet, and provides you with tools to take advantage of the information and communications they offer. Graphics software helps you create, edit, and manipulate images. These images could be photographs that you're planning to insert in a real estate brochure, a freehand portrait, a detailed engineering drawing of a motorcycle, or a cartoon animation. Presentation software provides all the tools you need for combining text, graphics, graphs, animations, and sound into a series of electronic slides to "present" to an audience. Table B-2 lists popular packages for each software category.

IN MORE DETAIL

- **Connectivity software** includes basic communications software, remote control software, e-mail, and Web browsers. **Communications software** interacts with your computer's modem to dial and establish a connection with a remote computer.

  Suppose you have a computer in your office and a notebook computer at home. You're home one evening and need some information that's stored on your office computer. If both computers have modems and the computer in your office is on, you can use **remote control software** to establish a connection between the two machines.

- **E-mail** is, perhaps, the heart of Internet activity. It helps you stay in touch with friends, relatives, colleagues, and business associates. **E-mail software** manages your computer mailbox.

- To access information on the Web, you need communications software and an additional software package called a Web browser. **Web browser software** allows you to view Web pages and manages the links that you use to jump from one document to the next. Browsers use add-on software called **plug-ins** to provide you with specialized data such as video, music, or realistic 3-D walkthroughs of buildings and fantasy worlds.

- The **graphics software** you select depends on the type of image you're creating. Once you know the type of image you need, you can read software descriptions and reviews to find the graphics software that's right for you.

Photos. Photo editing features of graphics software help you crop photos, modify colors, remove red eye, combine elements from more than one photo, and apply special effects.

Paintings. Painting features allow you to create and edit bitmapped images on screen that look like water colors, oil paint, chalk, ink, or charcoal.

Drawings and 3-D objects. Images composed of lines and filled shapes are called **vector graphics**. Their advantage is the relatively small amount of storage space they require. Vector graphic images are easy to manipulate as shown in Figure B-11.

Animations and videos. Animation software streamlines the process of creating a series of still frames that produce an animated sequence. You can use graphics software to capture videos from your television, camcorder, or VCR. The software helps you edit the video by cutting footage and adding sound.

- **Presentation software** uses the computer to create snazzy speeches and presentations. Most presentation software includes collections of graphics and sounds that can enhance your presentation. After you create your slides, use the presentation software to organize them into a compelling visual story for your audience, as shown in Figure B-12.

Web Browsers

Presentations

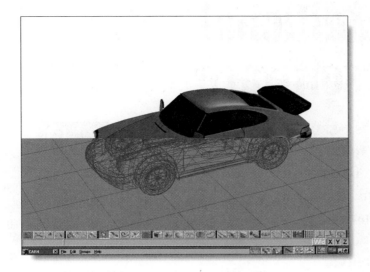

FIGURE B-12: *A projection device displaying slides on a screen*

◄ You can display slides on a color monitor for a one-on-one presentation or run a slide show for a group using a computer projection device.

You can output a presentation as overhead transparencies, paper copies, or 35 mm slides.

TABLE B-2: *Popular connectivity, graphics, and presentation software packages*

SOFTWARE CATEGORY	POPULAR PACKAGES
Remote control software	Procomm Rapid Remote, pcANYWHERE, ReachOut, LapLink, Remotely Possible
E-mail software	Qualcomm Eudora, Microsoft Internet Mail, Lotus Notes
Web browser software	Netscape Navigator, Microsoft Internet Explorer
Graphics software	Adobe Illustrator, CorelDRAW, Micrografx Graphics Suite
Presentation software	Microsoft PowerPoint, Lotus Freelance Graphics

The process of converting videos into a format that can be stored on a computer disk is called digitizing.

Exploring additional application software

DO YOUR KEYBOARDING SKILLS NEED a bit of polish? Do you want to help your children learn and have fun at the same time? Are you the head of human resources and find that your company's managers don't understand all the fuss about diversity? Where will you turn for help? You might very well find your answers in education and training software. Are computers changing the way we spend our spare time? Clearly, entertainment software is big business as well as fun business. Do you need to locate facts, figures, and other information? Information and reference software can help you do just that.

InfoWeb

Games Galore

IN MORE DETAIL

- **Education and training software** helps you learn and perfect new skills. Educational software teaches basic reading and counting skills. Instruction is presented as games, and different levels of play adapt to age and ability. **Exam preparation software**, such as that shown in Figure B-13 is available for standardized tests such as the SAT, GMAT, and LSAT. Software is available to help learn languages, learn how to play the piano, prepare for standardized tests, improve keyboarding skills, and even learn about managing in a diverse workplace. Education and training software is often called **edutainment software** because it blurs some of the lines between learning and game playing.

- **Entertainment software** includes games of all sorts, software toys, simulations, and software designed to help you enjoy hobbies and leisure activities. Generally, game software is divided into these main categories: action, adventure/role playing, classic/puzzle, simulations, and strategy/war games. Many of the most popular games are available in multiple formats. You can play them alone on your PC, in multiplayer environments via the Internet, or on a standalone game console, such as Nintendo.

- **Adventure/role playing software** has realistic 3-D graphics, allows players to interact with the environment, and has weapons and monsters galore. Action games like the one shown in Figure B-14 are similar to arcade games.

- **Simulation software** covers a broad range of interests. For example, with the simulation software, SimCity, you develop a city. The computer populates your city with *Simmies* that clog your streets, trash your parks, and threaten to remove you from office if you don't supply better city services.

- **Information and reference software** provides you with a collection of information and a way to access that information. The information and reference software category spans a broad range of applications from encyclopedias to medical reference, from map software to trip planners, and from cookbooks to telephone books. Information and reference software is generally shipped on a CD-ROM because of the quantity of information it includes. With many of these products, links between the CD-ROM and a Web site provide updates to information that has gone out of date. See Figure B-15 for an example of reference software.

- **Mapping and trip planning software** is useful for both individuals and business people. With software like Streetfinder from Rand McNally, you can type an address, then view and print a detailed map. With this type of software, you never again need to feel bewildered when you move to or travel to a new city.

FIGURE B-13: *Exam preparation software*

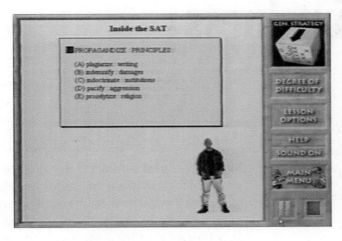

FIGURE B-14: *Adventure/role playing software*

FIGURE B-15: *Reference software*

▶ Select Phone claims to contain 100 million U.S. business and residential listings, which can be searched by name, address, city, state, zip code, phone number, geographic location, or county.

The fact that information and reference software includes massive amounts of data distinguishes it from data management software, which contains no data.

Examining business software

IN ADDITION TO PRODUCTIVITY software, another major category of application software is **business software**, which helps businesses and organizations efficiently accomplish routine tasks. The emphasis with business software is on organization-wide tasks such as accounting, personnel management, and inventory control. This software can help you keep track of your money and progress toward financial goals. Often, business software is divided into two categories: horizontal market software and vertical market software.

Money Management

IN MORE DETAIL

☞ **Horizontal market software:** A "horizontal market" is a group of different types of businesses that, despite their differences, have some of the same software needs. Horizontal market software refers to generic software packages that can be used by many different kinds of businesses. Accounting and payroll applications are good examples of horizontal market software. Accounting software helps businesses maintain a set of books to track income and expenses and to generate financial reports. Some accounting and finance software is geared toward very small businesses and even individuals. Figure B-16 shows a best selling personal finance software program. Payroll software keeps track of employee hours and produces the reports required by the government for income tax reporting.

☞ **Vertical market software:** A "vertical market" is a group of similar businesses—travel agencies, for example—that need specialized software. Vertical market software is designed for specialized tasks in a specific market or business. The construction industry has developed many specialized applications, as shown in Figure B-17. Vertical market software, such as estimating software designed specifically for construction businesses, can automate the task of gathering labor and materials costs as well as perform the calculations needed to arrive at a price estimate. Other examples of vertical market software include the software that handles billing and insurance for medical practices, and software that tracks the amount of time attorneys spend on each case.

Buying computers with bundled software

The price of most computers includes the operating system, so if you purchase an IBM-compatible computer, you can expect that the latest versions of DOS and Windows will be pre-installed on the hard drive. Many computer vendors also include applications software such as a word processor or personal finance manager. Multimedia computer systems usually include several CD-ROMs such as encyclopedias, fact books, and games. All other factors being equal, a system with bundled software will cost slightly more than a system without bundled software. However, if the software meets your needs, the slight increase in price is generally less than you would pay if you bought the software separately.

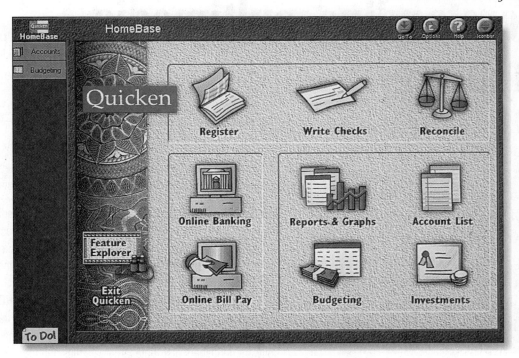

FIGURE B-17: *Vertical market software*

Understanding multimedia computing

THE TERM MULTIMEDIA ISN'T REALLY anything new. It refers to the integrated use of multiple media, such as slides, video tapes, audio tapes, records, CD-ROMs, and photos. Computer technology is replacing or controlling many of the technologies and media that were previously used for multimedia presentations. Advances in computer technology have made it possible to combine text, photo images, speech, music, animated sequences, and video into a single interactive computer presentation. To display realistic graphic and video, your computer system must have a high-resolution monitor and a CD-ROM drive. Figure B-18 shows a computer well-equipped for multimedia.

Multimedia

Computer History Hypermedia

Hypertext

MMX

IN MORE DETAIL

- **Multimedia**: This term is defined as an integrated collection of computer-based text, graphics, sound, animation, photo images, and video.

- **Multimedia applications**: One example of a multimedia application is a multimedia encyclopedia. It contains articles and pictures on a wide range of topics like a traditional encyclopedia, but a multimedia encyclopedia has more. A multimedia encyclopedia provides you with a rich selection of text, graphics, sound, animation, and video.

  Most multimedia applications are shipped on a CD-ROM because the graphics, sound, and video require large amounts of storage space. However, not everything shipped on CD-ROM is multimedia. Many software publishers distribute large data files and non-multimedia software on CD-ROM because one CD-ROM is more convenient and more cost effective than 20 or 30 floppy disks.

- **Multimedia kits**: If you already have a computer, but it is not equipped for multimedia, you can add multimedia capabilities by purchasing a multimedia kit that contains a CD-ROM drive and sound card.

- **Hypertext**: Hypertext is a key element of many multimedia products, and it has been used effectively in non-multimedia products as well. You are likely to use hypertext with many computer applications. The term hypertext was coined by Ted Nelson in 1965 to describe the idea of documents that could be linked to each other. Linked documents make it possible for a reader to jump from a passage in one document to a related passage in another document.

- **Hypermedia**: The links in today's applications often involve graphics, sound, and video, as well as text. This type of multimedia hypertext is referred to as hypermedia. Hypertext and hypermedia are important computer-based tools because they help you easily follow a path that makes sense to you through a large selection of text, graphical, audio, and video information. See Figure B-19 for an example of a multimedia encyclopedia with hypermedia.

  Multimedia has become so popular that many of today's computers have a special multimedia processor called an **MMX chip**. This chip speeds up multimedia features such as sound and video. However, only specially written software can take advantage of the special multimedia features on this chip.

A high-resolution color monitor displays graphics, animations, and videos.

A fast processor and lots of memory can speed up searches and video displays.

Earphones can be used as an alternative to speakers.

Speakers are attached to a sound card for audio playback.

A CD-ROM drive plays multimedia software.

FIGURE B-19: *A multimedia encyclopedia with hypermedia*

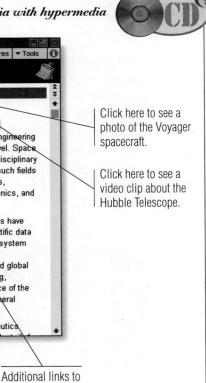

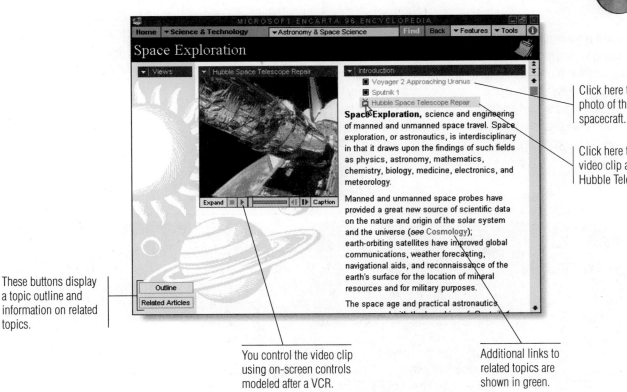

MICROSOFT ENCARTA 96 ENCYCLOPEDIA

Home ▾Science & Technology ▾Astronomy & Space Science Find Back ▾Features ▾Tools

Space Exploration

▾ Views | Hubble Space Telescope Repair | ▾ Introduction

■ Voyager 2 Approaching Uranus
■ Sputnik 1
☒ Hubble Space Telescope Repair

Space Exploration, science and engineering of manned and unmanned space travel. Space exploration, or astronautics, is interdisciplinary in that it draws upon the findings of such fields as physics, astronomy, mathematics, chemistry, biology, medicine, electronics, and meteorology.

Manned and unmanned space probes have provided a great new source of scientific data on the nature and origin of the solar system and the universe (*see* Cosmology); earth-orbiting satellites have improved global communications, weather forecasting, navigational aids, and reconnaissance of the earth's surface for the location of mineral resources and for military purposes.

The space age and practical astronautics

Expand | ◀ ▶ | Caption

Outline
Related Articles

Click here to see a photo of the Voyager spacecraft.

Click here to see a video clip about the Hubble Telescope.

These buttons display a topic outline and information on related topics.

You control the video clip using on-screen controls modeled after a VCR.

Additional links to related topics are shown in green.

SOFTWARE AND MULTIMEDIA APPLICATIONS ◀ B-21

Learning about purchasing and installing software

MANY MICROCOMPUTERS ARE SOLD WITH PRE-INSTALLED SYSTEM AND APPLICATION SOFTWARE, but eventually most computer users want to purchase and install additional software.

IN MORE DETAIL

☞ **Software compatibility**: Before you install software or a multimedia application, you must make sure it is compatible with your computer system. To be compatible, the software must be written for the type of computer you use and for the operating system that is installed on your computer. For example, Microsoft Word is available for both IBM-compatible and Apple Macintosh computers, but these are two separate versions of the software. You cannot use the Macintosh version of Microsoft Word on your IBM-compatible computer.

Once you know the software is compatible with the type of computer you use, you must make sure the software will work with your operating system. If your IBM-compatible computer uses the DOS operating system, you must select DOS software. If your computer uses the Microsoft Windows operating system, you can select DOS or Windows software because Windows can run software designed for both of these operating systems.

☞ **System requirements** specify the minimum hardware and operating system requirements needed for a software product to work correctly. You must also make sure your computer meets or exceeds the system requirements specified by the software. The system requirements are usually listed on the outside of the software package, as shown in Figure B-20, and might also be explained in more detail in the software reference manual.

☞ **Software distribution**: Computer software is usually shipped on 3.5" disks, called **distribution disks**, or on CD-ROMs. Instead of using software directly from the distribution disk, you usually install the software on your hard disk. During the installation process, programs and data files for the software are copied to the hard disk of your computer system.

☞ **Software installation**: There is not a consistent installation procedure for software, so each software application might require different steps. Figure B-21 shows an installation process.

☞ **CD-ROM software installation**: Installing software from a CD-ROM frequently differs from the installation process for software shipped on floppy disks. You should read the installation instructions to find out how to install software distributed on a CD-ROM. Because of the large size of CD-ROM software, you generally access the CD-ROM programs and data directly from the CD-ROM instead of from a hard disk. In this case, a very limited amount of information must be copied to your hard disk during the installation process.

Downward compatibility

Operating systems go through numerous versions. A higher version number indicates a more recent version; for example, DOS 6.0 is a more recent version than DOS 5.0. Windows 95 is a more recent version than Windows 3.1. Operating systems are usually **downwardly compatible**, which means that you can use application software designed for earlier versions of the operating system, but not those designed for later versions. For example, you can generally use software that requires Windows 3.1 if Windows 95 is installed on your computer. However, your software might not work correctly if it requires Windows 95 but you only have Windows 3.1 on your computer. If you want to use software that requires a newer version of your operating system, you must first purchase and install an operating system upgrade.

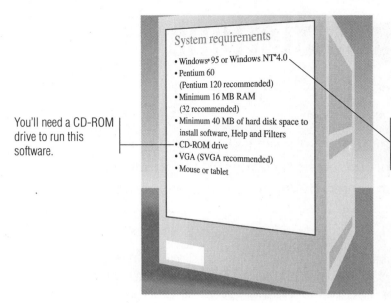

System requirements

- Windows® 95 or Windows NT®4.0
- Pentium 60
  (Pentium 120 recommended)
- Minimum 16 MB RAM
  (32 recommended)
- Minimum 40 MB of hard disk space to install software, Help and Filters
- CD-ROM drive
- VGA (SVGA recommended)
- Mouse or tablet

You'll need a CD-ROM drive to run this software.

Your computer must have Windows 95 or a newer operating system.

FIGURE B-21: *An installation process*

☒ **Full Installation**
☐ **Customized Installation**

▲ **1.** Insert the setup disk and start the setup program.

▲ **2.** Select Full or Customized Installation. For a full installation, the setup program copies all the files and data from the distribution disks to the hard disk of your computer system. A full installation provides you with access to all the features of the software.

During a customized installation, the setup program displays a list of software features for your selection. After you select the features you want, the setup program copies only the selected program and data files to your hard disk. A customized installation can save space on your hard disk.

▲ **3.** If the software includes multiple disks, insert each disk in the specified drive when the setup program tells you to do so.

▲ **4.** When the setup program is finished, start the program you have just installed to be sure it works.

▲ **5.** Fill out the registration card and send it in. When you send in the card, you become a registered user. The perks of being a registered user vary with each software publisher,

but they might include receiving free technical support, product information, or discounts on new versions of the software.

Reviewing legal restrictions on software

JUST BECAUSE YOU CAN COPY SOFTWARE DOESN'T MAKE IT LEGAL TO DO SO. LIKE BOOKS and movies, most computer software is protected by a copyright. In addition to copyright protection, computer software is often protected by the terms of a software license.

IN MORE DETAIL

☞ Copyrighted material: A **copyright** is a form of legal protection that grants certain exclusive rights to the author of a program or the owner of the copyright. The owner of the copyright has the exclusive right to copy the software, to distribute or sell the software, and to modify the software. If you are not the owner of the copyright, it is illegal to copy, distribute, or sell the software unless you obtain permission from the copyright owner.

☞ Copyright Act: The Copyright Act, a section of which is shown in Figure B-22, states under what circumstances you can and cannot legally copy copyrighted software. When you purchase copyrighted software, you do not become the owner of the copyright. Instead, you own only a copy of the software. Your purchase allows you to use the software on your computer, but you cannot make additional copies to give away or sell. The restrictions stated by the Copyright Act apply only to the programs and data included as part of the original software. The data you enter—the documents, files, and graphics you create—can be copied without restriction.

☞ Copyright symbol: Copyrighted materials, such as software, display a copyright notice that contains the word "Copyright" or the © symbol, the year of publication, and the name of the copyright holder. When you start a computer program, the copyright notice usually appears on the first screen; it is also usually printed in the reference manual.

☞ Licensed software: A **software license** is a legal contract that defines the ways in which you may use a computer program. For microcomputer software, you will find the license on the outside of the package, on a separate card inside the package, or in the reference manual. Mainframe software licenses are usually a separate legal document, negotiated between the software publisher and a corporate buyer.

It is important to distinguish the concept of licensing from that of purchasing a copy of software. When you pay for licensed software, you do not buy and then own a copy of the software. Instead, you are buying permission to use the software. You can think of it as renting software, rather than buying it. Refer to Table B-3 for a description of the various software licenses that are available.

☞ **Public domain software** is owned by the public rather than by the author. The program is available to everyone for use without restriction. Public domain software may be freely copied, distributed, and even resold. The primary restriction on public domain software is that you are not allowed to apply for a copyright on it. Public domain software is fairly rare. It is frequently confused with shareware, because it is legal to copy and distribute both public domain software and shareware.

☞ **Shareware** is copyrighted software marketed under a "try before you buy" policy. Shareware usually includes a license that allows you to use the software for a trial period. If you want to continue to use it, you must become a registered user by sending in a registration fee. When you send in the fee to become a registered shareware user, you are granted a license to use the software beyond the trial period. You might also receive a free copy of the latest version of the software or printed documentation for the program.

A typical shareware policy allows you to make copies of the software and distribute them to others. This is a fairly effective marketing strategy that provides low cost advertising. Unfortunately, registration fee payment is based on the honor system, so many shareware authors collect only a fraction of the payment they deserve for their programming efforts.

Copyright

Shareware

Anti-Piracy

Only the copyright owner can reproduce, sell, or distribute the copyrighted software. Note that this section was written before computer software copyright became an issue, thus the reference to phonorecords, but not software.

It is legal to copy the software from distribution disks to the hard disk of your computer system so you can access the software from the hard disk.

It is legal to make an extra copy of the software in case the copy you are using becomes damaged.

Section 117 - Right to Copy or Adapt Computer Programs in Limited Circumstances

Section 106. Exclusive Rights in Copyrighted Works

Subject to sections 107 through 118, the owner of copyright under this title has the exclusive rights to do and to authorize any of the following:

(1) to reproduce the copyrighted work in copies or phonorecords;

(2) to prepare derivative works based upon the copyrighted work;

(3) to distribute copies or phonorecords of the copyrighted work to the public by sale or other transfer of ownership, or by rental, lease, or lending…

Notwithstanding the provisions of section 106, it is not an infringement for the owner of a copy of a computer program to make or authorize the making of another copy or adaptation of the computer program provided:

1. that such a new copy or adaptation is created as an essential step in the utilization of the computer program in conjunction with a machine that is used in no other manner; or

2. that such new copy or adaptation is for archival purposes only and that all archival copies are destroyed in the event that continued possession of the computer program should cease to be rightful. Any exact copies prepared in accordance with the provisions of this section may be leased, sold or otherwise transferred, along with the copy from which such copies were prepared, only as part of the lease, sale, or other transfer of all rights in the program. Adaptations so prepared may be transferred only with the authorization of the copyright owner.

If you give away or sell the software, you cannot legally keep a copy.

You cannot legally sell or give away modified copies of the software without permission.

FYI

People who illegally copy, distribute, or modify software are sometimes referred to as software pirates, and the illegal copies they create are referred to as pirated software.

TABLE B-3: *License agreements*

TYPE OF LICENSE	DESCRIPTION
Shrink wrap license	When you purchase computer software, the disks or CD-ROM in the package are usually sealed in an envelope or plastic shrink wrapping; opening the wrapping signifies your agreement to the terms of the software license; shrink wrap licensing is one of the most frequently used methods for providing legal protection for computer software.
Single-user license	Limits the use of the software to one user at a time. Most commercial software is distributed under a single-user license.
Multiple-user license	Allows more than one person to use a particular software package. This type of license is useful in cases where users each have their own personalized version of the software. It is generally priced per user, but the price for each user is typically less than the price of a single-user license.
Concurrent-use license	Allows a certain number of copies of the software to be used at the same time. For example, if an organization with a computer network has a concurrent-use license for five copies of a word processor, at any one time up to five employees may use the software. Concurrent-use licenses are usually priced in increments.
Site license	Generally allows the software to be used on any and all computers at a specific location, such as within a corporate office building or on a university campus. A site license is priced at a flat rate, for example, $5,000 per site.

Concepts Review

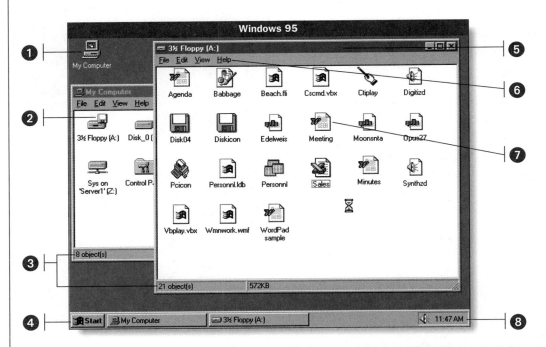

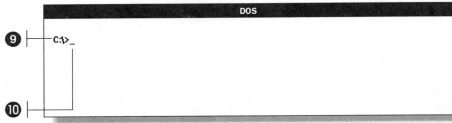

Label each element shown in Figure B-23.

1. _____

2. _____

3. _____

4. _____

5. _____

6. _____

7. _____

8. _____

9. _____

10. _____

Match each statement with the term it describes:

11. ___ Software
12. ___ Copyright notice
13. ___ Windows
14. ___ Utilities
15. ___ CD-ROM
16. ___ Public domain

a. © 1998 Course Technology, Inc.

b. Stores multimedia software

c. System software used for tasks such as formatting a disk

d. Author relinquished copyright to software

e. Operating system for an IBM computer

f. Instructions and associated data stored in electronic format

Fill in the best answer:

17. When you type a report or enter the information for a mailing list, you are creating a(n) _____.

18. _____ software helps the computer carry out its basic operating tasks; _____ software helps the computer user carry out a task.

19. The set of instructions that tell a computer how to convert inches to centimeters is called a computer _____.

20. If you want to run more than one program at a time, you must use an operating system with _____ capabilities.

21. The DOS, Windows, and Mac OS operating systems are typically used on _____ systems.

22. _____ software helps the computer accomplish such tasks as preparing a disk for data, providing information about the files on a disk, copying data from one disk to another, and retrieving data from damaged disks.

23. Examples of _____ software include word-processing, spreadsheet, data management, and scheduling.

24. Multimedia applications combine media such as _____, _____, _____, _____, _____, and _____.

25. You can add multimedia capabilities to your computer by purchasing a(n) _____ that contains a CD-ROM drive and sound card.

26. The "try before you buy" policy refers to _____ licenses.

27. A(n) _____ allows the software to be used by any and all computers at a specific location and is priced at a flat rate.

INDEPENDENT CHALLENGE 1

In this unit you learned how utility software helps you direct the operating system to accomplish tasks such as formatting a disk. This is a good time to try it out. If your lab computers have the Windows 95 operating system, you can do this independent challenge on your own by referring to Figure B-7. Otherwise, your instructor will need to help you.

To complete this independent challenge:

1. Write down the steps you followed to format a disk.

2. Be sure to include any steps to insert or swap disks.

3. Write down any screen messages that appear during the format process.

INDEPENDENT CHALLENGE 2

In this unit you learned how to identify microcomputer operating systems by looking at the main screen and prompt. In this independent challenge you will explore more about the operating system in your school computer lab. If you have more than one lab or your computer uses more than one operating system, your instructor should tell you which one to use for the independent challenge.

To complete this independent challenge:

1. Find out which operating system is used in your school computer lab. Be sure you find out the type and version. You can obtain this information online from one of the computers. If you see a command-line user interface, try typing **ver** and then pressing **Enter**. If you see a graphical user interface, try clicking the Apple menu or click the Help menu, then select Help About.

2. Once you know the operating system used in your school lab, use the operating system reference manual and library resources to answer the following questions:

   a. Which operating system and version is used in your school lab?

   b. What company publishes the operating system software?

c. When was the first version of this operating system introduced?

d. Does this operating system have a command-line user interface or a graphical user interface?

e. Does this operating system support multi-tasking?

f. Do you need a password to use the computers in your school lab? Even if you do not need to use a password, does the operating system provide some way to secure access to the computers?

g. How much does the publisher of this operating system usually charge for upgrades if you are a registered user?

INDEPENDENT CHALLENGE 3

Using a computer to maintain your schedule—what could be better? The computer warns you if you try to make two appointments at the same time, gives you advance notice of your appointments, and keeps track of your "To Do" list by bringing forward the tasks you didn't complete yesterday. Well, one slight problem...where is your computer when your friend sees you in the "caf" and sets up a date, or your colleague stops you in the hall to let you know about the sales meeting next Tuesday? Better switch to one of those pocket schedulers, right? Nope. Too limiting...not enough memory and a really small screen. So why not carry around a small device that communicates to your computer using an infrared beam? Is this the solution? What other solutions have been tried? Can you think of a better one?

This independent challenge is a good idea for a term paper. You will need to research the software packages that give you scheduling capabilities, along with some of the hardware innovations that provide you with the option to run scheduling software on something other than a desktop computer. When you write your paper, be sure you include references to the resources you use.

You learned in this unit that most users do not need to write programs in order to use their computers. But you also learned that computer programming is a challenging career field. In this independent challenge you will find out more about computer programming careers.

Computer programming jobs are often listed on the back pages of computer magazines, in professional journals, and on career bulletin boards on the Internet. Some of the best sources of information are:

Infoworld magazine
The professional journal, *Communications of the ACM*
The newspaper *San Jose Mercury News* and its Internet site at **http://www.sjmercury.com**
The Internet Monster Board at **http://www.monster.com**
The Internet Career Mosaic at **http://www.careermosaic.com**
The Internet site at **http://www.jobweb.com** has a list of other Internet job listings

To complete this independent challenge:

1. Locate three advertisements for computer programming jobs. Photocopy or get a computer printout of the ads. Create a table like the one that follows, and fill it in for each of the three job openings you found.

	Job 1	Job 2	Job 3
Educational requirements			
Work experience required			
Programming languages required			
Mainframe, mini, or microcomputer			
Company name			
Starting salary			

There are so many software packages that it is difficult to get an idea of what's available unless you take a look through current computer magazines and software catalogs. This independent challenge has two parts. You can do either one or both as your instructor assigns. Part 1 helps you discover the breadth of available software applications. Part 2 helps you research an application or operating system in more depth. You will be able to find the information for this independent challenge in computer magazines in your library. If you have access to the Internet, check out Computer Express at **http://www.cexpress.com**.

To complete this independent challenge:

1. Find an ad for a computer vendor that sells a large variety of software. Jot down the name of the vendor and where you found the ad. List the categories the vendor uses to classify software and the number of software packages in each category.

2. Select one type of software from the following categories: operating systems, utilities, document production, graphics, presentation, electronic mail, desktop publishing, spreadsheet, database, accounting, or web authoring.

3. Read a comparison review of software packages in the category you select.

4. Next try to locate and photocopy ads for each of the products in the review. Look through the software vendor ads to find the best price for each product.

5. Finally, write a one- or two-page summary explaining your purchase recommendation.

INDEPENDENT CHALLENGE 6

What application software would you recommend? In this independent challenge you will decide what application software is most appropriate for a task. You can do this independent challenge on your own or discuss it in a small group.

To complete this independent challenge:

For each of the scenarios that follow, decide which application software would accomplish the task most effectively:

a. You want to keep track of your monthly expenses and try to figure out ways to save some money.

b. As the leader of an international team of researchers studying migration patterns of Canada geese, you want all the team members to communicate their findings to each other quickly.

c. You are the office manager for a department of a large Fortune 500 company. One of your responsibilities is to arrange meetings and schedule facilities for the employees in your department.

d. As a partner in a law firm, you need to draft and modify legal briefs.

e. You are in charge of a fund-raising campaign, and you need to track the names, addresses, phone numbers, and donations made by contributors.

f. You are going to design and produce the printed program for a community theater play listing the actors, director, lighting specialists, and so on.

g. A sales manager for a cosmetics company wants to motivate the sales force by graphically showing the increases in consumer spending over the past five years.

h. The marketing specialist for a new software company wants to send out announcements to 150 computer magazines.

i. The owners of five golf courses in Jackson County want to design a promotional brochure that can be distributed to tourists in restaurants and hotels.

j. The owner of a small business wants to keep track of ongoing income and expenses and print out monthly profit and loss statements.

k. The superintendent of a local school system wants to prepare a press release explaining why student test scores were 5 percent below the national average.

l. A contractor wants to calculate his cost for materials needed to build a new community center.

m. A college student wants to send out customized letters addressed to 20 prospective employers.

n. The parents of three children want to decide whether they should invest money for their children's education in the stock market or whether they should buy into their state's prepaid tuition plan.

o. The director of fund-raising for a large nonprofit organization wants to keep a list of prospective donors.

MULTIMEDIA LAB

Multimedia brings together text, graphics, sound, animation, video, and photo images. If you are using the CD version of this book, you have already seen multimedia in action. In this Lab you will learn how to apply multimedia and then have the chance to see what it might be like to design some aspects of multimedia projects.

1. Click the Steps button to learn about multimedia development. As you proceed through the Steps, answer the Quick Check questions. After you complete the Steps, you will see a Quick Check Report. Follow the instructions on the screen to print this report.

2. In Explore, browse through the STS-79 Multimedia Mission Log. How many videos are included in the Multimedia Mission Log? The image on the Mission Profile page is a vector drawing, what happens when you enlarge it?

3. Listen to the sound track on Day 3. Is this a WAV file or a MIDI file? Why do you think so? Is this a synthesized sound or a digitized sound? Listen to the sound track on page 8. Can you tell if this is a WAV file or a MIDI file?

4. Suppose you were hired as a multimedia designer for a multimedia series on targeting fourth- and fifth-grade students. Describe the changes you would make to the Multimedia Mission Log so it would be suitable for these students. Also, include a sketch showing a screen from your revised design.

5. When you view the Mission Log on your computer, do you see palette flash? Why or why not? If you see palette flash, list the images that flash.

6. Multimedia can be effectively applied to projects, such as Encyclopedias, atlases, and animated storybooks; to computer-based training for foreign languages, first aid, or software applications; for games and sports simulations; for business presentations; for personal albums, scrapbooks, and baby books; for product catalogs and Web pages.

Suppose you were hired to create one of these projects. Write a one-paragraph description of the project you would be creating. Describe some of the multimedia elements you would include. For each of the elements indicate its source and whether you would need to obtain permission for its use. Finally, sketch a screen or two showing your completed project.

COMPUTER HISTORY HYPERMEDIA LAB

The Computer History Hypermedia Lab is an example of a multimedia hypertext, or hypermedia that contains text, pictures, and recordings that trace the origins of computers. This Lab provides you with two benefits: first, you learn how to use hypermedia links, and second, you learn about some of the events that took place as the computer age dawned.

1. Click the Steps button to learn how to use the Computer History Hypermedia Lab. As you proceed through the Steps, answer all the Quick Check questions that appear. After you complete the Steps, you will see a Quick Check Summary Report. Follow the instructions on the screen to print this report.

2. Click the Explore button. Find the name and date for each of the following:

   a. First automatic adding machine

   b. First electronic computer

   c. First fully electronic stored-program computer

   d. First widely used high-level programming language

   e. First microprocessor

   f. First microcomputer

   g. First word-processing program

   h. First spreadsheet program

3. Select one of the following computer pioneers and write a one-page paper about that person's contribution to the computer industry: Grace Hopper, Charles Babbage, Augusta Ada, Jack Kilby, Thomas Watson, or J. Presper Eckert.

4. Use this Lab to research the history of the computer. Based on your research, write a paper explaining how you would respond to the question, "Who invented the computer?"

Productivity in the Office, Home, and School

Unit C

COMPUTER USERS GLADLY TACKLE THE COMPLEX interface of word-processing software so they can create professional-looking documents. Spreadsheet software seems to make it relatively painless for novices to set up complex numerical calculations. Computer users organize their information by creating and maintaining databases. This chapter takes a look at how these software tools affect the computing you do today and how they have affected our society.

OBJECTIVES

Introduce document production software

Improve the quality of writing

Present documents

Examine the power of publishing

Automate document production

Introduce spreadsheets and worksheets

Understand spreadsheet intelligence

Present numerical data

Understand databases

Search databases for information

Put it all together

Introducing document production software

DESPITE THE POPULARITY OF RADIO, television, and film, documents remain an integral part of our society and culture and an important component of our everyday lives. Initially, documents were hand-copied. See Figure C-1. As literacy has increased throughout the world, the tools of document production have changed. Typing was once a special-ized skill practiced mainly by women in secretarial positions, but it is now a skill possessed to some degree by a sizable percentage of the population in highly literate nations. The perva-siveness of this skill stems from the popularity of computerized document production.

Literacy

IN MORE DETAIL

☞ **Document production software** includes word-processing software, desktop publishing software, e-mail editors, and the software that helps you create home pages and hypertext documents for the Internet's World Wide Web. Document production software facilitates correcting typing and spelling errors and makes it easy to let your ideas flow because it automati-cally handles many of the writing tasks. See Figure C-2 for reasons to use a computer for writing.

☞ Steps in creating a document using a word processor:
* Type the text.
* Edit the document until you are satisfied with the content and writing style.
* Format and print the document.
* Transfer your document to desktop publishing software to complete the layout printing.

☞ **Word wrap** takes care of where to break lines so you don't need to worry about typing off the edge of the paper. Even after you have typed an entire document, adjusting the size of your right, left, top, and bottom **margins** is simple. The lines will break automatically, readjusting for the new margins.

☞ Sections of your document are referred to as **blocks**. You can easily insert text, cut sections of text, and move entire paragraphs or pages to improve the structure and logical flow of a document. Deleting or moving blocks are sometimes referred to as **block operations**.

☞ Some writers find that the limited amount of text displayed on the screen prevents them from getting a good look at the overall flow of ideas throughout the document. An **outliner** helps you develop a document as a hierarchy of headings and subheadings.

FIGURE C-1: *Technology has had a significant impact on document production tools*

FIGURE C-2: *Some reasons for using a computer for your writing*

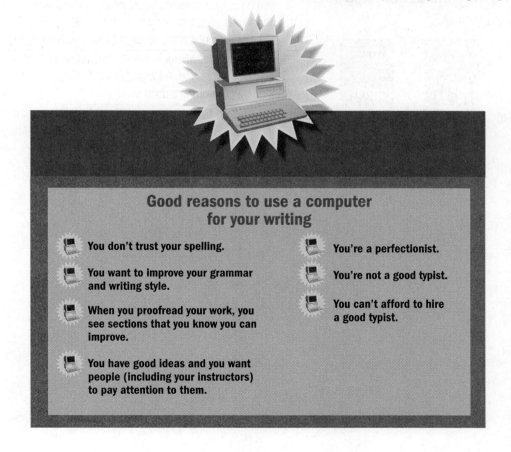

Good reasons to use a computer for your writing

- You don't trust your spelling.
- You want to improve your grammar and writing style.
- When you proofread your work, you see sections that you know you can improve.
- You have good ideas and you want people (including your instructors) to pay attention to them.
- You're a perfectionist.
- You're not a good typist.
- You can't afford to hire a good typist.

Improving the quality of writing

CRITICS HAVE IMPLIED THAT INSTEAD of helping writers, computers have somehow lowered literary standards. However, people, not computers, create documents. When used skillfully, computerized document production tools can help you improve the quality of your writing. With such tools, it is easy to edit the first draft of your document to refine its overall structure, and then zero in to make detailed improvements to your sentence structure and word usage.

Word Processing

Improve Your Writing

Grammar

IN MORE DETAIL

- Once you have taken care of the overall structure of your document, you can turn to the details of spelling, grammar, and word usage. A document with spelling and grammar errors reflects poorly on the writer. An **in-line spell checker** checks the spelling of each word as you type, as shown in Figure C-3. A **spell checker** looks through your entire document any time you activate it. You would generally use this type of spell checker when you have completed your first draft, and then again just before you print. See Figure C-4. A spell checker works by looking for each word from your document in a list called a dictionary. If the word from your document is in the dictionary, the spell checker considers the word correctly spelled. If the word is not in the dictionary, the word is identified as misspelled.

- A **grammar checker** is a feature of most word processors that coaches you on correct sentence structure and word usage. Think of a grammar checker as an assistant that will proofread your document, point out potential trouble spots, and suggest alternatives. Refer to Figure C-5.

- The online **thesaurus** helps you find more descriptive words to clarify and enliven your writing. A thesaurus will find synonyms and antonyms for a highlighted word in a document.

- The **search feature** is used to hunt for all the occurrences of any problem word. For each occurrence, you can decide to leave it or revise it. **Search and replace** is useful if you want to substitute one word or phrase for another.

FIGURE C-3: *The in-line spell checker*

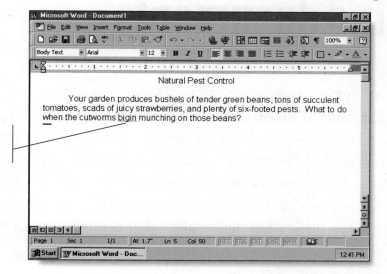

A wiggly red line indicates a possible spelling error.

FIGURE C-4: *Using a spell checker*

The spell checker finds a misspelled word and highlights it.

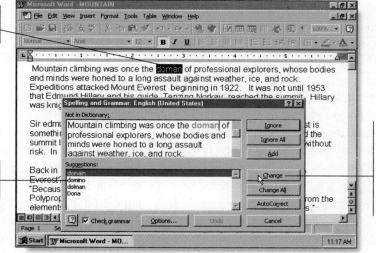

The spell checker offers some correctly spelled options.

You can select one of the options to replace the misspelling using the Change button. To leave the word as is, you would click the Ignore button.

FIGURE C-5: *Using a grammar checker*

The grammar checker highlights the sentence it is currently checking.

The problem is indicated in green.

A suggestion for improvement is provided.

If requested, the grammar checker explains the basis for its suggestion.

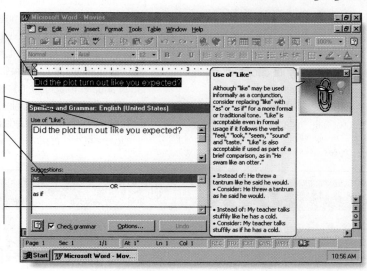

QUICK TIP

At first, focus on expressing your ideas. When you're satisfied with the content of your document, you can shift your focus to the details of how your document will look on paper.

Presenting documents

BEFORE THE PRINTING PRESS, DOCUMENTS WERE HAND COPIED. MANY OF THE HAND-COPIED documents called **illuminated manuscripts** were works of art in addition to being a means of communicating information. Today modern printing techniques make it cost effective to produce beautiful documents that are available to everyone in libraries, bookstores, and newsstands. Document production software includes formatting tools such as document templates, wizards, fonts, styles, borders, and clip art, which make it possible for individuals to produce professionally formatted and illustrated documents.

IN MORE DETAIL

- A **document template** is a preformatted document into which you type your text. Format settings such as margins, line spacing, heading fonts, and type size have all been set up for you. Figure C-6 shows some of the document templates typically available with today's word-processing software.

- Some software goes a step further than templates by furnishing you with **document wizards** that not only provide you with a document format, but take you step-by-step through the process of entering the text for a wide variety of documents. For example, to create an entry-level resume, you might find it easy to use a resume wizard like the one shown in Figure C-7.

- A **font** is a typeface or style of lettering. Fonts are designed by typesetters and artists. Your document production software generally supplies you with many fonts. Typeset fonts, such as Times New Roman and Arial, make your document look formal and professionally produced. Research studies show that sans serif fonts are easier to read on the computer screen. See Table C-1.

- You can manipulate the look of your document by adjusting the line spacing, margins, indents, tabs, and borders. Larger margins and double-spacing generate white space, make your document appear less dense, and make your document seem easier to read. The margins for most papers and reports should be set at 1 inch or 1.5 inches. Most word processors set the line spacing at an appropriate distance for the font size.

- **Justification** defines how the letters and words are spaced across each line. Typeset documents can be fully justified so the text on the right margin as well as on the left margin is aligned evenly.

- **Columns** enhance readability and **tables** organize data. In document production terminology, columns generally mean newspaper-style layout of paragraphs of text. Tables arrange data in a grid of rows and columns. Tables are more appropriate than columns for numeric data and for lists of information.

- When you summarize or list information, or even when you type your answers to homework questions, your points will stand out if you use **hanging indents**, **bulleted lists**, or **numbered lists**. The details on this textbook page are an example of a bulleted list with hanging indents.

- To add visual interest to your documents, incorporate borders, rules, and graphics. A **border** is a box around text or graphics, usually around a title, heading, or table. A **rule** is a line, usually positioned under text. Rules can be horizontal, vertical or diagonal. The thinnest rule is one pixel thick and called a **hairline rule**. A **frame** is an invisible box that can contain text or graphics. You can position it anywhere on the page. Generally you can flow text around the frame and layer frames one on top of another to achieve complex layout effects, as shown in Figure C-8. **Graphics** are pictures and illustrations. **Clip-art collections** provide hundreds of images that you have permission to use in non-commercial works.

TABLE C-1: *Understanding font styles*

CHARACTER	FONT STYLE	FONTS WITH THIS STYLE
E	serif	Times New Roman, Courier, Garamond
E	sans serif	Helvetica, Arial, **Impact**

Serif

Serif

FIGURE C-6: *Document templates*

Template categories include letters, memos, reports, and publications.

Within each category you can choose from several different templates.

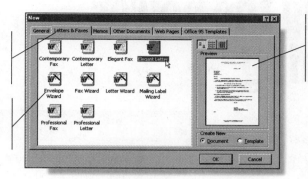

The preview shows you an example of a document created using the selected template.

FIGURE C-7: *Entry-level resume wizard*

The Resume Wizard prompts you to enter your name, address, and phone number, which it uses to create the heading for your resume.

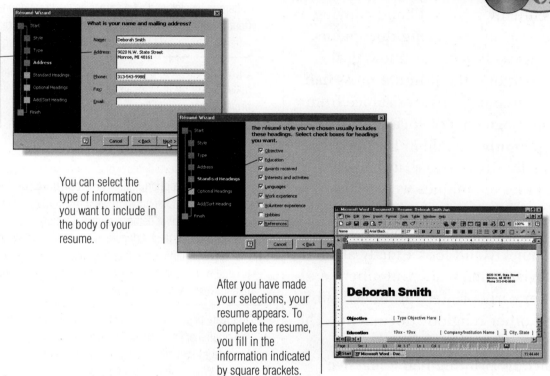

You can select the type of information you want to include in the body of your resume.

After you have made your selections, your resume appears. To complete the resume, you fill in the information indicated by square brackets.

FIGURE C-8: *Frames*

Frames can contain graphics or text.

A frame can be positioned anywhere on the page—even in the top margin.

Text runs around this frame set in the middle of the page.

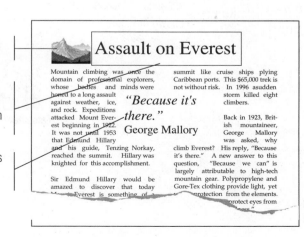

Assault on Everest

Mountain climbing was once the domain of professional explorers, whose bodies and minds were honed to a long assault against weather, ice, and rock. Expeditions attacked Mount Everest beginning in 1922. It was not until 1953 that Edmund Hillary and his guide, Tenzing Norkay, reached the summit. Hillary was knighted for this accomplishment.

Sir Edmund Hillary would be amazed to discover that today Mount Everest is something of a

"Because it's there."
George Mallory

summit like cruise ships plying Caribbean ports. This $65,000 trek is not without risk. In 1996 a sudden storm killed eight climbers.

Back in 1923, British mountaineer, George Mallory was asked, why climb Everest? His reply, "Because it's there." A new answer to this question, "Because we can" is largely attributable to high-tech mountain gear. Polypropylene and Gore-Tex clothing provide light, yet ... protection from the elements. ... protect eyes from ...

You can find graphics on the Internet. With the right equipment, you can also scan pictures from books and magazines. Be sure you check for permission before you borrow any graphic for your documents.

Examining the power of publishing

PRINTING WITH MOVEABLE TYPE existed in Asia as early as 1000 A.D. However, until Johann Gutenberg demonstrated his moveable type printing press in 1448, this technology did not exist in Europe. Printing eventually replaced hand copying as a means of producing documents, but as with many technological innovations, the printing press had to overcome initial resistance from some segments of society. Apparently, people in Europe were initially suspicious that the new printing techniques were black magic. How, they wondered, could copies of documents be produced so quickly and look exactly alike? To alleviate such fears, Gutenberg and other early printers produced Bibles and other religious documents. The change from hand copying to machine printing had a massive effect on Western culture and civilization by making information available to all who could read.

IN MORE DETAIL

☞ Thomas Paine harnessed the power of the printed word in 1776 when he sold 500,000 copies of a 50-page pamphlet, *Common Sense*. This document asserted that it was just common sense for the American colonies to become independent from Great Britain. Six months later, the Declaration of Independence was signed. Thomas Paine and his compatriot, Thomas Jefferson, envisioned a free press as the cornerstone of a free society. They hoped that publishing would spread ideas, foster dialogues among diverse interest groups, and help to establish a common social agenda.

☞ Early expectations were that computerized document production would make it easy for individuals, not just publishing companies, to produce professional-quality books and pamphlets. Word processors have made it possible for individuals to create more documents, such as newsletters and manuscripts.

☞ The expedient development of a worldwide data communications network has opened up opportunities for **electronic publishing**. Electronic documents are easy to send, store, and manipulate. They might even bring us closer to the global democracy that Thomas Paine envisioned. Today virtually anyone can post a document on the World Wide Web, send an e-mail message, or participate in online discussion groups. The power of the printed word seems to be evolving into the power of the electronically published word as demonstrated in Figure C-9.

☞ To create pages for the World Wide Web, many word processors and desktop publishers automatically generate an HTML (HyperText Markup Language) formatted document from any document you have entered and stored. When you create a Web page, your goal should be to effectively combine and format basic Web elements to create a visual display that enhances the content of your page. The basic elements of a Web page are shown in Figure C-10.

Computer History

FIGURE C-9: *Electronic document on the Web*

▶Many activists believed that certain provisions of the U.S. Telecommunications Act of 1996 would limit freedom of speech on the Internet. Massive protests on electronic forums and a well-engineered law-suit prompted the Supreme Court to declare that many parts of the Act were unconstitutional.

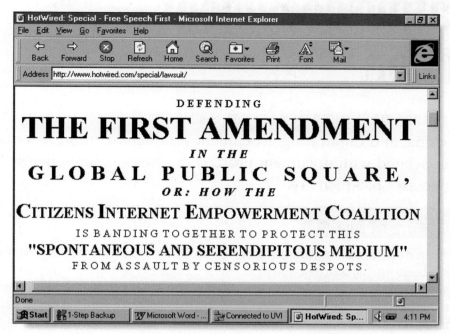

FIGURE C-10: *Web page elements*

Address for the Web page

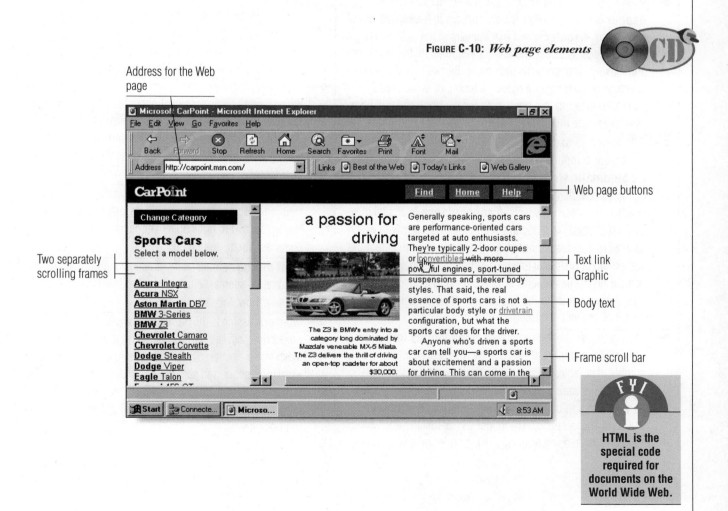

Web page buttons

Two separately scrolling frames

Text link

Graphic

Body text

Frame scroll bar

HTML is the special code required for documents on the World Wide Web.

Automating document production

Who Wrote It?

COMPUTERS ARE PRETTY TALENTED WHEN IT COMES TO REPETITIVE TASKS SUCH AS COUNTING, numbering, searching, and duplicating. Document production automates many of the repetitive tasks associated with document production. Automating repetitive tasks saves time and increases productivity.

IN MORE DETAIL

- As you edit a document and change its format, you might remove or insert large sections of text, reducing or expanding the page count. Or you may decide to double space the document, doubling the page count. **Automatic page numbering**, sometimes called **pagination**, means the computer numbers and renumbers the pages as you edit and format your document.

- Page numbers are often included in a header or footer. A **header** is text that automatically appears in the top margin of every page. A **footer** is text that appears in the bottom margin of every page. Headers and footers help identify the document and make your documents look more like published works which often have either a header, a footer, or both on each page. The footer in this book includes the book and unit titles as well as page numbers.

- If it's important to determine the number of words in a document, your computer can count the words in a document with the **automatic word count** feature of your document production software. Another use for a computer's ability to count words is for literary analysis. A **concordance** is an alphabetized list of words in a document and the frequency with which each word appears. Concordance has been used to determine authorship of historical and contemporary documents by comparing the frequencies of words used in a document by an unknown author to the frequencies of words used in a document of known authorship.

- Most grammar checkers have built in **readability formulas** that count the number of words in each sentence and the number of syllables per word. Most writers aim for a seventh- or eighth-grade reading level on documents for the general public. As you write, you can use readability formulas to target your writing to your audience. The longer your sentences and words, the higher the reading level required to understand your writing.

- Scholarly documents often require **footnotes** that contain citations for works mentioned in the text. As you revise your text, the footnotes need to stay associated with their source in the text and must be numbered sequentially. Your document production software includes footnoting facilities that position and number the footnotes even if you move blocks of text. Some software can gather citations at the end of a document creating **end notes** and print them in order of their appearance in the document or in alphabetical order. Some word processors even have wizards that help you enter your citations in the correct format depending on whether they are books or magazine articles.

- Many people have come to expect that all documents, not just those created by professional publishers, have **indexes** and **tables of contents**. Most document production software will automatically generate an index and table of contents, and then automatically update them as you edit your document.

- **Boilerplate text** refers to information that remains constant from one document to the next. Law offices frequently use boilerplate text to draw up legal documents for wills, divorces, trusts, and so on.

- **Mail merge** automates the process of producing customized documents such as letters and advertising flyers. Figure C-11 explains how it works.

- Word processing is the most commonly-used document production software. Word-processing technology includes inexpensive electronic typewriters, more expensive personal word processors, and personal computers, which are the most versatile and most costly of the three. You can use Figure C-12 to compare the features of today's word-processing technologies.

FIGURE C-11: *A mail merge*

► To set up a mail merge, you create a document containing specially marked "blanks." You also create a file of information that goes in the blanks each time the document is printed. Your document production software will merge the document and the information.

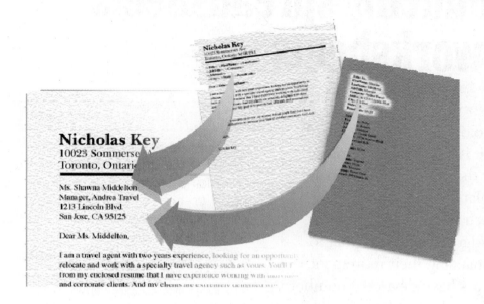

FIGURE C-12: *Word-processing technology*

◄ A **personal computer** set up for word processing includes hard and floppy disk drives, and a screen. Word-processing software and a printer might need to be purchased separately.

▼ A **personal word processor** includes a larger screen, floppy disk drive, and printer, but does not run a large variety of other software.

▼ An **electronic typewriter** has a 3 to 5 line screen display, stores a few pages in memory, and has a built in printer.

Introducing spreadsheets and worksheets

THE UNITED STATES IS ONE OF THE most technological societies on earth. Therefore, it is somewhat surprising to find that there are people who are afraid to balance their checkbooks, calculate their tax returns, work out expense budgets, or decide what to do about financing their retirement. Entrepreneurs have devised a number of tools to ease the burden of making calculations. To date, the most ambitious of these tools is the computerized spreadsheet.

Spreadsheet software is applicable in most professions. Here are but a few examples of professionals who use spreadsheets and how they use them: educators to keep grades and analyze test scores; farmers to keep track of crop yields, to calculate the amount of seed to purchase, and to estimate expenses and profits for the coming year; contractors to make bids on construction projects; scientists to analyze data from experiments. Spreadsheets can even be used at home to help you balance your checkbook, keep track of household expenses, track your savings and investments, and calculate your taxes.

Spreadsheet Tips

Spreadsheets

IN MORE DETAIL

☞ A **spreadsheet** is a numerical model or representation of a real situation. For example, your checkbook register is a sort of spreadsheet because it is a numerical representation of the cash flowing in and out of your bank account. One expert describes spreadsheets as "intuitive, natural, usable tools for financial analysis, business and mathematical modeling, decision making, simulation, and problem solving."

☞ A handheld calculator might be useful for simple calculations, but it becomes less convenient as you deal with more numbers and as your calculations get more complex. The biggest disadvantage of most calculators is that the numbers you entered are stored, but you can't see them. You can't verify if they're accurate. Also, it is difficult to change the numbers you have entered without starting the whole calculation over again. See Figure C-13. By contrast, if you use spreadsheet software, all your numbers are visible on the screen, and they are easy to change. You can print your results as a nicely formatted report, you can convert your numbers into a graph, and you can save your work and revise it later. You can easily incorporate your calculations and results into other electronic documents, post them as Web pages, and e-mail them to your colleagues.

☞ You use spreadsheet software to create an on-screen spreadsheet called a worksheet. A **worksheet** is based on a grid of columns and rows. Each **column** is lettered and each **row** is numbered. The intersection of a column and row is called a **cell**. Each cell has a unique **cell address** derived from its column and row location. For example, the upper-left cell in a worksheet is cell A1 because it is in column A of row 1. Figure C-14 illustrates a simple worksheet.

☞ A cell can contain a number, text, or a formula. A **number** is a value that you want to use in a calculation. **Text** is used for the worksheet title, for labels that identify the numbers, and for numbers used as text, such as social security numbers. A **formula** tells the computer how to use the contents of cells in calculations. You can use formulas to add, subtract, multiply, and divide numbers.

☞ Building a worksheet from scratch requires thought and planning so that you end up with an accurate and well-organized worksheet. When you create your own worksheets, use these guidelines: determine the main purpose of the worksheet; list the information available to solve the problem; make a list of the calculations you'll need; enter numbers and labels in the cells; enter the formulas; test the worksheet; save and print the worksheet. Figure C-15 shows a completed worksheet before printing.

FIGURE C-13: *Using a calculator*

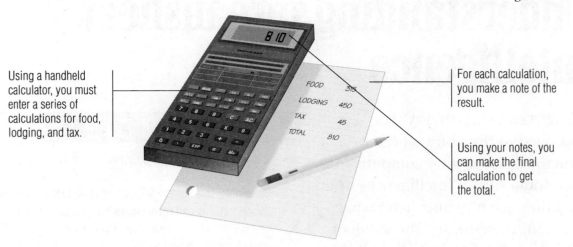

Using a handheld calculator, you must enter a series of calculations for food, lodging, and tax.

For each calculation, you make a note of the result.

Using your notes, you can make the final calculation to get the total.

FIGURE C-14: *A typical worksheet displays numbers and text in a grid of rows and columns*

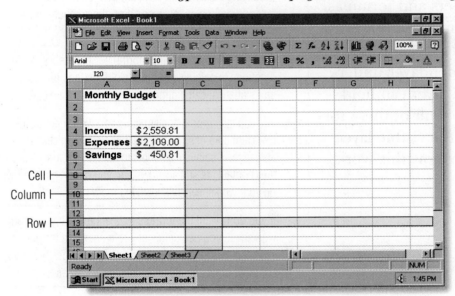

Cell

Column

Row

FIGURE C-15: *A completed worksheet*

Every worksheet should have a title.

Documentation helps you keep track of revisions and explains how the sheet was created in case someone else needs to revise it.

Labels identify data.

These numbers are used in the formulas in column C.

In the cells that contain formulas, only the results appear.

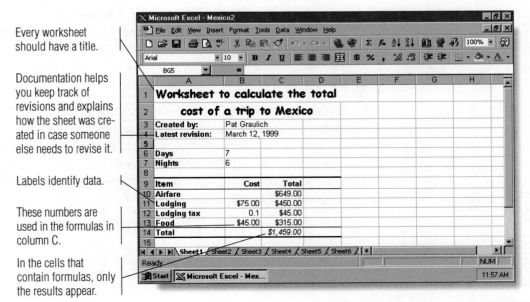

Understanding spreadsheet intelligence

COMPUTER TECHNOLOGY HAS improved to the point where it sometimes seems that computers do have some sort of intelligence—or at least they seem to anticipate what you want them to do. The value of spreadsheet software is the way it handles the numbers and formulas in a worksheet. Think of the worksheet as having two layers—the layer you see and a hidden layer underneath. The hidden layer can hold formulas, but the result of these formulas appears on the visible layer. Figure C-16 shows how this works.

▭━ Whenever you add or change something in a cell, the spreadsheet calculates all the formulas. This means that the results displayed on your worksheet always reflect the current figures contained in the cells. **Formulas** can include numbers and **references** to other cells. This is what gives a spreadsheet such flexibility. If you have a formula that says "subtract the contents of cell B5 from the contents of B4," it doesn't matter what those cells contain. Modifying the text, numbers, and formulas in a worksheet is easy. When you enter new numbers in a worksheet, the computer recalculates all the formulas, keeping the results up-to-date.

▭━ A **function** is a predefined formula. Spreadsheet software has built-in functions to calculate hundreds of functions for mathematical, financial, and statistical calculations.

▭━ You can also modify the structure of a worksheet by inserting and deleting rows and columns, or moving the contents of cells to other cells. The spreadsheet software attempts to adjust your formulas so the cell references they contain are still accurate, and you do not have to revise all the formulas on your worksheet, as shown in Figure C-17.

▭━ If you don't want the formula to change when you change the structure of a worksheet, you can define any reference in a formula as an absolute reference. An **absolute reference** never changes when you insert rows or columns or when you copy or move formulas.

▭━ **Shortcuts** are another example of spreadsheet intelligence. Spreadsheet software contains many handy shortcuts to help simplify the process of creating, editing, and formatting a worksheet. **Fill operations** continue a series you have started. Type "January" in one cell and "February" in the next, and then use a fill operation, and the spreadsheet will automatically enter the rest of the months in the next 10 cells. Figure C-18 shows an example of a fill operation.

▭━ **Testing**, called **auditing** in spreadsheet jargon, is an important step in creating worksheets. To test a worksheet, you can enter some test data for which you already know the result. Most spreadsheet software includes auditing features to help you find references to empty cells, cells not referenced, formulas that reference themselves and cause a never-ending calculating loop, or values that fall outside specified limits for certain calculations.

FIGURE C-16: *Formulas work behind the scenes*

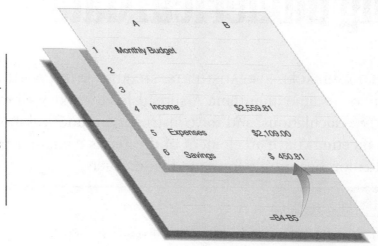

The formula =B4-B5 works behind the scenes to tell the computer to subtract the number in cell B5 from the number in cell B4. The formula is located in cell B6. What appears in cell B6 is not the formula but its results.

FIGURE C-17: *Formulas adjust when you insert or delete cells*

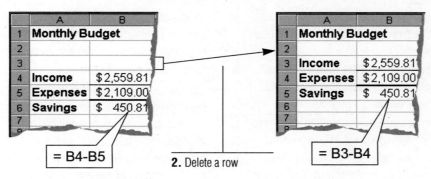

= B4-B5

2. Delete a row

= B3-B4

3. The spreadsheet software automatically changes the formula, which is now in B5, to reflect the new location of the Income and Expenses numbers.

1. A formula in cell B6 calculates savings based on numbers in cells B4 and B5.

FIGURE C-18: *Filling cells with data*

Type the first few numbers in a series.

The spreadsheet software will fill in the rest of the series.

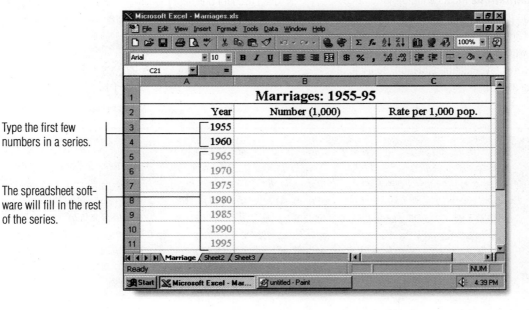

QUICK TIP

You are responsible for the accuracy of spreadsheets you create. Don't rely on your worksheet until you test it.

Presenting numerical data

AS THE BUSINESS WORLD EMBRACED SPREADSHEETS, SHARING THEM WITH COLLEAGUES, employees, and customers became important. A spreadsheet works well for recording and graphing data, for making calculations, and for constructing numerical models of the real world. Today business meetings have an element of theater as computer projection devices display full-screen, full-color, beautifully formatted worksheets.

IN MORE DETAIL

☞ A **template** is a worksheet form created by professionals who have done all the formatting and formulas for you. If you decide to use a template, you simply select the template you want and then fill it in with your numbers. One popular spreadsheet program offers templates for the following tasks: tracking a household budget, creating purchase orders, deciding on the best car lease option, calculating monthly loan payments, creating a business plan, recording business expenses while you travel, invoicing customers, providing customers with a sales quote, and tracking the time you work on various projects.

☞ Spreadsheet software provides you with formatting options to improve the appearance of your worksheet. Worksheets that you intend to print might be formatted differently from worksheets that you intend to view only on the screen. Worksheets that you want to project for presentations often require a format different from printed worksheets. Worksheets for routine calculations are much handier to use if you can see all the information without scrolling. Figure C-19 provides some tips for improving a printed worksheet.

☞ Worksheets for **presentations** must be legible when displayed by a projection device. You might consider a larger type size—one that can be easily viewed from the back of the room in which your worksheet will be projected. Scrolling is usually not desirable in a presentation situation, so try to fit the worksheet on one screen.

☞ The use of color will make your presentation more interesting and help to highlight important data on the worksheet. However, if you are also planning to print your worksheet in black and white, select your colors carefully. Colors appear in shades of gray on a black-and-white printout. Some colors produce a dark shade of gray that obscures labels and numbers. Figure C-20 provides some examples of worksheets formatted for presentations.

☞ Spreadsheet software is characterized by its ability to easily create professional-looking graphs and charts. **Graphs** provide a quick summary or overview of a set of data. Trends that might be difficult to detect in columns of figures come into focus when skillfully graphed. When you design graphs, you have a responsibility to your audience to create a visual representation of the truth. Although you might not intentionally design a graph to "lie," it is all too easy to design a graph that implies something other than the truth.

☞ **Spreadsheet modeling** means setting up numbers in a worksheet to describe a real-world situation. Spreadsheets are often used for business modeling. The process of setting up a model and experimenting with different numbers is often referred to as **what-if analysis**.

INFOWEB

Numbers Can Lie

How did it all begin?

Computerized spreadsheet software was invented in 1978 by a Harvard Business School student, Dan Bricklin. Many computer historians believe that his software, called VisiCalc, not only launched a new genre of computer software, but also put a rocket under the fledgling microcomputer industry and launched the Digital Age. Before the availability of VisiCalc, consumers couldn't think of much use for a personal computer. VisiCalc provided business people with a handy tool for making calculations without visiting a statistician or accountant. It contained all the basic elements of today's electronic spreadsheets— a screen-based grid of rows and columns, predefined functions, automatic calculations, formatting options, and rudimentary "intelligence" for copying and replicating formulas.

FIGURE C-19: *Formatting for a printed worksheet*

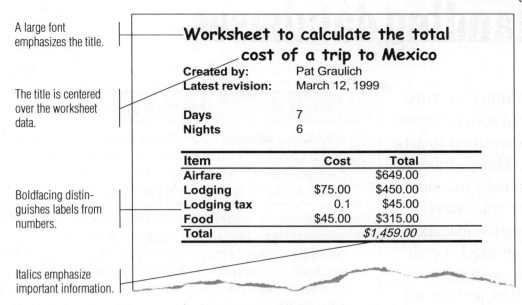

A large font emphasizes the title.

The title is centered over the worksheet data.

Boldfacing distinguishes labels from numbers.

Italics emphasize important information.

Worksheet to calculate the total cost of a trip to Mexico

| Created by: | Pat Graulich |
| Latest revision: | March 12, 1999 |

| Days | 7 |
| Nights | 6 |

Item	Cost	Total
Airfare		$649.00
Lodging	$75.00	$450.00
Lodging tax	0.1	$45.00
Food	$45.00	$315.00
Total		*$1,459.00*

FIGURE C-20: *Worksheets for presentations*

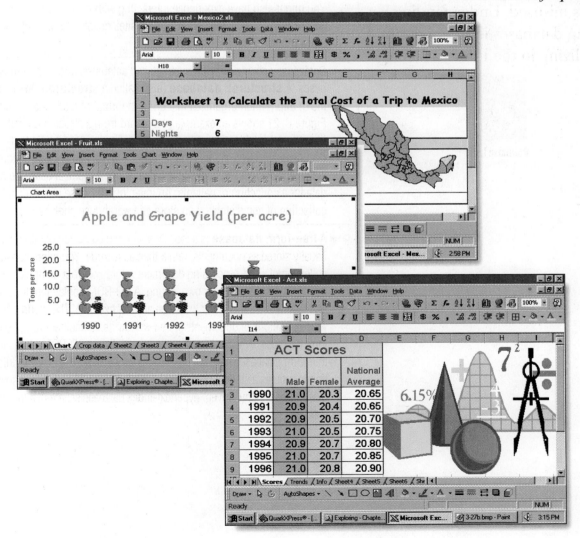

Understanding databases

SOMETIME IN THE MIDDLE OF THIS century our industrial society began to evolve into an information society. The way we live has changed in many ways. We more frequently interact with information, we enter careers connected to information management, we increasingly attach a cash value to information, we tend to depend on information, and we are becoming aware of the potential problems that can occur when information is misused. Understanding and using databases is an important skill for living in the Information Age.

Database Lab

FIGURE C-21: *A structured database*

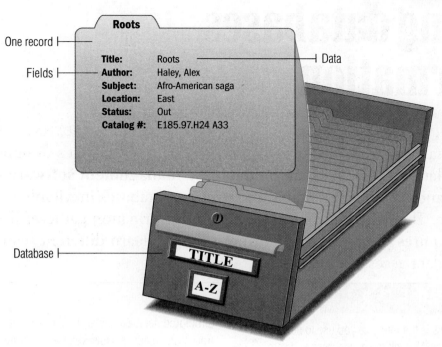

One record
Fields
Data

Roots

Title: Roots
Author: Haley, Alex
Subject: Afro-American saga
Location: East
Status: Out
Catalog #: E185.97.H24 A33

Database

TITLE
A-Z

FIGURE C-22: *Menu-driven database search of a free-form database*

Select News and Media.

From the News and Media list, select Politics.

From the list of political information, select Today's White House Press Releases.

Searching databases for information

Search Engines

IT'S MORE LIKELY THAT YOU'LL BE LOOKING FOR INFORMATION, NOT CREATING OR ADDING information to a database. The focus of this lesson is on software that's designed to search for information in databases, rather than on **database management software** that's designed to create and manipulate databases. Different databases inevitably use different data access software. Therefore becoming an effective information gatherer in the Information Age requires you to be flexible and willing to learn different searching procedures for different data access software.

IN MORE DETAIL

- **Data access software** is the interface you use to search for information in a database. You tell the data access software what you're looking for, and it will attempt to find it. The data access software understands the structure and details of the database, so you don't need to. Depending on your data access software, you might enter your search specifications using a menu, a hypertext index, a keyword search engine, a query by example, a query language, or a natural language.

- The collection of choices you're given to interact with a database is referred to as a **menu**. Database menus are similar to those you use in most other software, they can be screen-based or audio. Menus are typically arranged as a hierarchy, so that after you make a choice at the first level of the menu, a second series of choices appears. Screen-based menus have become a popular format for providing access to information via the Internet. Some screen-based menus include a feature called a hypertext index that links you to information and categories, such as education, entertainment, and business.

- A **keyword search engine**, as shown in Figure C-23, lets you access data by **keyword**, instead of by topic or through a menu of subject categories. Keyword search engines are especially popular for searching through the many documents stored in a free-form database such as the World Wide Web. To use a keyword search engine, you simply type in a word and the search engine locates related information. Almost every search engine lets you enter topics, define expert searches, and specify the strength of the match.

- When the information in a database needs to be accessed quickly, it is usually stored as a structured database. Because of its structure, a computer can generally locate data in a

structured database faster than it can locate information in a free-form database. However, the structure in structured databases can cause a problem for users who might not know the format for the records in a database. One way to help users search structured databases is by providing a **query by example (QBE)** user interface like the one shown in Figure C-24.

- A **query language** is a set of command words that you can use to direct the computer to create databases, locate information, sort records, and change the data in those records. To use a query language, you need to know the command words and the grammar or syntax that will let you construct valid query sentences. For example, the **SQL (structured query language)** command word to find records is "select."

  Advances in artificial intelligence have made some progress in the ability of computers to understand queries formulated in a **natural language** such as English, French, or Japanese. To make such natural language queries you don't need to learn an esoteric query language. Instead, you just enter questions such as: "What Byzantine statues are in the museum collection?" Computers still have some interpretation difficulties arising from ambiguities in human languages, so the use of natural language query software is not yet widespread.

- Information you find in databases can be copied to a document or worksheet. Figure C-25 shows how to copy information from a database. Whether you print, import, copy, save, or transmit the data you find in databases, it is your responsibility to use it appropriately. Respect copyrights by giving credit to the original author in a footnote or end note.

FIGURE C-23: *A keyword search*

Enter your search topic here, then click the Go Get It button to begin the search.

FIGURE C-24: *QBE interface*

◄ When you use a QBE interface, you see a blank record on the screen. You enter examples of what you want the computer to find into this record. In this case, the user is looking for books published in 1993 or later that includes "Economics" in the title.

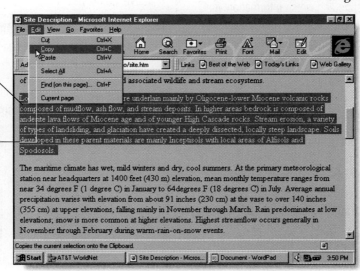

FIGURE C-25: *Using search results*

Highlight the text you want to copy.

Click the Edit menu, then select Copy. The text is copied to a special area of computer memory called the Clipboard. You can now switch to your word-processing software and paste the text into a document.

Putting it all together

YOU SHOULDN'T FINISH THIS UNIT WITH THE IMPRESSION THAT YOU USE ONLY ONE software tool per project. It is true that word-processing, spreadsheet, and database software tools each have their own strengths. But you often can be more productive if you use the tools together. This lesson looks at using the tools you've learned about to gather information, organize it, analyze it, and report your results. Table C-2 provides an overview of how to integrate your applications.

IN MORE DETAIL

☞ Choose your topic. Then browse around your library and the Internet to find sources of information. Whereas most research once took place in library buildings, the trend today is to use a computer to search online. From your home or office you can look through millions of Web documents and search through the card catalogs of many libraries, including the Library of Congress.

☞ You might want to make photocopies of interesting articles, check out relevant books, and save any information you find on the Web. Make sure you keep track of where you obtain your information. For information you gather from the Internet, make note of its source. Every document on the World Wide Web has a unique address called a **uniform resource locator** (URL). Most Web browser software has a setting to include the URL on any Web pages you send to your printer. Figure C-26 illustrates a Web page URL.

☞ Make sure that as part of your information-gathering activities, you have a way to distinguish which information you copy verbatim and which information you have paraphrased using your own words. For example, you might simply put quotes around the material that you copied verbatim and be sure to cite the source.

☞ Begin a new document using your word-processing software. Type in your main point. The next step is to create an outline of items that will support your main point. Use the outlining feature of your word processor to type in the headings and subheadings for your report. Work on your document until you're satisfied, and then run a spell checker and a grammar checker if one is available. Don't forget to proofread it.

☞ Before you finalize the content of your paper, you might consider if some sections would be clearer if you included a graph or other illustration. You can use spreadsheet software to create graphs for data you have gathered. You can use graphics

software to access or modify images for your report. You can use your copy and paste commands to insert the graphs or images into your document.

☞ When you're happy with the content of your document, save it on disk. Make an extra copy of your work on a different disk, just to be safe. You might also want to print your paper, even though you have not formatted it yet. If you lose your electronic copies, you can still reconstruct it from the printout.

☞ If you have not been provided with style guidelines from your instructor or boss, you should follow a standard style manual, such as *The Chicago Manual of Style,* or the *Publication Manual of the American Psychological Association,* or Turabian's *Guide to Style*. These manuals tell you how large to make your margins, what to include in headers and footers, how to label graphs and illustrations, how to format your footnotes or end notes correctly, and so forth. Use the formatting features of your word-processing software to follow the style guidelines.

☞ Enhance your report with visual aids, such as handouts or computer-generated slides generated using presentation software. See Figure C-27.

☞ If you're going to present your report, you need some speaker notes and some visual aids. Create your speaker notes using your word-processing software or insert the notes directly in your presentation using this feature in your presentation software.

Online Card Catalogs

Internet Citations

FIGURE C-26: *A Web page URL*

FIGURE C-27: *Using presentation software*

TABLE C-2: *Putting it all together*

WHAT TO USE	WHEN
Database and data access software	To search the World Wide Web and other databases for resources and data To collect and organize information such as a database of resources
Word-processing software	To create an outline To write a rough draft To improve the quality of your writing using tools such as a spell checker, a grammar checker, and a thesaurus
Spreadsheet software	To analyze data To add graphics and charts To represent data in your report
Presentation software	To present your report to a large audience To make handouts of your report
Communication software	To publish your report electronically To broaden your research, for example, by using e-mail to contact resources

Concepts Review

FIGURE C-28

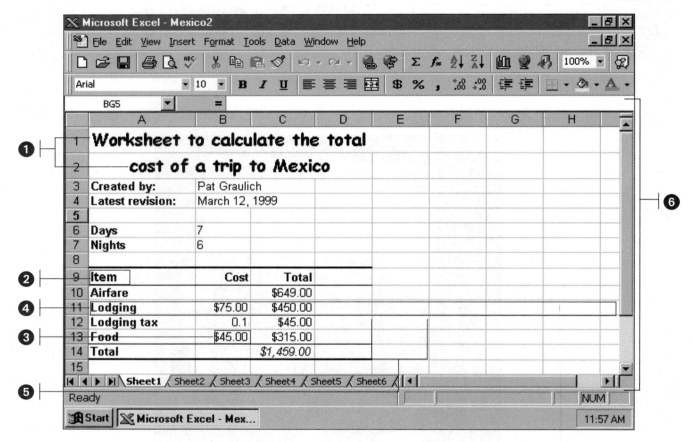

Label each element shown in Figure C-28.

1. _____

2. _____

3. _____

4. _____

5. _____

6. _____

Match each statement with the term it describes:

7. ___ In-line spell checker

8. ___ QBE

9. ___ Document template

10. ___ Document production software

11. ___ Database

12. ___ Grammar checker

13. ___ Cell reference

14. ___ What-if analysis

15. ___ Spreadsheet

16. ___ Document wizards

a. Take you step-by-step through a template to create a document

b. A preformatted document

c. Names a location in a spreadsheet

d. Search method in a database that finds information by example

e. Helps you with your writing style in a document

f. Immediately identifies misspelled words in a document

g. Category of software that includes e-mail editors, word processors, and desktop publishing software

h. A library catalog

i. A numerical model or representation of a real situation

j. The process of setting up a model and experimenting with different numbers

True or False?

17. When you first type a document, it is best not to get distracted by how the final product will look. Instead, you should concentrate on expressing your ideas. True or False?

18. The spell checker feature of word-processing software would alert you if you accidentally used the word "see" instead of "sea" when referring to a large body of water. True or False?

19. Spreadsheet software never adjusts formulas when you insert or delete cells. True or False?

20. The spreadsheet software publisher is responsible for the validity of the figures and formulas in your worksheets. True or False?

21. When you move or copy a cell, a spreadsheet typically adjusts any formulas in that cell relative to their original position. You must use an absolute reference if you don't want a cell address in the formula to change. True or False?

22. A worksheet that will be viewed on the screen would generally be formatted differently than a worksheet that will be printed in black and white. True or False?

23. To use a keyword search engine, you simply type in a word, such as music, and the search engine locates all related information in the database. True or False?

24. Once you locate information in a database, you can print it, export it to other software packages, copy and paste it into other software, save it for future reference, or transmit it. True or False?

25. You can generate computer slide shows using presentation software. True or False?

Fill in the best answer:

26. The spread of literacy went hand-in-hand with technology developments, culminating in today's use of computers and _____ software.

27. A feature of word-processing software called _____ takes care of where to break lines of text.

28. A(n) _____ provides preset formats for a document, whereas a _____ is a feature that coaches you step-by-step through the process of entering text into a document.

29. One of the most significant effects of computerized document production has been to encourage _____ publishing.

30. Web pages, which are documents posted on the World Wide Web, are in _____ format.

31. _____ has been used to establish the authorship of historical and contemporary documents.

32. In a spreadsheet grid, each _____ is lettered, each _____ is numbered.

33. B3 and B4 are called cell _____.

34. Most spreadsheet software includes hundreds of predefined formulas called _____ for mathematical, financial, and statistical calculations.

35. The process of setting up a model and experimenting with different numbers is often referred to as _____ analysis.

36. In popular terminology, a(n) _____ is a collection of information stored on one or more computers.

37. A(n) _____ database is a file of information organized in a uniform format of records and fields, whereas a(n) _____ database is a loosely structured collection of information.

38. Menus, keyword searches, query by example, a query language, and natural language are all methods used to _____ information in a database.

39. When using a(n) _____ user interface to search a database, you use a blank record to enter examples of the data you want the computer to find.

40. A(n) _____, such as SQL, consists of a set of command words that you can use to direct the computer to create databases, locate information, sort records, and change the data in those records.

INDEPENDENT CHALLENGE 1

One of the most commonly used document production software applications is word processing. You should have a good understanding as to why this tool is so valuable in our society today. Use your word processor to create a report that covers these important concepts.

To complete this independent challenge:

1. List the features of word-processing software that make it easy for you to enter the text of your documents.

2. Make a list of editing tasks that word-processing software can help you accomplish.

3. Explain the difference between a document template, a font, a style, and a document wizard.

4. Explain the difference between serif and sans serif as they apply to fonts.

5. In document production terminology, what is the difference between a column and a table?

6. Conclude your report with your reaction to this statement: "Word processing has improved the quality of writing in our society today."

INDEPENDENT CHALLENGE 2

Most word-processing software includes a grammar checker that helps you locate potential problems with sentence structure, punctuation, and word usage. When you use a grammar checker, it is important to remember that you must evaluate its suggestions and decide whether to implement them. In this project you'll use a grammar checker to revise some of your own writing.

To complete this independent challenge:

1. Begin with a first draft of one of your reports. The report should be at least one page of your writing. You can use something you have previously composed, or you can write something new. You'll need to type your document using word-processing software with grammar checker capabilities. Print your first draft.

2. After you've printed your first draft, activate the grammar checker. Consider each of its suggestions, and implement those you think will improve your writing.

3. Make sure you proofread your document after you've completed the changes to make sure it still flows well.

4. Print your revised document, and then mark the first draft copy by using a highlighter to indicate the changes you made. Submit both drafts of your document to your instructor.

Spreadsheet software is a widely used numeric analysis tool. Your neighbor just bought a new computer and is deciding which applications to install on the computer. You have to put together a report explaining the benefits of spreadsheet software.

To complete this independent challenge:

1. Write one or two paragraphs describing how a spreadsheet works to someone who has never seen one or used one.

2. Explain the difference between the following spreadsheet terms: a number, a formula, a function, and a cell reference.

3. Make a list of five careers, and then write a brief description of a spreadsheet application that would be useful in each.

4. Make a list of tips for formatting worksheets. Divide your tips into three categories: on-screen, printed, and projected.

5. Explain what happens to the cell references in a formula when you copy that formula to a different column. How does this relate to absolute references?

6. What does it mean to audit a spreadsheet? Describe techniques for auditing a worksheet.

A new neighbor just bought a modem and subscribed to a local Internet service provider. He wants to begin research on the Web. You have to become the resident database expert for this person and write a report that he can use to help him learn about databases and the Web.

To complete this independent challenge:

1. Explain the difference between a structured database and a free-form database.

2. List and describe at least four search procedures that you might use to locate information in a database.

3. Describe five different ways you can use search results.

4. List five different databases you encounter each day.

5. Describe the types of information gathering that you do each day, and detail the techniques you use to gather information.

6. List different search engines available on the Web and what their differences are.

7. Explain how you can use search results. Include a few ideas on what responsibilities you have as you use the information you find.

INDEPENDENT CHALLENGE 5

Although close to 80 percent of the population for most industrialized countries has completed high school, journalists supposedly write for an audience with only an eighth-grade reading level. Is this true? To find out, you can use your word-processing software to discover the reading level of typical articles in popular magazines and newspapers.

To complete this independent challenge

1. Locate two articles you think are typical of the writing style for the magazines or newspapers you read.

2. Using your word processor, enter at least 10 sentences from the first article.

3. Use your word processor's reading-level feature to find the reading level for the passage you typed.

4. Print the passage and on it note the reading-level statistics you obtained from your word processor.

5. Do the same with the second article. Submit both of your printouts to your instructor. Be sure to include full bibliographical data on both articles.

INDEPENDENT CHALLENGE 6

How to use a search engine is becoming a pivotal skill for the Information Age. Most keyword search engines include instructions or short tutorials on their use. For this independent challenge, you'll connect to one of the Web search engines and learn how to use it. To do this challenge, you must have access to the Internet, and you must have a Web browser such as Netscape Navigator or Microsoft Internet Explorer.

To complete this independent challenge:

1. Start your browser and connect to one of the following sites:

   www.lycos.com   **www.altavista.com**
   www.yahoo.com   **www.excite.com**
   www.hotbot.com

2. Read through the instructions carefully, paying close attention (and maybe taking notes) on the options available for advanced searches, exact matches, and Boolean operators (AND, OR, NOT). Next try a few searches to make sure you've got the hang of it.

3. Finally write a mini-manual about how to use your keyword search engine, providing examples of different types of searches.

INDEPENDENT CHALLENGE 7

Because computerized databases have become such an integral part of our society, we don't often consider what life would be like without them. However, without computerized databases, banking, shopping, communications, entertainment, education, and health care would probably be far different from what they are today. To complete this independent challenge:

1. Make a list of assumptions about how your life would be different if there were no computerized databases. For example, one of your assumptions might be: "Without computerized databases, we would have to pay for everything in cash because banks couldn't process enough checks by hand, nor could credit card companies verify charges."

2. After you have a list of assumptions, write a short story about one day in the life of a person who lives in a society where there are no computerized databases. In your story, try to depict how this person's life is different from what we think of as "normal."

3. Submit your list of assumptions and your short story to your instructor.

WORD PROCESSING LAB

Word-processing software is the most popular computerized productivity tool. In this Lab you will learn how word-processing software works. When you have completed this Lab, you should be able to apply the general concepts you learned to any word-processing package you use at home, at work, or in your school lab.

1. Click the Steps button to learn how word-processing software works. As you proceed through the Steps, answer all of the Quick Check questions that appear. After you complete the Steps, you will see a Quick Check Summary Report. Follow the instructions on the screen to print this report.

2. Click the Explore button to begin. Click File, then click Open to display the Open dialog box. Click the file Timber.tex, then press the Enter key to open the letter to Northern Timber Company. Make the following modifications to the letter, then print it out. You do not need to save the letter.

  a. In the first and last lines of the letter, change "Jason Kidder" to your name.

  b. Change the date to today's date.

  c. The second paragraph begins, "Your proposal did not include." Move this paragraph so it is the last paragraph in the text of the letter.

  d. Change the cost of a permanent bridge to $20,000.

  e. Spell check the letter.

3. In Explore, open the file Stars.tex. Make the following modifications to the document, then print it out. You do not need to save the document.

  a. Center and boldface the title.

  b. Change the title font to 16-point Arial.

  c. Boldface DATE, SHOWER, and LOCATION.

  d. Move the January 2-3 line to the top of the list.

  e. Double-space the entire document.

4. In Explore, compose a one-page double-spaced letter to your parents or to a friend. Make sure you date the letter and check your spelling. Print the letter and sign it. You do not need to save your letter.

SPREADSHEETS LAB

Spreadsheet software is used extensively in business, education, science, and humanities to simplify tasks that involve calculations. In this Lab you will learn how spreadsheet software works. You will use spreadsheet software to examine and modify worksheets, as well as to create your own worksheets.

1. Click the Steps button to learn how spreadsheet software works. As you proceed through the Steps, answer all of the Quick Check questions that appear. After you complete the Steps, you will see a Quick Check Summary Report. Follow the instructions on the screen to print this report.

2. Click the Explore button to begin this assignment. Click OK to display a new worksheet. Click File, then click Open to display the Open dialog box. Click the file Income.xls, then press the Enter key to open the Income and Expense Summary worksheet. Notice that the worksheet contains labels and values for income from consulting and training. It also contains labels and values for expenses such as rent and salaries. The worksheet does not, however, contain formulas to calculate Total Income, Total Expenses, or Profit. Do the following:

   a. Calculate the Total Income by entering the formula =sum(C4:C5) in cell C6.

   b. Calculate the Total Expenses by entering the formula =sum(C9:C12) in C13.

   c. Calculate Profit by entering the formula =C6-C13 in cell C15.

   d. Manually check the results to make sure you entered the formulas correctly.

   e. Print your completed worksheet showing your results.

3. You can use a spreadsheet to keep track of your grade in a class. In Explore, click File, then click Open to display the Open dialog box. Click the file Grades.xls to open the Grades worksheet. This worksheet contains all the labels and formulas necessary to calculate your grade based on four test scores. Suppose you receive a score of 88 out of 100 on the first test. On the second test, you score 42 out of 48. On the third test, you score 92 out of 100. You have not taken the fourth test yet. Enter the appropriate data in the Grades.xls worksheet to determine your grade after taking three tests. Print out your worksheet.

4. Worksheets are handy for answering "what if" questions. Suppose you decide to open a lemonade stand. You're interested in how much profit you can make each day. What if you sell 20 cups of lemonade? What if you sell 100? What if the cost of lemons increases?

   In Explore, open the file Lemons.xls and use the worksheet to answer questions a through d, then print the worksheet for question e:

   a. What is your profit if you sell 20 cups a day?

   b. What is your profit if you sell 100 cups a day?

   c. What is your profit if the price of lemons increases to $.07 and you sell 100 cups?

   d. What is your profit if you raise the price of a cup of lemonade to $.30? (Lemons still cost $.07 and assume you sell 100 cups.)

   e. Suppose your competitor boasts that she sold 50 cups of lemonade in one day and made exactly $12.00. On your worksheet adjust the cost of cups, water, lemons, and sugar, and the price per cup to show a profit of exactly $12.00 for 50 cups sold. Print this worksheet.

5. It is important to make sure the formulas in your worksheet are accurate. An easy way to test this is to enter 1's for all the values on your worksheet, then check the calculations manually. In Explore, open the worksheet Receipt.xls, which calculates sales receipts. Enter 1 as the value for Item 1, Item 2, Item 3, and Sales Tax %. Now, manually calculate what you would pay for three items that cost $1.00 each in a state where sales tax is 1% (.01). Do your manual calculations match those of the worksheet? If not, correct the formulas in the worksheet and print formula report of your revised worksheet.

6. In Explore, create your own worksheet showing your household budget for one month. You may use real or made up numbers. Make sure you put a title on the worksheet. Use formulas to calculate your total income and your total expenses for the month. Add another formula to calculate how much money you were able to save. Print a formula report of your worksheet. Also, print your worksheet showing realistic values for one month.

DATABASES LAB

The Database Lab demonstrates the essential concepts of file and database management systems. You will use the Lab to search, sort, and report the data contained in a file of classic books.

1. Click the Steps button to review basic database terminology and to learn how to manipulate the classic books database. As you proceed through the Steps, answer the Quick Check questions that appear. After you complete the Steps, you will see a Quick Check Summary Report. Follow the instructions on the screen to print this report.

2. Click the Explore button. Make sure you can apply basic database terminology to describe the classic books database by answering the following questions:

   a. How many records does the file contain?

   b. How many fields does each record contain?

   c. What are the contents of the Catalog # field for the book written by Margaret Mitchell?

   d. What are the contents of the Title field for the record with Thoreau in the Author field?

   e. Which field has been used to sort the records?

3. In Explore, manipulate the database as necessary to answer the following questions:

   a. When the books are sorted by title, what is the first record in the file?

   b. Use the Search button to search for all books in the West location. How many do you find?

   c. Use the Search button to search for all books in the Main location that are checked in. What do you find?

4. In Explore, use the Report button to print out a report that groups the books by Status and sorted by title. On your report, circle the four field names. Put a box around the summary statistics showing which books are currently checked in and which books are currently checked out.

Computer
Files and
Data Storage

Unit

IN THIS UNIT YOU WILL LEARN ABOUT COMPUTER files and data storage. You will learn that there are different types of files, and you will find out how to use each type. This unit explains how computers store and retrieve data and provides you with a practical foundation for using a computer to manage your own data. You will find out how to create a valid filename that the computer will accept. You will learn how DOS or Windows organizes the files on your disk so they are easy to locate. You will also learn what happens when you save, retrieve, or modify a file.

OBJECTIVES

Understand computer files

Define storage technology

Understand magnetic storage: floppy disks

Use floppy disk drives

Understand magnetic storage: hard disk drives

Understand magnetic storage: tape

Examine optical storage

Understand physical file storage

Learn about file management

Understand logical file storage

Learn about using files

Learn more about using files

Understanding computer files

IN EVERYDAY CONVERSATION, PEOPLE USE THE TERMS *DATA* AND *INFORMATION* INTERCHANGEABLY. Computer professionals have special definitions for the terms *data, information,* and *file.* Although we might refer to these as technical definitions, they are not difficult to understand. **Data** is defined as the words, numbers, and graphics that describe people, events, things, and ideas. Data becomes information when you use it as the basis for initiating some action or for making a decision. **Information**, then, is defined as the words, numbers, and graphics used as the basis for human actions and decisions. A **file** is defined as a named collection of program instructions or data that exists on a storage medium such as a hard disk, a floppy disk, or a CD-ROM.

There are several kinds of files such as executable files, source files, batch files, and data files. A typical computer user deals mainly with data files when using application software, which includes all types of files. This lesson takes a closer look at file types.

IN MORE DETAIL

☞ Data files: A **data file** contains words, numbers, and pictures that you can view, edit, save, send, and print. Typically, you create data files when you use application software. For example, you create a data file when you store a document you have written using word-processing software or when you store a picture, graph, a sound clip, or a video. In addition, word-processing software often includes a dictionary data file that contains a list of words the software uses to check spelling.

Whether you create or purchase a data file, you typically use it in conjunction with application software, which you use to manipulate the data in the file. You usually view, revise, and print a data file using the same software you used to create it.

☞ Executable files: An **executable file** contains the instructions that tell a computer how to perform a specific task. For example, the word-processing program that tells your computer how to display and print text is stored on disk as an executable file. Other executable files on your computer system include the operating system, utilities, and programs for application software.

To use some executable files, you *run* them. Most operating systems help you identify the executable files you can run. To run an executable file in DOS you type the filename of the program; in Windows 3.1 you click a program icon, and in Windows 95 and Windows 98 you can either select the program from a menu or click the program icon. The Windows 95 screen shown in Figure D-1 illustrates the use of icons to indicate which files you can run.

The programs you run are one type of executable file. Your computer also has executable files that are executed at the request of a computer program, not the user. For example, a word-processing program might request that the computer use an executable file called Grammar.dll to check the grammar in a document. The instructions are stored in a format that the computer can interpret, but this format is not designed to be readable to users.

☞ Source files: A **source file** contains instructions that a computer user can understand and that must be translated before a computer can execute them. A computer user can request that a specific source file be run. The computer does the translation, so it seems as if the source program is being executed just like an executable file. But this is not the case; behind the scenes, a translation program is busy converting the source program into commands the computer can execute.

You cannot run folders

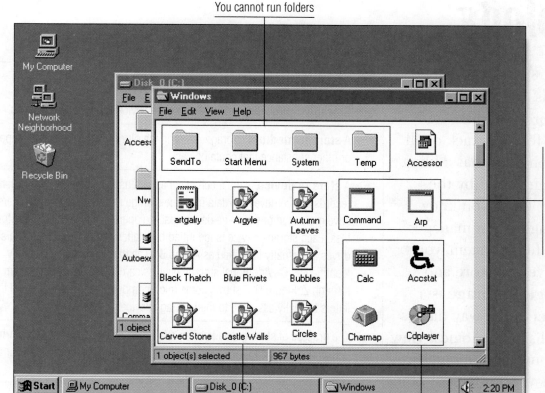

Some files you can run do not have unique icons. Instead, they use a "generic" icon of a blank window. The label indicates the name of the file.

Some files are represented by icons that look like pages. These icons represent data files.

Many of the files you can run are indicated by unique icons. Each icon has a label that tells you the name of the application.

You can think of executable files as *active*: The instructions stored in the file cause the computer to do something. Think of data files as *passive*: The computer processes the data, but the data generally does not direct the process.

Batch files

INFOWEB

Autoexec

*One type of source file is a batch file. A **batch file** is a series of operating system commands that you use to automate tasks you want the operating system to perform. When you first turn on an IBM-compatible computer, it looks for a batch file called Autoexec.bat. If it finds this file,*

the computer automatically executes any instructions the file contains. Usually the Autoexec.bat file contains instructions that customize your computer configuration. A batch file, such as Autoexec.bat, contains instructions that can be read and modified by computer

users. The commands in a batch file must go through a translation process before they can be executed.

Defining storage technology

YOUR COMPUTER SYSTEM MIGHT contain hundreds, or even thousands, of files stored on disks and storage devices. To keep track of all these files, the computer has a filing system that is maintained by the operating system. Once you know how the operating system manages your computer's filing system, you can use it effectively to store and retrieve files. **Logical storage** is a conceptual model of the way data is stored on your disk. This logical view of storage is a convenient mental model that helps you understand the computer's filing system; however, it is not how the data is actually stored. **Physical storage** refers to how data is actually stored on the physical disk. Take a closer look at storage technology and what it means.

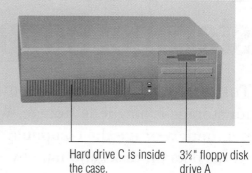

▶ This desktop computer has a basic storage configuration: a 3½" floppy disk drive as drive A and a hard disk drive C inside the case.

Hard drive C is inside the case.

3½" floppy disk drive A

▶ This tower model has an impressive selection of storage devices, including disk, CD-ROM, and tape drives. The tape drive does not have a letter because it is not a device that you can use to store individual files from your applications.

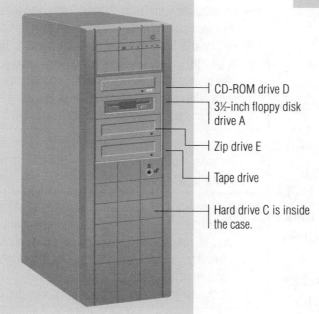

⊣ CD-ROM drive D

⊣ 3½-inch floppy disk drive A

⊣ Zip drive E

⊣ Tape drive

⊣ Hard drive C is inside the case.

▶ This notebook computer has one 3½" floppy disk drive as drive A. The hard disk drive C is inside the case. There is no drive B. Because of space restrictions it is difficult to fit many storage devices in a notebook computer.

Hard drive C is inside the case.

3½" floppy disk drive A

Magnetic and optical storage technologies are used for the majority of today's micro, mini, and mainframe computers.

To differentiate between physical and logical file storage, remember that physical storage refers to the way data is electronically stored on the storage medium. Logical storage refers to the metaphor you use to visualize the organization of your files.

The time it takes to get the data

Access time *is the average time it takes a computer to locate data on the storage medium and read it. Access time for microcomputer storage devices, such as a disk drive, is measured in milliseconds. One* ***millisecond*** *(ms) is a thousandth of a second. When you read, for example, that disk access time is 11 ms, it means that on average, it takes the computer eleven thousandths of a second to locate and read data from the disk.*

Understanding magnetic storage: floppy disks

INFOWEB

Floppies and Zips

Unit D

THE MOST COMMONLY USED MEDIUM for storage is magnetic storage. With **magnetic storage** the computer stores data on disks and tape by magnetizing selected particles of an oxide-based surface coating. The particles retain their magnetic orientation until that orientation is changed, thereby making disks and tape fairly permanent but modifiable storage media. See Figure D-3. The two most popular types of magnetic storage media are floppy disks and hard disks. Magnetic tape provides a third type of magnetic storage.

A **floppy disk** is a flexible mylar plastic disk covered with a thin layer of magnetic oxide. Floppy disks get their name from this thin mylar disk. If you cut open the disk casing (something you should never do unless you want to ruin the disk), you would see that the mylar disk inside is thin and, well, floppy. Floppy disks are also called floppies or diskettes.

IN MORE DETAIL

☞ Physical characteristics: Floppy disks come in several sizes. Today's microcomputers typically use 3½" disks. A 3½" circular disk made of flexible mylar is housed inside a protective case of rigid plastic. When the disk is inserted in the disk drive, the spring-loaded access cover slides to the side to expose the disk surface for reading and writing data. Figure D-4 shows the construction of a 3½" disk. A special high-capacity floppy disk manufactured by Iomega Corporation is called a **Zip disk**.

☞ Double-sided disks: In the past floppy disks stored data only on one side; but today most floppy disks store data on both sides. A **double-sided disk** stores twice as much data as a single-sided disk.

☞ Disk density: Disk density refers to the size of the magnetic particles on the disk surface. The disk density limits the amount of data you can reliably store on the disk. **Double-density disks**, abbreviated as DD, are also referred to as *low-density* disks. A **high-density disk**, abbreviated as HD, stores more data than a double-density disk. The higher the disk density, the smaller the magnetic particles it stores, and the more data it can store.

☞ Formatted disks: The amount of data a computer can store on each side of a disk depends on the type of disk it is, its density, and on the way the disk is formatted. The formatting process, which was described in Unit B, creates a series of concentric **tracks** on the disk, and each track is divided into smaller segments called **sectors**, as shown in Figure D-5. Most of today's computers use a double-sided disk that is formatted with 80 tracks per side and 18 sectors per track creating 1,440 sectors. On IBM-compatible computers, each sector of a track holds 512 bytes of data, so a file that is 512 bytes or less fits in a single sector. Larger files are stored in more than one sector.

Protecting your data

You can intentionally change or erase files stored on magnetic media. If you run out of storage space on a disk, you can erase files you no longer need to make more space available. Data stored on magnetic media such as floppy disks can also be unintentionally altered by the environment, and by device or media failure. In the environment, magnetic fields, dust, mold, smoke particles, and heat are the primary culprits causing data loss. Placing a magnet on your disk is a sure way of losing data. Even though the metal detectors in an airport use a magnetic field, the field is not strong enough to disrupt the data on your floppy or hard disks. In fact, you are more likely to damage your disks by leaving them on the dashboard of your car in the sun or by carrying them around in your backpack where they will pick up dust and dirt.

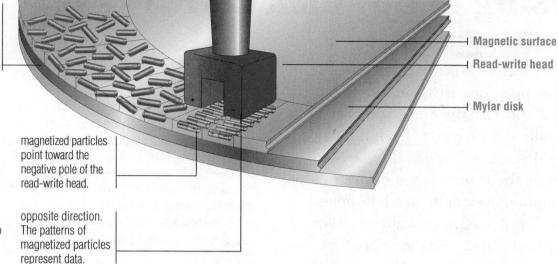

Before data is stored, the particles in the magnetic surface of the disk are scattered in random patterns.

Magnetic surface

Read-write head

Mylar disk

The read-write head magnetizes the particles. The positive poles of the

magnetized particles point toward the negative pole of the read-write head.

The read-write head can reverse polarity to align the next row of particles in the

opposite direction. The patterns of magnetized particles represent data.

FIGURE **D-4:** *A 3½" floppy disk*

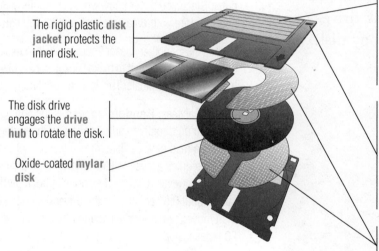

Only high-density disks have this **high-density indicator hole**.

The rigid plastic **disk jacket** protects the inner disk.

The spring-loaded **access cover** slides to the left when the disk is inserted in the drive. When the disk is in the drive, this head aperture is aligned with the opening in the access cover to expose the disk surface to the read-write head.

The disk drive engages the **drive hub** to rotate the disk.

Oxide-coated **mylar disk**

The **disk label** often wraps around to the underside of the disk. When you affix the label, make sure it does not stick to the access cover.

When the **write-protect window** is open, the disk is write protected and the computer cannot write data on the disk. Here the write-protect window is closed.

The **disk liner** removes dirt and dust from the disk surface.

FIGURE **D-5:** *A formatted disk*

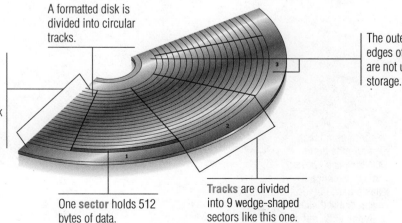

A formatted disk is divided into circular tracks.

A double-density floppy disk is formatted for 40 tracks per side. A high-density disk is formatted for 80 tracks per side.

The outer and inner edges of the disk are not used for data storage.

One **sector** holds 512 bytes of data.

Tracks are divided into 9 wedge-shaped sectors like this one.

Using floppy disk drives

FLOPPY DISK STORAGE IS USED FOR three purposes: distribution, storing data, and backup. Since you don't usually run programs from floppy or Zip disks, a 3½" or Zip drive would not be the main storage device in a computer system. Instead, floppies and Zip disks are typically used for transporting or shipping data files. In order to use floppy disks or Zip disks, your computer must have the appropriate disk drive. Figure D-6 shows both types of disk drives. This lesson looks at floppy disk drives in more detail.

IN MORE DETAIL

☞ Floppy disk drives: The storage device that records and retrieves data on a floppy disk is the **floppy disk drive**. Refer to Figure D-7 to find out how the rotation of the disk, combined with the lateral movement of the read-write head, allows the drive mechanism to access any sector of the disk.

☞ Distribution: Newer technologies are decreasing the use of floppy disks. In the past, software was distributed on floppy disks. Now, most software vendors use CD-ROMs instead. Local computer networks and the Internet have made it easy to share data files, so floppy disks are shipped less frequently.

☞ Storing data: In the university setting, floppy disks are often used to store student data. If you have your own computer, you would tend to store your data on the hard disk. But in a student lab, you don't have your own computer. Since you never know which computer you will be assigned, you need to store your data on a disk so that you can carry your data with you.

☞ Backup files: Another use for floppy disks is to make duplicate copies of your data files. It is important to make backup copies of your work in case something happens to the originals. This is a process known as backing up your files.

☞ Random access: **Random access** is the ability of a disk-based storage device to go directly to any location on the storage medium. The read-write head can read or write data from any sector of the disk, in any order. This provides quick access to files anywhere on a disk. Even with random access, however, a floppy disk drive is not a particularly speedy device. It takes about 0.5 seconds for the drive to spin the disk up to speed and then move the read-write head to a particular sector. A Zip drive is about 20 times faster.

A common use for floppy disks is to share data with other computer users. For example, if you want to give a copy of a report to several colleagues, you can copy the report to floppy disks and give them to your colleagues. Today, instead of floppy disks, many computer users use computer networks or electronic mail to share data.

A common misconception is that a 3½" disk is a "hard disk" because it has a hard plastic case. A 3½" disk is a floppy disk, not a hard disk.

▲ A 3½" disk drive has an eject button to release the disk and a drive light to indicate when the drive is in use. You insert the disk so the label goes in last. Virtually every computer has a 3½" disk drive.

▲ A Zip drive uses special Zip disks that are slightly larger than a 3½" floppy disk. The green light indicates that the drive is ready. A yellow light indi- cates that the drive is in use. Insert the Zip disk so the label enters last. Zip disks are increasing in popularity and use.

FIGURE **D-7**: *How a 3½" floppy disk drive works*

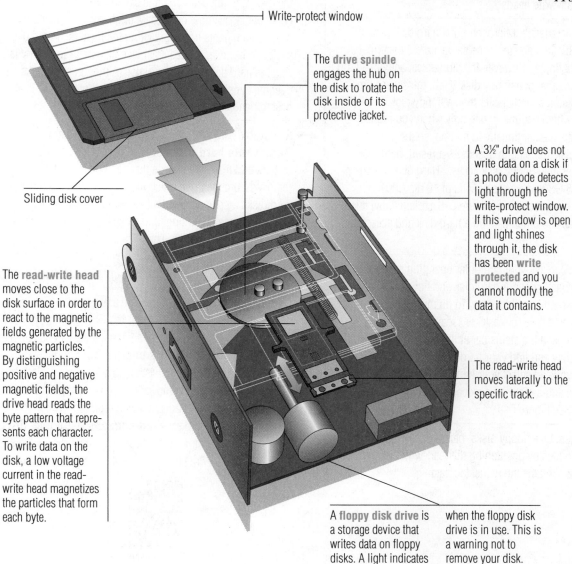

Write-protect window

Sliding disk cover

The **drive spindle** engages the hub on the disk to rotate the disk inside of its protective jacket.

A 3½" drive does not write data on a disk if a photo diode detects light through the write-protect window. If this window is open and light shines through it, the disk has been **write protected** and you cannot modify the data it contains.

The **read-write head** moves close to the disk surface in order to react to the magnetic fields generated by the magnetic particles. By distinguishing positive and negative magnetic fields, the drive head reads the byte pattern that repre- sents each character. To write data on the disk, a low voltage current in the read- write head magnetizes the particles that form each byte.

The read-write head moves laterally to the specific track.

A **floppy disk drive** is a storage device that writes data on floppy disks. A light indicates when the floppy disk drive is in use. This is a warning not to remove your disk.

Understanding magnetic storage: hard disk drives

Hard disk storage provides faster access to files than a floppy or zip disk drives and is the preferred type of storage for most computer systems. You will frequently see the terms *hard disk* and *hard disk drive* used interchangeably. You might also hear the term *fixed disk* used to refer to hard disks.

IN MORE DETAIL

- Microcomputer disk storage: A **hard disk platter** is a flat, rigid disk made of aluminum or glass and coated with a magnetic oxide. A **hard disk** is one or more **platters** and their associated read-write heads.

- Physical characteristics: Microcomputer hard disk platters are typically 3½" in diameter—the same size as the circular mylar disk in a floppy. However, the storage capacity of a hard disk far exceeds that of a floppy disk. Also, the access time of a hard disk is significantly faster than a floppy disk. Unlike floppy disks, which begin to rotate only when you request data, hard disks are continually in motion, so there is no delay as the disk spins up to speed. As a result, hard disk access is faster than floppy disk access. Hard disk storage capacities of 5 GB and access speeds of 10 ms (.001 seconds) are not uncommon. Figure D-8 explains how it is possible to pack so much data on a hard disk and access it so quickly.

- Capacity: You can ask your computer operating system to tell you the capacity of your hard disk and how much of the capacity is currently used for data. To do this in DOS, at the C:\> prompt you'd type "chkdsk" or "scandsk". In Windows 3.1, you can look at the status bar at the bottom of the File Manager window and find your hard disk's capacity. In Windows 95 you can select your hard disk drive icon under My Computer, and a graph of disk capacity and utilization is displayed. See Figure D-9.

- Random access: Like floppy disks, hard disks provide random access to files by positioning the read-write head over the sector that contains the requested data.

- Head crash: The read-write heads in a hard disk hover a microscopic distance above the disk surface. If a read-write head runs into a dust particle or some other contaminant on the disk, it might cause what is called a **head crash**. A head crash damages some of the data on the disk. To help eliminate contaminants from contacting the platters, a hard disk is sealed in its case. A head crash can also be triggered by jarring the hard disk while it is in use. Although hard disks have become considerably more rugged in recent years, it is still best to handle and transport them with care.

- Removable hard disks: Some hard disks are removable. **Removable hard disks** or hard disk cartridges contain platters and read-write heads that can be inserted and removed from the drive much like a floppy disk. Removable hard disks increase the potential storage capacity of your computer system, although the data is available on only one disk at a time. Removable hard disks also provide security for your data by making it possible for you to remove the hard disk cartridge and store it separately from the computer.

- Mainframe disk storage: Mainframe users refer to disk storage as DASD (pronounced "daz-dee"). DASD stands for direct access storage device. Many mainframe installations still use removable disk packs. A **disk pack** contains from six to twenty hard disks. Each disk is a little larger than 10 inches. The entire pack can be removed and replaced with another pack. Disk packs are gradually being replaced by high-capacity fixed disk drives. **High-capacity fixed disk drive** technology is similar to a microcomputer hard disk with its platters and read-write heads, but with higher storage capacity.

Speed Update

► Like a floppy disk, a hard disk is a random (or direct) access storage device. To locate data, the disks spin to the specified sector and the heads move to the specified cylinder.

The **drive spindle** supports one or more **hard disk platters**. Both sides of the platter are used for data storage. More platters mean more surface area and more data storage capacity. Hard disk platters rotate as a unit on the drive spindle to position a specific sector under the read-write heads. The platters spin continuously at 3,600 revolutions per minute.

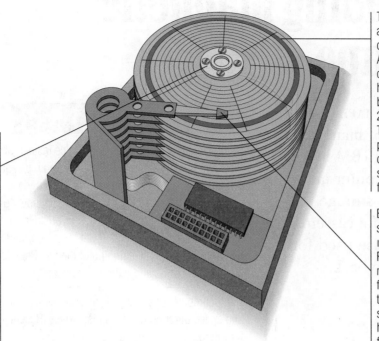

The platter surfaces are formatted into cylinders and sectors. A **cylinder** is a vertical stack of tracks. A hard disk could have between 312 and 2,048 cylinders. To find a file, the computer must know the cylinder, platter, and sector in which the file is stored.

Each data storage surface has its own **read-write head**. Read-write heads move in and out from the center of the disk to locate a specific track. The head hovers only five microinches above the disk surface so the magnetic field is much more compact than on a floppy disk. As a result, more data is packed into a smaller area on a hard disk platter.

FIGURE D-9: *Hard disk capacity and utilization in Windows 95 and Windows 98*

To view disk utilization statistics double-click the **My Computer** icon to open the My Computer window.

Click the storage device icon for which you want information.

Click **File**, then click **Properties** to display the properties of the storage device.

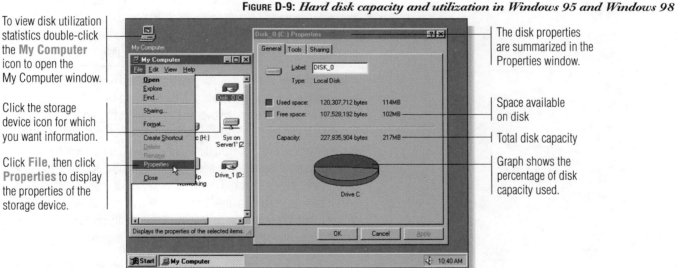

The disk properties are summarized in the Properties window.

Space available on disk

Total disk capacity

Graph shows the percentage of disk capacity used.

How a disk cache helps speed things up

*To further increase the speed of data access, your computer might use a disk cache. A **disk cache** (pronounced "cash") is a special area of computer memory into which the computer transfers the data that you are likely to need from disk storage. Suppose your computer retrieves the data from a particular sector of your disk. There is a high probability that the next data you need will be from an adjacent sector—the remainder of a program file, for example, or the next section of a data file. So, the computer reads the data from nearby sectors and stores it in the cache. If the data you need next is already in the cache, the computer doesn't need to wait while the mechanical parts of the drive locate and read the data from the disk. A disk cache speeds up the performance of your computer system, because accessing data from the cache is an electrical operation.*

Understanding magnetic storage: tape

IN THE 1960S, MAGNETIC TAPE WAS the most popular form of mainframe computer storage. When IBM introduced its first microcomputer in 1981, the legacy of tape storage continued in the form of a cassette tape drive, similar to those used for audio recording and playback.

Tape

☞ Using tape as a primary storage device instead of a hard disk would be slow and inconvenient because tape requires sequential access rather than random access. With **sequential access**, data is stored and read as a sequence of bytes along the length of the tape. To find a file stored on a microcomputer tape storage device, you advance the tape to the approximate location of the file, then wait for the computer to slowly read each byte until it finds the beginning of the file. Refer to Figure D-10 to learn how data is stored and retrieved from tape.

☞ Microcomputer users quickly abandoned tape storage for the convenience and speed of random access disk drives. Recently, however, tape storage for microcomputers has experienced a revival—not as a principal storage device, but for making backup copies of the data stored on hard disks. The data on magnetic storage can be easily destroyed, erased, or otherwise lost. Protecting the data on the hard disk is of particular concern to users because it contains so much data—data that would be difficult and time-consuming to reconstruct. Therefore, it is a good idea to have a copy of the data tucked safely away somewhere as a backup.

☞ A **tape backup** is a copy of the data from a hard disk, stored on magnetic tape, and used to restore lost data. A tape backup is relatively inexpensive and can rescue you from the overwhelming task of trying to reconstruct lost data. If you lose the data on your hard disk, you can copy the data from the tape backup onto the hard disk. Typically, you do not use the data directly from the tape backup because the sequential access is too slow to be practical. For a backup device, access time is less important than the time it takes to copy data from your hard disk to tape. Drive manufacturers do not usually supply such performance specifications, but most users can expect a tape drive to back up 100 MB in 15–20 minutes.

☞ The most popular types of tape drives for microcomputers also use tape cartridges, but there are several tape specifications and cartridge sizes. A **tape cartridge** is a removable magnetic tape module similar to a cassette tape. See Figure D-11. **QIC** (quarter-inch cartridge) is a tape cartridge that contains quarter-inch wide tape. Depending on tape length, QIC tape capacities range from 340 MB to 2 GB. **DAT** (digital audio tape) was originally an audio recording format, but is now also used for data storage. The 4 mm wide DAT tape format storage capacity ranges from 2 GB to 12 GB. When you purchase tapes, check the tape drive manual to make sure the tapes you purchase are the correct type for your tape drive.

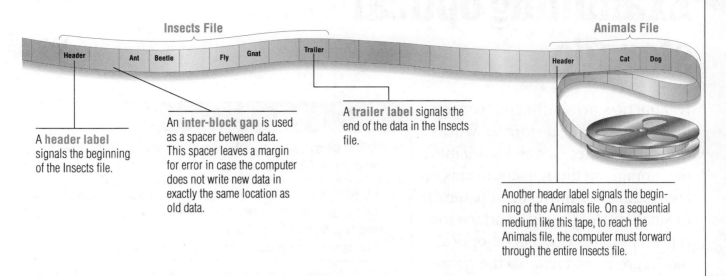

Insects File

| Header | Ant | Beetle | Fly | Gnat | Trailer |

Animals File

| Header | Cat | Dog |

A **header label** signals the beginning of the Insects file.

An **inter-block gap** is used as a spacer between data. This spacer leaves a margin for error in case the computer does not write new data in exactly the same location as old data.

A **trailer label** signals the end of the data in the Insects file.

Another header label signals the beginning of the Animals file. On a sequential medium like this tape, to reach the Animals file, the computer must forward through the entire Insects file.

FIGURE **D-11**: *Cartridge tape storage*

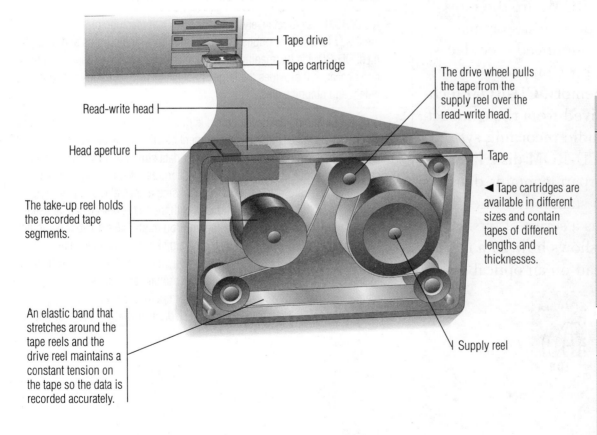

Tape drive

Tape cartridge

Read-write head

Head aperture

The take-up reel holds the recorded tape segments.

An elastic band that stretches around the tape reels and the drive reel maintains a constant tension on the tape so the data is recorded accurately.

The drive wheel pulls the tape from the supply reel over the read-write head.

Tape

◄ Tape cartridges are available in different sizes and contain tapes of different lengths and thicknesses.

Supply reel

QUICK TIP

After the initial time-consuming backup of the hard drive, most tape backup software allows you to selectively back up only the files that have changed, making subsequent backups quicker.

FYI

Even though tape storage is sequential, most tape backup software will allow you to back up and restore individual files and directories.

Examining optical storage

IN ADDITION TO MAGNETIC STORAGE, there is also optical storage. With **optical storage**, data is *burned* into the storage medium using beams of laser light. The burns form patterns of small pits in the disk surface to represent data. The pits on optical media are permanent, so the data cannot be changed. Optical media are very durable, but do not give you the flexibility of magnetic media for changing the data once it is stored. CD-ROMs are the most popular type of optical storage. **CD-ROM** (pronounced "cee dee rom") stands for Compact Disc Read Only Memory. CD-ROM technology is derived from the compact disc digital-audio recording system. A computer CD-ROM disk, like its audio counterpart, contains data that has been stamped on the disk surface as a series of pits. Figure D-12 shows how data is stored and read on an optical disk.

CD-R

▫━ To read the data on a CD-ROM, an optical read head distinguishes the patterns of pits that represent bytes.

▫━ CD-ROM disks provide tremendous storage capacity. A single CD-ROM disk holds up to 680 megabytes, equivalent to over 300,000 pages of text, and these disks are quite durable. The surface of the disk is coated with a clear plastic, making the data permanent and unalterable.

▫━ CD-ROM disks are limited by the fact that they are *read only*. **Read only** means that the computer can retrieve data from a CD-ROM but cannot save any new data on it. In this respect, CD-ROM technology differs markedly from hard disk storage, on which you can write, erase, and read data. A CD-ROM drive supplements a hard disk drive because a CD-ROM is a read-only device. Figure D-13 shows a CD-ROM drive.

▫━ A CD-ROM disk is relatively inexpensive to manufacture, making it an ideal way for software publishers to distribute large programs and data files. CD-ROM is the medium of choice for delivery of multimedia applications because it provides the large storage capacity necessary for sound, video, and graphics files.

▫━ A recent technological development is the creation of CD-R disks on which you can write data. Until the development of CD-Rs, the data stored on optical media could not be changed. The data stored on magnetic media can be changed. **CD-R** (compact disc-recordable) technology allows the computer to record data on a CD-R disk using a special CD-R recording device. Disks that have been produced with the CD-R device can be used on a regular CD-ROM drive, like the one you might have on your computer. As with regular CD-ROMs the data on the disk cannot be erased or modified. Therefore, CD-R is a useful technology for archiving data. **Archiving** refers to the process of moving data off a primary storage device to a supplemental storage device when that data is not frequently accessed. CD-R technology will not replace your hard disk drive anytime in the near future.

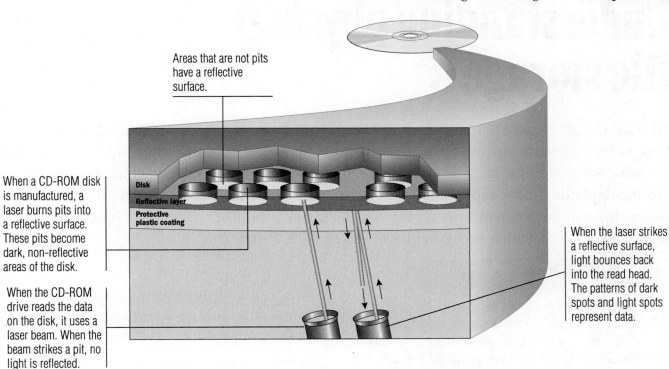

Areas that are not pits have a reflective surface.

When a CD-ROM disk is manufactured, a laser burns pits into a reflective surface. These pits become dark, non-reflective areas of the disk.

When the CD-ROM drive reads the data on the disk, it uses a laser beam. When the beam strikes a pit, no light is reflected.

Disk
Reflective layer
Protective plastic coating

When the laser strikes a reflective surface, light bounces back into the read head. The patterns of dark spots and light spots represent data.

FIGURE D-13: *CD-ROM drive*

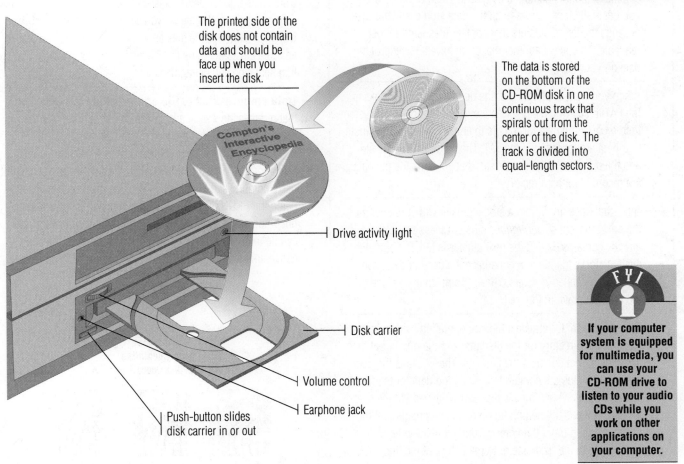

The printed side of the disk does not contain data and should be face up when you insert the disk.

Compton's Interactive Encyclopedia

The data is stored on the bottom of the CD-ROM disk in one continuous track that spirals out from the center of the disk. The track is divided into equal-length sectors.

Drive activity light

Disk carrier

Volume control

Earphone jack

Push-button slides disk carrier in or out

FYI
If your computer system is equipped for multimedia, you can use your CD-ROM drive to listen to your audio CDs while you work on other applications on your computer.

Understanding physical file storage

NOW THAT YOU UNDERSTAND HOW A STORAGE DEVICE STORES DATA ON A STORAGE MEDIUM, LET'S look at how files are stored. Files are stored in clusters. A **cluster** is a group of sectors and is the smallest storage unit the computer can access. The number of sectors that form a cluster depends on the type of computer and capacity of the disk. IBM-compatible computers form a cluster from two sectors. Each cluster is numbered and the operating system maintains a list of which sectors correspond to each cluster.

IN MORE DETAIL

- When the computer stores a file on a disk, the operating system records the cluster number that contains the beginning of the file in a file allocation table, or FAT. The **FAT** is an operating system file that helps the computer store and retrieve files from disk storage by maintaining a list of files and their physical location on the disk. The FAT is such a crucial file that if it is damaged by a head crash or other disaster, you generally lose access to all the data stored on your disk because the list of clusters that contain files is no longer readable. This is yet another reason to have a backup of the data on your hard drive.

- When you want to store a file, the operating system looks at the FAT to see which clusters are empty. The operating system then records the data for the file in empty clusters. The cluster numbers are recorded in the FAT. The name of the new file and the number of the first cluster that contains the file data are recorded in the directory.

- A file that does not fit into a single cluster will spill over into the next adjacent or *contiguous* cluster unless that cluster already contains data. If the next cluster is full, the operating system stores the file in a nonadjacent cluster and sets up instructions called *pointers*. These "point" to each piece of the file, as shown in Figure D-14.

- When you want to retrieve a file, the operating system looks through the directory for the filename and the number of the first cluster that contains the file data. The FAT tells the computer which clusters contain the remaining data for the file. The operating system moves the read-write head to the cluster that contains the beginning of the file and reads it. If the file is stored in more than one cluster, the read-write head must move to the next cluster to read more of the file. It takes longer to access a file stored in nonadjacent clusters than one stored in adjacent clusters because the disk or head must move farther to find the next section of the file.

- With random-access storage, files tend to become **fragmented**, that is, each file is stored in many nonadjacent clusters. Drive performance generally declines as the drive works harder to locate the clusters that contain the parts of a file. To regain peak performance, you can use a **defragmentation utility** to rearrange the files on a disk so that they are stored in adjacent clusters. Figure D-15 explains more about fragmentation and defragmentation.

- **Data compression** or **file compression** is a technique that reduces the size of a large file by using fewer bits to represent the data that the file contains on the disk. PKZIP, a popular data compression utility, creates files with the **.zip** extension that are sometimes called "zipped" files. You cannot use a compressed file directly—the file must be "unzipped" using the PKUNZIP utility. File compression is reversible by uncompressing, extracting, or expanding the file so the data can be returned to its original form. Compressing files is a convenient way to archive, back up, or transmit large files.

Defragmentation and Disk Operations

FAT

Storage Basics

Past & Future

► Each sector is listed in the FAT along with a number that indicates the status of the cluster.

Looking at the FAT entry for cluster 7, you see that the Jordan.wks file continues in cluster 8.

Looking at the FAT entry for cluster 8, you see that the Jordan.wks file continues in cluster 10.

The FAT entry for cluster 10 shows that this is the end of the Jordan.wks file. The file is stored in **non-contiguous clusters** 7, 8, and 10.

Fat		
Cluster	Status	Comment
1	1	Reserved for operating system
2	1	Reserved for operating system
3	4	First cluster of Bio.txt. Points to cluster 8 which holds more data for Bio.txt.
4	999	Last cluster of Bio.txt
5	0	Empty
6	0	Empty
7	8	First cluster for Jordan.wks. Points to cluster 8 which holds more data for the Jordan.wks file.
8	10	Points to cluster 10 which holds more data for the Jordan.wks file.
9	999	First and last cluster containing Pick.wps
10	999	Last cluster of Jordan.wks

If status is "1" the cluster is reserved for technical files. If status is "0," the cluster is empty, so new data can be stored there. If the status is "999," the cluster contains the end of a file. Other status numbers indicate the sector that holds more data for a file.

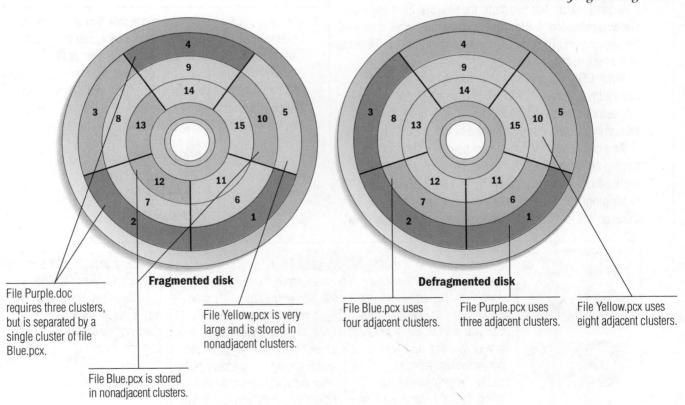

Fragmented disk

Defragmented disk

File Purple.doc requires three clusters, but is separated by a single cluster of file Blue.pcx.

File Yellow.pcx is very large and is stored in nonadjacent clusters.

File Blue.pcx is stored in nonadjacent clusters.

File Blue.pcx uses four adjacent clusters.

File Purple.pcx uses three adjacent clusters.

File Yellow.pcx uses eight adjacent clusters.

Learning about file management

You have been learning about physical storage. In this lesson, you will learn more about logical storage, which is the conceptual way data is stored on your disk. Specifically, this lesson looks at filenames and filenaming conventions.

IN MORE DETAIL

- A **filename** is a unique set of letters and numbers that identifies a file and usually describes the file contents.

- A **valid filename** is created by following specific rules. The rules for creating a valid filename are referred to as **filenaming conventions**. Each operating system has a unique set of filenaming conventions. It is sometimes difficult to select a DOS or Windows 3.1 filename that is unique and descriptive within the eight-character limit. You should try, however, to choose filenames that help you remember what is in the file. The filenaming conventions used by several operating systems are listed in Table D-1.

- A filename usually has two parts: the filename itself and the filename extension. A **filename extension** further describes the file contents. The extension is separated from the filename with a period, called a *dot*.

  When DOS was originally introduced, many computer users added a three-letter extension to each filename to further describe the file contents. Increasingly, however, the file extension is automatically assigned by the software.

  As a computer user, you are not usually responsible for naming executable files. These files are included with the application software you purchase, and the files are named by the programmers who write them. It is useful to know, however, that the executable files you can run generally have either a .COM (for *command*) extension or .EXE (for *executable*) extension.

  As you will recall from a previous lesson, there are some executable files that the computer runs without your intervention. These files have extensions such as .SYS, .DLL, .DRV, and .VBX.

- Generic file extensions: Some file extensions do not tell you what application was used to create the file, but instead tell you a general file category. For example, a .TXT extension tells you that the file is in the general category of text data files. A useful computing skill is the ability to look at a file extension and understand what it tells you about the file. Refer to Table D-2 for a list of generic file extensions.

- Many application programs create data files with a specific extension. This helps the program later locate the files it created, so you don't have to look through a list of files created by all the programs on your computer. If you are familiar with these extensions, you will know which application to use when you want to revise a file. Table D-3 lists the extensions typically used in DOS and Windows environments.

Filename Extensions

Wildcards: what's *.*?

Wildcards are used in most operating systems to make it easier to manipulate a collection of files. For example, suppose you want to list all the files on your disk that have an .exe extension. You can specify *.exe. (pronounced "star dot e x e") The asterisk is a **wildcard character** used to represent a group of characters. For example, *.exe means all the files with an .exe extension.

.exe can represent Excel.exe or Spell.exe; and Excel. can represent Excel.exe and Excel.cfg. *.* (pronounced "star dot star") means all files. Using wildcards, you can delete all the files on a disk in one operation, instead of deleting each file individually. When you use DOS, the command DEL *.* will delete all the files in a directory. Be careful if you use this command.

TABLE D-1: *Filenaming conventions*

	DOS AND WINDOWS 3.1	WINDOWS 95	Mac OS	UNIX
Maximum length of filename	8 character filename plus the 3 character extension	255 characters including 3 character extension	31 character filename; no extensions used	256 characters (depends on the version of UNIX); includes an extension of any length
Character to separate filename from extension	. (period)	. (period)	no extensions	. (period)
Spaces allowed	No	Yes	Yes	No
Numbers allowed	Yes	Yes	Yes	Yes
Characters NOT allowed	/ [ ] ; = " \ : , | * ?	\ ? : " < > |	None	!@#$%^&* ( )[ ]{}'"V|;<>
Reserved words	AUX, COM1, COM2, COM3, COM4, CON, LPT1, LPT2, LPT3, PRN, or NUL	AUX, COM1, COM2, COM3, COM4, CON, LPT1, LPT2, LPT3, PRN, or NUL	None	Depends on version of UNIX
Case sensitive	No	No	Yes	Yes—use lowercase

TABLE D-2: *Generic file extensions*

FILE TYPE	FILE EXTENSION	FILE TYPE	FILE EXTENSION
Text	.txt	**Graphics**	.bmp .pcx .tif .wmf .jpg .gif
Sound	.wav .mid	**Animation/video**	.flc .fli .avi .mpg
Executable	.exe .com .dll .vbx	**Compressed**	.zip
Batch	.bat	**Web documents**	.html .htm

TABLE D-3: *Application specific file extensions*

DATABASE APPLICATIONS	FILE EXTENSION	SPREADSHEET APPLICATIONS	FILE EXTENSION	WORD-PROCESSING APPLICATIONS	FILE EXTENSION
Microsoft Access	.mdb	Lotus 1-2-3	.wk4	WordPerfect	.wpd
Microsoft Works	.wdb	Microsoft Excel	.xls	Microsoft Word/Wordpad	.doc
Claris FileMaker Pro	.fm	Microsoft Works	.wks	Microsoft Works	.wps
Lotus Approach	.apr	Quattro Pro	.wb1	Lotus Word Pro	.sam

Understanding logical file storage

IN ADDITION TO KNOWING FILENAMING conventions, it is important to know how files are stored on the disk. Understanding both logical and physical file storage will help you maintain solid file management. Metaphors of directory structures are sometimes called logical models because they represent the way you logically conceive them. For example, you can think of files being stored in file folders nested inside one another or as a tree with many branches. Figure D-16 provides illustrations of three metaphors to help you understand how files are stored.

DOS Directories and File Managemnent

Windows Directories, Folders, and Files

Directories

When you type directory names, don't confuse the backslash \ with the regular slash /, which slants a different way.

IN MORE DETAIL

○━━ The **directory** is a list of files for each disk or CD-ROM that is maintained by the operating system. The directory contains information about each file such as the filename, the file extension, the date and time the file was created, and the file size for every file on a storage device. You can use an operating system command to view the directory of a disk.

○━━ The **file size** is the number of characters a file contains.

○━━ The **root directory**, which is the main directory of a disk, provides a useful list of files. It could be difficult, however, to find a particular file if your directory contains several hundred files.

○━━ **Subdirectories** or **folders** divide your directory into smaller lists, which help you organize a large number of files. Most operating systems allow you to divide your directory into subdirectories. For example, you can create one subdirectory to hold all your word-processing documents and another subdirectory to hold all your files that contain graphical images.

A subdirectory name is separated from a drive letter and a filename by a special symbol. In DOS and Microsoft Windows, this symbol is the backslash \. For example, the root directory of drive C might have a subdirectory called Graphics, written as C:\Graphics.

○━━ A **file specification** is the drive letter, subdirectory, and filename that identifies a file. Suppose you create a subdirectory on drive A named Word for your word-processing documents. Now suppose you create a file of a list of things to do named To-do.doc and put it on drive A in the Word subdirectory. The file specification for that document would be A:\Word\To-do.doc.

FIGURE D-16: *A logical view of the directory "tree"*

You can mentally visualize the directory of a disk as a tree on its side. The trunk and branches are directories and the leaves are files.

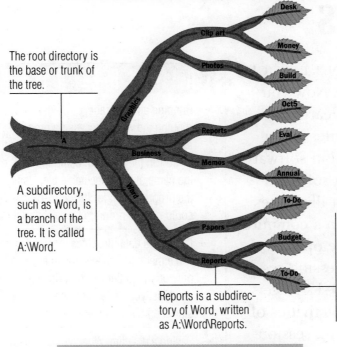

The root directory is the base or trunk of the tree.

A subdirectory, such as Word, is a branch of the tree. It is called A:\Word.

Reports is a subdirectory of Word, written as A:\Word\Reports.

Files, such as To-Do and Budget, are the leaves of the tree. To-Do and Budget are in the Reports subdirectory. The file specification for To-Do is A:\Word\Reports\To-Do.

A hierarchical metaphor uses a diagram to show how files are arranged in folders on each storage device.

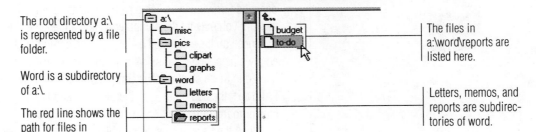

The root directory a:\ is represented by a file folder.

Word is a subdirectory of a:\.

The red line shows the path for files in a:\word\reports.

The files in a:\word\reports are listed here.

Letters, memos, and reports are subdirectories of word.

A boxes-within-boxes metaphor uses nested windows to represent the contents of folders.

The window for the root directory of 3½ Floppy (A:) holds the file folders Pics, Word, and Misc.

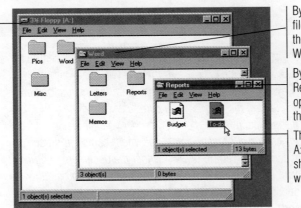

By clicking the Word file folder, you open the window for the Word directory.

By clicking the Reports folder, you open the window for the Reports directory.

The files in A:\Word\Reports are shown in the Reports window.

COMPUTER FILES AND DATA STORAGE ◄ **D-21**

Learning about using files

YOU HAVE LEARNED ABOUT PHYSICAL and logical file storage. Now you can apply what you've learned to how you typically use files when you work with application software. Using word-processing software to produce a document illustrates the way you use files on a computer, so take a look at the file operations for a typical word-processing session. Examine Figure D-17 to get an overview of the file activities of a typical word-processing session.

Using Files

☞ Running an application: You generally begin a word-processing session by running the word-processing program. The word-processing program is an executable file and would be shown in the directory with an .exe extension.

    To run the program using the DOS operating system, you would type in the name of this executable file. Using Windows 3.1, you would click on the program icon for the word-processing program. With Windows 95, you could run the program by selecting it from a menu or by clicking an icon.

☞ Creating a data file: Once the word-processing program is running, you can either begin a new document or retrieve a document that was created previously. To begin a new document, you usually just start typing. As you type, your data is placed in memory. Usually, your data is not stored on disk, until you initiate the save command.

☞ Saving a data file: When you are ready to save the data for the first time, you must give it a name. You will select a name that conforms to the filenaming conventions of the operating system on your computer as described previously in Table D-1. If you are using the Windows operating system, you may let the computer assign a filename extension.

    Once you have selected a filename, the computer checks the FAT to find empty clusters on the disk. When you save a file, the data for the file is copied to these clusters. The computer records the cluster numbers in the FAT. Next, the computer adds the filename and the address of the starting cluster to the directory.

    When the save process is complete, your data has been saved as a data file on your disk. With most word-processing software, the data for your document remains in memory even after the save process is completed. When you no longer want to work on the document, you need to close the document or exit the word-processing program.

The document-centric approach to files

In addition to opening a file through the application, another way to open a data file is by selecting the file itself. This approach is the document-centric approach. The term document-centric or docucentric is derived from two words: document and centric. **Document-centric** *means that the document is central to the way you use a computer. The operating system on your computer determines whether you can use the document-centric approach. Under the document-centric approach, once you identify the document you want to revise, the computer automatically starts the appropriate application program and opens the data file you selected.*

◄ Running an appli-
cation: you decide to
create a document
about the summer
vacation packages
your company offers.
The program file is
copied from the hard
drive to the memory
of the computer.

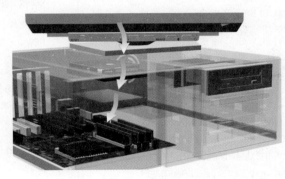

◄ Creating a data file:
Your data is stored
in memory while
you type.

► Saving a data file:
You name the file
so you can later
retrieve it by name.
A:Vacation.doc is
copied from memory
to the floppy disk.
Once you have saved
your file, you can exit
the Word program or
work on another
document.

Learning more about using files

ONCE YOU HAVE CREATED AND SAVED A FILE, SUCH AS A WORD-PROCESSING FILE, YOU CAN continue to work with that file. Refer to Figure D-18 as you look at some more ways you can use the file.

IN MORE DETAIL

☞ Retrieving a data file: To retrieve a data file, you must first find it. If the file you want is not in the list, you might have to tell the computer to look in a different subdirectory or folder. The application only shows you files in one folder at a time. Once the file is found, the computer copies the file from the storage device into the memory of the computer.

☞ Revising a data file: When your data is in the memory of your computer—you can add, delete, or change the words in your document. Changes are not reflected on the data that is stored on the disk, however, until you save the file again.

☞ Saving a revised file: When you have completed your revisions, you must save the document if you want the revised version of the document stored on the disk. Most software provides you with two options for saving your revised document.

The first option lets you save your revised document over the existing document. This means that the only document stored on the disk is the most current, revised version.

The second option lets you save your revised file using a new filename. Your original file will remain unchanged. If you ever want to go back to the original file, you can find it by using the original filename. In Windows this is the Save As option. In DOS, you activate this option by responding with No to the question "Do you want to replace the file?" When you save a file under this option, your revision is saved as a new file and you must give it a name that is different from a previous version of the file.

☞ Copying files: You can copy a file from one storage medium to another, from one folder to another, or from one directory to another. When you copy a file, the original file remains intact.

☞ Deleting files: If you want to eliminate a file that you have saved on disk, you **delete** or **erase** the file. As additional files are stored on the disk, the sectors that formerly contained the deleted file are gradually overwritten.

What really happens when you erase a file

When you erase a file, the operating system changes the status of the appropriate clusters in the FAT. For example, if a file is stored in clusters 1, 2, 5, and 7 and you erase it, the operating system changes the status for those four clusters to "empty." The data is not physically removed or erased from those clusters. Instead, the old data remains in the clusters until a new file is stored there. This rather interesting situation means that if you inadvertently erase a file, you might be able to get it back using the operating system's undelete utility. Of course, you can only undelete a file if you haven't recorded something new over it, so it's best to discover and correct mistakes immediately. Not all operating systems provide an undelete utility. To find out if one is available, you can consult the reference manual for your operating system.

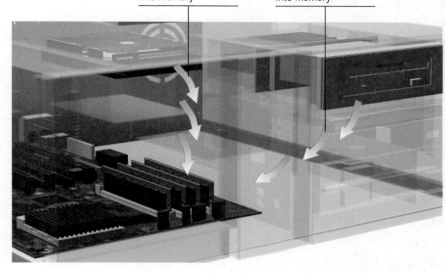

Word.exe is loaded into memory

A:\Vacation.doc is copied from disk into memory

◀ Retrieving a file: Now suppose that a few days later, you decide that you want to revise your file. You start Microsoft Word. Once the Word program is running, you can retrieve the Vacation.doc file from the disk on which it is stored. Once the operating system has retrieved the file, the word-processing software displays it on the screen.

▶ Revising a data file: When you see the Vacation.doc file on the screen, you can make modifications to it. Each character that you type and each change that you make is stored temporarily in the main memory of the computer, but not on the disk. When you are finished revising your document, save it.

When you revise the document, the changes you make to Vacation.doc are stored in memory until you save it to disk.

If you accidentally erase a file, you should stop using the computer immediately. Do not store anything else on the drive that contains the erased file until after you have used an undelete utility program to try to restore the file.

You do not need two floppy disk drives to copy a disk. Both Windows and DOS allow you to make a copy of an entire disk by reading the data from the source disk into memory, then inserting the destination disk and copying the data from memory to the new disk.

Concepts Review

Examine Figure D-19 and answer the following questions.

1. The figure is showing the directory for which drive?

2. Name the two program files shown in the directory window.

3. Name two data files shown in the directory window.

4. Identify two files that were created with the same program.

5. How much storage space is used by all the files in the directory?

6. How many files are in the directory?

7. Which operating system is this directory for?

8. Name two generic files in this directory.

9. What type of style directory is this?

10. Is there a file extension listed?

11. If there is a file extension, name the file and extension.

12. What would happen if you double-click the file Jv-mem?

13. What would happen if you double-click the icon labeled Q-mail?

FIGURE D-19

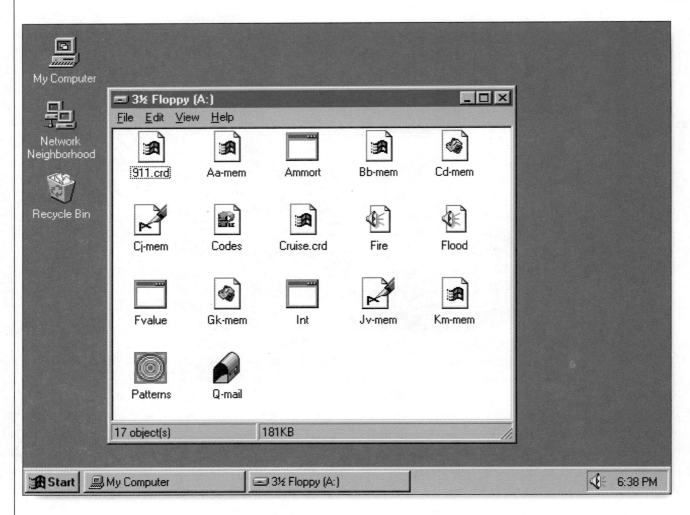

Circle the filenames in the following list that are not valid under the operating system used in your school's computer lab. Describe the filenaming convention that each nonvalid filename violates.

14. WP.EXE _____

15. PRN _____

16. WIN.EXE _____

17. AUTOEXEC.BAT _____

18. RESULTS*.WKS _____

19. MONTHLY.WK1 _____

20. REPORT#1.TXT8. _____

21. SMITH&SMITH.DOC _____

22. SEP/94.WRI _____

23. ASIA MAP.DOC _____

24. OCEAN.TIF_____

25. MN43-44.DBF _____

Match each statement with the term it describes:

26. ___ Magnetic storage

27. ___ Optical storage

28. ___ Data

29. ___ Document-centric

30. ___ .txt

31. ___ FAT

32. ___ File specification

a. Maintains a list of files and their physical location on the disk

b. Filename extension for general category of text file

c. Magnetized particles of oxidized-based surface coating

d. The drive letter, subdirectory, and filename that identifies a file

e. Document is central to way you use computer

f. Data burned into medium with laser light

g. Words, numbers, and graphics

Fill in the best answer:

33. To differentiate between data and information, use the rule: _____ is used by computers; _____ is used by humans.

34. Storage capacity is measured in _____, and access time is measured in _____.

35. A magnet can disrupt data on _____ storage, but _____ storage technology is more durable.

36. The formatting process creates a series of concentric _____ and pie-shaped _____ on the disk.

37. Data files which are entered by the user, changed often, or shared with other users are generally stored on _____ media.

38. The computer can move directly to any file on a _____ access device, but must start at the beginning and read through all the data on a _____ access device.

39. Newer technologies are decreasing the use of _____ for distribution; instead vendors are using _____ to distribute software.

40. The primary storage device on a microcomputer is _____.

41. The _____ keeps track of the physical location of files on a disk.

42. Executable files that YOU can run have _____ or _____ extensions.

43. When you use Windows application software to create a data file, you don't always have to add a(n) _____.

44. Nested file folders and directory trees are ways of representing _____ storage.

Many software applications use a specific file extension for data files created with that application. Determine the extensions used by five applications on your own or a lab computer.

To complete this independent challenge:

1. Run each software application and attempt to retrieve a file. If the software application uses a specific file extension, you will usually see the extension indicated in a box on the screen. For example, you might see *.DOC if you are using Microsoft Word.

2. For each of the five programs you select, specify the program name, sketch a picture of the program icon (if you are using Windows), indicate the executable filename (if you are using DOS), and indicate the filename extension the program uses. If the program does not use a specific filename extension, indicate that this is the case.

INDEPENDENT CHALLENGE 2

You should be aware of the storage devices on the computer you use so you use the best device for each task. You will need to take a hands-on look at either your computer at home or a computer in your school lab.

Answer the following questions to complete this independent challenge:

1. Where is this computer located?
2. What is the hard disk capacity?
3. What is the hard disk drive letter?
4. What is the floppy disk size?
5. What is the floppy disk capacity?
6. What is the floppy disk drive letter?
7. Is there a Zip disk drive?
8. Is there a tape storage device?
9. Is there a CD-ROM drive?
10. Which storage device do you usually use for the data files you create?
11. Which storage device holds most of the applications software that you use?
12. Which device would you use for backups?

INDEPENDENT CHALLENGE 3

Calculating Hard Disk Capacity Most manufacturers list the storage capacity of their hard disk drives on the drive itself or in the user manual.

To complete this independent challenge:

1. The manufacturer calculates storage capacity in bytes using the formula:

   capacity = cylinders $\times$ surfaces $\times$ sectors $\times$ 512

   The 512 in the formula is the number of bytes stored in each sector of each cylinder. Suppose you have a hard disk with 615 cylinders, 4 surfaces (two platters), and 17 sectors. What is the capacity in bytes of this disk?

2. How much storage space would your computer textbook require? Calculate approximately how many bytes of storage space the text (not pictures) of this book would require.

3. Count the number of lines on a typical page.

4. Count the number of characters (including blanks) in the longest line of text on the page.

5. Multiply the number of lines by the number of characters in the longest line to calculate the average number of characters (bytes) per page.

6. Multiply this figure by the number of pages in the book.

7. What do you estimate is the computer storage space

INDEPENDENT CHALLENGE 4

Use a recent computer magazine or an Internet site, such as Computer Express at **http://www.cexpress.com** or **http://www.warehouse.com.**

To complete this independent challenge:

1. Create a chart, such as the following:

Shopping list item	Brand name	Merchant	Price

2. Fill in shopping list item, brand name, merchant, and price for each of the following:

- Package of 10 3½" floppy disks
- High-density 3½" floppy disk drive
- Hard disk drive
- Tape cartridges
- Tape drive
- Zip disk
- Zip disk drive
- CD-ROM drive
- CD-R disk

INDEPENDENT CHALLENGE 5

File Extensions Many software applications use a specific file extension for data files created with that application.

To complete this independent challenge:

1. Suppose you have a disk with the following files:

Minutes.doc	Report.doc	Budget.xls
Jacsmemo.doc	Report1.doc	Shipjan.xls
Shipfeb.xls	Shipmar.xlx	Shipapr.xls
Minutes.txt	Roger.txt	Roadmap.bmp

If you could specify all the files with a .doc extension by *.doc. How would you specify the following files?

a. All the files with .txt extensions

b. All the files that contain "minutes"

c. All the files that begin with "Ship"

d. All the files on the disk

e. All the files that begin with the letter "R"

2. Suppose you need to retrieve a file from Sarah's computer. She tells you that the file is stored as D:\Data\Payables.xls.

a. What is the filename?

b. What is the file extension?

c. On which drive is the file stored?

d. In which directory is the file stored?

e. What type of file is it likely to be?

f. Will you need a specific software program to retrieve and view the file?

3. Suppose you need to defragment the files manually on the disk shown below. Using the disk on the right, show how the files are arranged after you complete the defragmentation. Use colored pencils or different patterns to show each file clearly.

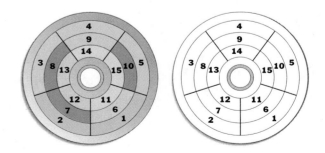

DOS DIRECTORIES AND FILE MANAGEMENT LAB

DOS is an operating system used on millions of computers. Even if your computer has a graphical user interface, such as Microsoft Windows, understanding DOS commands helps you grasp the basic concepts of computer file management. In this Lab, you learn how to use basic DOS commands.

1. Click the Steps button to learn basic DOS commands. As you proceed through the Steps, answer all of the Quick Check questions that appear. After you complete the Steps, you will see a Quick Check Summary Report. Follow the instructions on the screen to print this report.

2. Go through the Steps for this Lab once again. This time, create a mini DOS manual by listing each DOS command and its function. For each command, you should also provide a sample of a valid command, for example:

   DIR   Provides a listing of all the files on a disk

   Example: DIR A:

3. Click the Explore button and make a new disk. (You can copy over the disk you used for the Steps.) Do each of the following tasks and record the command you used:

   a. Display the directory for drive A.

   b. Display only those files on drive A that begin with the letter "T."

   c. Erase all the files that have names beginning with "New."

   d. Create a directory called PAPERS.

   e. Move all the files with .DOC extensions into the PAPERS directory.

   f. Rename OPUS27.MID to SONG.MID.

   g. Delete all the files with names that start with "Budget."

4. In Explore, make a new disk. (You can copy over the disk you used for earlier Lab activities.) Do each of the following tasks, then give your disk to your instructor. Don't forget to put your name on the disk label.

   a. Make two subdirectories on your disk: PICS and BUDGETS.

   b. Move all the files with .BMP extensions into the PICS directory.

   c. Move all the files with .WKS extensions into the BUDGETS directory.

   d. Delete all the files except README.TXT from the root directory. (Do not delete the files from PICS or BUDGETS.)

   e. Rename the file README.TXT to READ.ME1.

5. Use the TYPE command to view the contents of the START.BAT file. Describe the file contents. Use the TYPE command to view the contents of OPUS27.MID. Describe what you see. Explain the different results you obtained when you used the TYPE command with START.BAT and OPUS27.MID.

WINDOWS DIRECTORIES, FOLDERS, AND FILES LAB

Graphical user interfaces such as Mac OS, Windows 3.1, and Windows 95 use a filing system metaphor for file management. In this Lab, you will learn the basic concepts of these file system metaphors. With this background, you will find it easy to understand how to manage files with graphical user interfaces.

1. Click the Steps button to learn how to manipulate directories, folders and files. As you proceed through the Steps, answer all of the Quick Check questions that appear. After you complete the Steps, you will see a Quick Check Summary Report. Follow the instructions on the screen to print this report.

2. Make sure you are in Explore. Change to drive c: as the default drive. Double-click the c:\ folder to display its contents, then answer the following questions:

   a. How many data files are in the root directory of drive c:?

   b. How many program files are in the root directory of drive c:?

   c. Does the root directory of drive c: contain any subdirectories? How can you tell?

   d. How many files are in the DOS folder?

   e. Copy and complete the diagram in Figure D-20 to show the arrangement of folders on drive c:. Do not include files.

FIGURE D-20

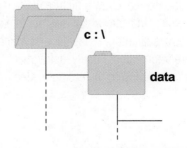

3. Click the Explore button. Make sure drive a: is the default drive. Double-click the a:\ folder to display the folder contents, then answer the following questions:

    a. How many files are in the root directory of drive a:?

    b. Are the files on drive a: data files or program files? How can you tell?

    c. Does the root directory of drive a: contain any subdirectories? How can you tell?

4. Open and close folders, and change drives as necessary to locate the following files. After you find the file, write out its file specification:

    a. config.sys   b. win.ini   c. toolkit.wks
    d. meeting.doc e. newlogo3.bmp f. todo.doc

DEFRAGMENTATION AND DISK OPERATIONS LAB

In this Lab you will format a simulated disk, save files, delete files, and undelete files to see how the computer updates the FAT. You will also find out how the files on your disk become fragmented and what a defragmentation utility does to reorganize the clusters on your disk.

1. Click the Steps button to learn how the computer updates the FAT when you format a disk and save, delete, and undelete files. As you proceed through the Steps, answer all of the Quick Check questions that appear. After you complete the Steps, you will see a Quick Check Summary Report. Follow the instructions on the screen to print this report.

2. Click the Explore button. Click the Format button to format the simulated disk. Try to save files 1, 2, 3, 4, and 6. Do they all fit on the disk?

3. In Explore, format the simulated disk. Try to save all the files on the disk. What happens?

4. In Explore, format the simulated disk. Save FILE-3, FILE-4, and FILE-6. Next, delete FILE-6. Now, save FILE-5. Try to undelete FILE-6. What happens and why?

5. In Explore, format the simulated disk. Save and erase files until the files become fragmented. Draw a picture of the disk to show the fragmented files. Indicate which files are in each cluster by using color, crosshatching, or labels. List which files in your drawing are fragmented. Finally, defragment the disk and draw a new picture showing the unfragmented files.

USING FILES LAB

In this Lab you manipulate a simulated computer to view what happens in memory and on disk when you create, save, open, revise, and delete files. Understanding what goes on "inside the box" will help you quickly grasp how to perform basic file operations with most application software.

1. Click the Steps button to learn how to use the simulated computer to view the contents of memory and disk when you perform basic file operations. As you proceed through the Steps, answer all of the Quick Check questions that appear. After you complete the Steps, you will see a Quick Check Summary Report. Follow the instructions on the screen to print this report.

2. Click the Explore button and use the simulated computer to perform the following tasks.

    a. Create a document containing your name and the city in which you were born. Save this document as NAME.

    b. Create another document containing two of your favorite foods. Save this document as FOODS.

    c. Create another file containing your two favorite classes. Call this file CLASSES.

    d. Open the FOODS file and add another one of your favorite foods. Save this file without changing its name.

    e. Open the NAME file. Change this document so it contains your name and the name of your school. Save this as a new document called SCHOOL.

    f. Write down how many files are on the simulated disk and the exact contents of each file.

3. In Explore, use the simulated computer to perform the following tasks.

    a. Create a file called MUSIC that contains the name of your favorite CD.

    b. Create another document that contains eight numbers and call this file LOTTERY.

    c. You didn't win the lottery this week. Revise the contents of the LOTTERY file, but save the revision as LOTTERY2.

    d. Revise the MUSIC file so it also contains the name of your favorite musician or composer, and save this file as MUSIC2.

    e. Delete the MUSIC file.

    f. Write down how many files are on the simulated disk and the exact contents of each file.

Computer Architecture

Unit E

IN THIS UNIT, YOU'LL TAKE A MORE DETAILED look inside the case of a modern computer system. The basic concepts you learn in this unit apply to micro, mini, and mainframe computers. You'll learn some technical concepts about how computers store and process data. You'll learn how, when, and why you should expand your computer system. Once you understand how a computer works, you will have more success troubleshooting problems you encounter in the lab, at work, or at home. After reading this unit, you'll also be better equipped to understand much of the computer jargon you hear in conversations and read in computer ads.

OBJECTIVES

Examine the inside of a system unit

Define data representation and transport

Understand data representation

Understand computer memory: RAM

Explore categories of computer memory

Define the central processing unit (CPU)

Understand CPU architecture

Understand CPU performance

Learn about input/output (I/O)

Plan for expansion

Learn about the boot process

Examining the inside of a system unit

COMPUTER ARCHITECTURE REFERS to the design and construction of a computer system. The architecture of any computer can be broadly classified by considering two characteristics: what the computer uses for power, and how the computer physically represents, processes, stores, and moves data.

Computers are electronic devices that are powered by electricity. Computers use electrical signals and circuits to represent, process, and move data. In order to help you understand the importance of these two characteristics, this lesson looks at computer architecture.

Inside the System Case

Integrated Circuits

Motherboards

Today, most integrated circuits are manufactured on a chip sliced from a silicon crystal. Silicon Valley in California got its name because so many of the computer companies located there use silicon chips in their products.

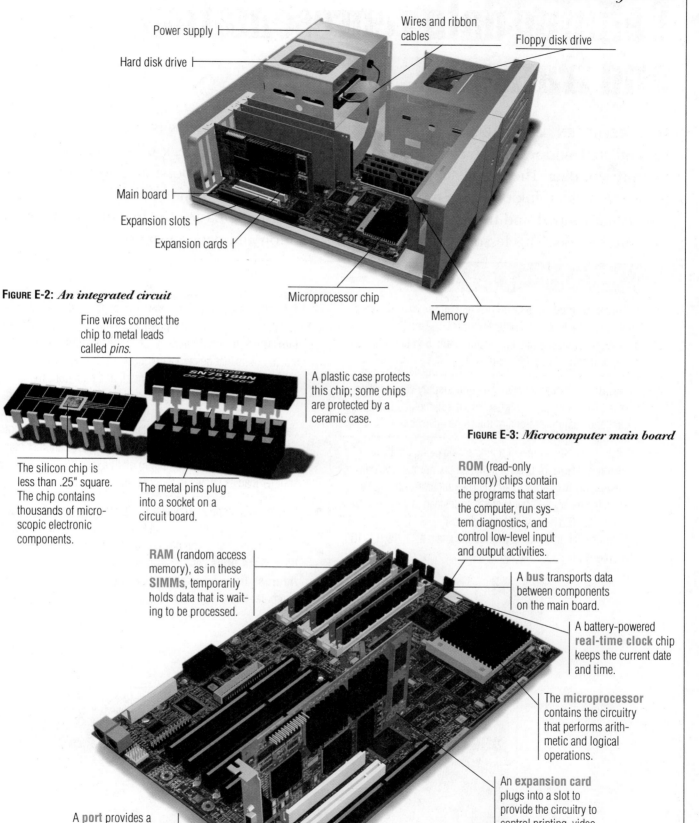

Power supply

Wires and ribbon cables

Floppy disk drive

Hard disk drive

Main board

Expansion slots

Expansion cards

Microprocessor chip

Memory

FIGURE E-2: *An integrated circuit*

Fine wires connect the chip to metal leads called *pins*.

SN 75188N

A plastic case protects this chip; some chips are protected by a ceramic case.

The silicon chip is less than .25" square. The chip contains thousands of microscopic electronic components.

The metal pins plug into a socket on a circuit board.

FIGURE E-3: *Microcomputer main board*

ROM (read-only memory) chips contain the programs that start the computer, run system diagnostics, and control low-level input and output activities.

RAM (random access memory), as in these SIMMs, temporarily holds data that is waiting to be processed.

A bus transports data between components on the main board.

A battery-powered real-time clock chip keeps the current date and time.

The microprocessor contains the circuitry that performs arithmetic and logical operations.

A port provides a plug for a cable that leads to a device, such as a printer, monitor, disk drive, or modem.

An expansion slot provides a way to add devices to a computer system.

An expansion card plugs into a slot to provide the circuitry to control printing, video display, disk storage, or telecommunications.

Defining data representation and transport

DATA REPRESENTATION REFERS TO THE FORM IN WHICH INFORMATION IS CONCEIVED, manipulated, and recorded. Since a computer is an electronic device, it uses electrical signals to represent data. The circuits in a digital computer have only two possible states. For convenience, you can think of one of those states as "on" and the other state as "off." If you equate the on state with 1 and the off state with 0, you can grasp the basic principle of how a digital computer works. This lesson looks at data representation and data transport.

IN MORE DETAIL

- A **digital device** works with discrete numbers or digits, such as 0 and 1. In this context, *discrete* means the numbers are distinct and separate. For example, the number 0 is discrete, or distinct, from the number 1.

- An **analog device** operates on continuously varying data. Figure E-4 can help you understand the difference between digital and analog versions of the same devices.

- Digital computers represent numeric data using the **binary number system**, or base 2. In the binary number system, there are only two digits: 0 and 1. The numeral 2 cannot be used in the binary number system, so instead of writing 2, you would write 10. The first eight numbers 1, 2, 3, 4, 5, 6, 7, and 8 are represented in the binary number system as 1, 10, 11, 100, 101, 110, 111, 1000. See Figure E-5.

Binary Numbers

- Typically, data travels from one location to another within the computer on an electronic pathway, or circuit, called a **data bus**. The term *bus* figuratively describes its function. Picture a school bus that goes to a neighborhood and picks up a load of children, drops them off at school, and then goes to the next neighborhood on its route to pick up a second bus load.

  A computer data bus works in a similar way. A computer data bus "picks up" a load of data from one of the components on the main board, and then transfers the data to another main board component. After dropping off this load, the bus collects another load as shown in Figure E-6.

- In terms of computer architecture, the data bus is a series of electronic circuits that connect the various electrical elements on the main board. The bus contains data lines and address lines. **Data lines** carry the signals that represent data. **Address lines** carry the location of the data to help the computer find the data it needs to process.

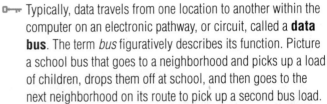

Why zeros and ones?

In a digital computer, each number or letter is represented by a series of electrical signals. Think about the way Morse code uses dashes and dots to represent letters. In a similar way, digital computers represent numbers, letters, and symbols with a code that uses a series of 0s (zeros) and 1s (ones). Data that is represented digitally can be easily moved or stored electronically as a series of "ons" and "offs."

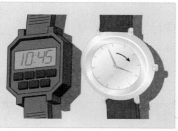

◄ The readout on a digital thermometer jumps in .1 degree increments, but the mercury in an analog thermometer creeps slowly up the temperature scale.

▲ A digital watch changes incrementally every minute, but the hands of an analog watch sweep continuously through a time interval.

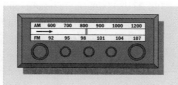

▲ A digital tuner jumps from one broadcast frequency to another, but the dial on an analog radio tuner sweeps through a continuous range of stations.

Decimal		Binary			
Place	Place	Place	Place	Place	Place
10	**1**	**8**	**4**	**2**	**1**
0					0
1					1
2				1	0
3				1	1
4			1	0	0
5			1	0	1
6			1	1	0
7			1	1	1
8		1	0	0	0
9		1	0	0	1
1	0	1	0	1	0

FIGURE E-6: *How a data bus works*

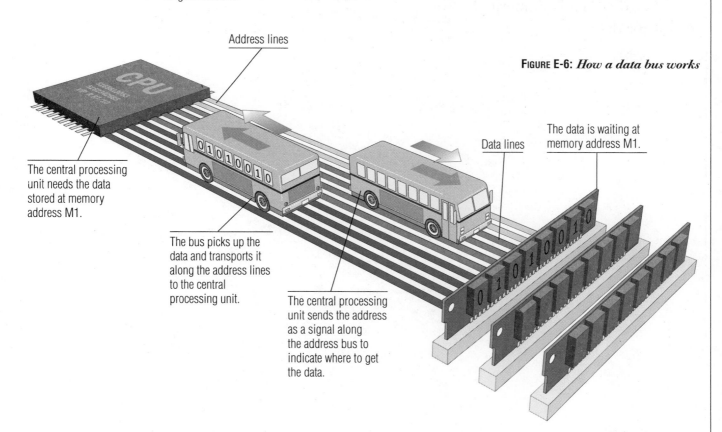

Address lines

Data lines

The data is waiting at memory address M1.

The central processing unit needs the data stored at memory address M1.

The bus picks up the data and transports it along the address lines to the central processing unit.

The central processing unit sends the address as a signal along the address bus to indicate where to get the data.

Understanding data representation

YOU NOW KNOW THAT DATA EXISTS IN the computer as a series of electronic signals represented as 0s and 1s. Each 0 or 1 that represents data is referred to as a **bit**. Most computer coding schemes use 8 bits to represent each number, letter, or symbol. A series of 8 bits is referred to as a **byte**. Study Figure E-7 to make sure you understand how the term *byte* is related to the terms *bits* and *characters*.

Digital computers use many different **coding schemes** to represent data. The coding scheme the computer uses depends on whether the data is numeric data or character data.

IN MORE DETAIL

○━ **Numeric data** consists of numbers that represent quantities and that might be used in arithmetic operations. For example, your annual income is numeric data. You use it in arithmetic operations every April when you calculate your income taxes.

○━ **Character data** is composed of letters, symbols, and numerals that will not be used in arithmetic operations. Examples of character data include your name, hair color, phone number, and social security number. Because you are not going to use your social security number or your phone number in arithmetic operations, they are considered character data.

○━ Digital computers typically represent character data using either the ASCII (pronounced "ASK ee") code or EBCDIC (pronounced "EB seh dick") code. **ASCII** stands for American Standard Code for Information Interchange. It is used to represent symbols and numerals as well as uppercase and lowercase letters. ASCII is a 7-bit data representation code used on most microcomputers, on many minicomputers, and on some mainframe computers. **EBCDIC** stands for Extended Binary Coded Decimal Interchange Code. IBM-brand mainframe computers often use the 8-bit EBCDIC code. Figure E-8 shows the ASCII and the EBCDIC codes.

► The smallest unit of information in a computer is a bit. A bit can be a 0 or a 1. The electronic circuits in a computer carry 1 bit as a pulse of electricity through an open switching circuit.

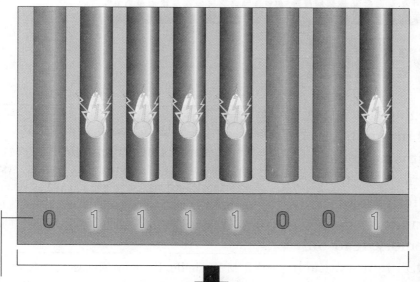

A collection of eight bits is called a **byte**. This byte is composed of the eight bits 01111001.

A byte represents one **character**—a letter, numeral, or punctuation symbol. This byte, 01111001, represents a lower-case *y*.

y

FIGURE E-8: *ASCII and EBCDIC codes*

SYMBOL	ASCII	EBCDIC	SYMBOL	ASCII	EBCDIC	SYMBOL	ASCII	EBCDIC
(space)	0100000	01000000	?	0111111	01101111	^	1011110	
!	0100001	01011010	@	1000000	01111100	_	1011111	
"	0100010	01111111	A	1000001	11000001	a	1100001	10000001
#	0100011	01111011	B	1000010	11000010	b	1100010	10000010
$	0100100	01011011	C	1000011	11000011	c	1100011	10000011
%	0100101	01101100	D	1000100	11000100	d	1100000	10000100
&	0100110	01010000	E	1000101	11000101	e	1100101	10000101
'	0100111	01111101	F	1000110	11000110	f	1100110	10000110
(	0101000	01001101	G	1000111	11000111	g	1100111	10000111
)	0101001	01011101	H	1001000	11001000	h	1101100	10001000
*	0101010	01011100	I	1001001	11001001	i	1101001	10001001
+	0101011	01001110	J	1001010	11010001	j	1101010	10010001
,	0101100	01101011	K	1001011	11010010	k	1101011	10010010
−	0101101	01100000	L	1001100	11010011	l	1101000	10010011
.	0101110	01001011	M	1001101	11010100	m	1101101	10010100
/	0101111	01100001	N	1001110	11010101	n	1101110	10010101
0	0110000	11110000	O	1001111	11010110	o	1111111	10010110
1	0110001	11110001	P	1010000	11010111	p	1110100	10010111
2	0110010	11110010	Q	1010001	11011000	q	1110001	10011000
3	0110011	11110011	R	1010010	11011001	r	1110010	10011001
4	0110100	11110100	S	1010011	11100010	s	1110011	10100010
5	0110101	11110101	T	1010100	11100011	t	1110100	10100011
6	0110110	11110110	U	1010101	11100100	u	1110101	10100100
7	0110111	11110111	V	1010110	11100101	v	1110110	10100101
8	0111000	11111000	W	1010111	11100110	w	1110111	10100110
9	0111001	11111001	X	1011000	11100111	x	1111000	10100111
:	0111010	01111010	Y	1011001	11101000	y	1111001	10101000
;	0111011	01011110	Z	1011010	11101001	z	1111010	10101001
<	0111100	01001100	[	1011011	01001010	{	1111011	
=	0111101	01111110	\	1011100		}	1111101	
>	0111110	01101110	]	1011101	01011010			

Understanding computer memory: RAM

MEMORY IS ELECTRONIC CIRCUITRY that holds data and program instructions when it is not being transported from one place to another. There are four major types of memory: random access memory, virtual memory, read-only memory, and CMOS memory. Each type of memory is characterized by the kind of data it contains and the technology it uses to hold the data.

Memory is sometimes called **primary storage**, but this term is easily confused with disk storage. It is preferable to use the term *memory* to refer to the circuitry that has a direct link to the processor and to use the term *storage* to refer to media, such as disks, that are not directly linked to the processor.

Memory Technology   **Grace Hopper**

IN MORE DETAIL

- **Random access memory**, or **RAM**, is an area in the computer system unit that temporarily holds user data, operating system instructions, and program instructions. Every time you turn on your computer, a set of operating system instructions is copied from disk into RAM. These instructions, which help control basic computer functions, remain in RAM until you turn the computer off.

- RAM is **volatile**. This is the term used to refer to memory that holds data only as long as the computer power is on. If the power goes off, the data in RAM disappears.

- The contents of RAM are necessary for the computer to process data. The results of processing are kept temporarily in RAM until they are needed again or until they are stored on disk.

- In RAM, microscopic electronic parts called **capacitors** hold the electronic signals for the ASCII, EBCDIC, or binary code that represents data. A charged capacitor represents an "on" bit. A discharged capacitor represents an "off" bit.

- You can visualize the capacitors arranged in banks of eight. Each bank of capacitors holds eight bits, or one byte of data. A **RAM address** on each bank helps the computer locate the data contained in the bank. Figure E-9 shows how RAM works.

- Today the storage capacity of RAM is measured in megabytes (MB). Microcomputers typically have between 16 and 64 MB of RAM, which means they can hold between 16 and 64 million bytes of data.

   The speed of RAM is also important. The processor works at a certain speed, but would be forced to slow down if it had to wait for data from RAM. Most RAM today has an access speed of 60 nanoseconds. Slower, older memory has access speeds of 70 or 80 nanoseconds.

- A **SIMM** (single in-line memory module) is a small circuit board that contains three to nine DIPS. It is the memory module of choice on today's microcomputers. Figure E-10 shows a SIMM that is available for microcomputers.

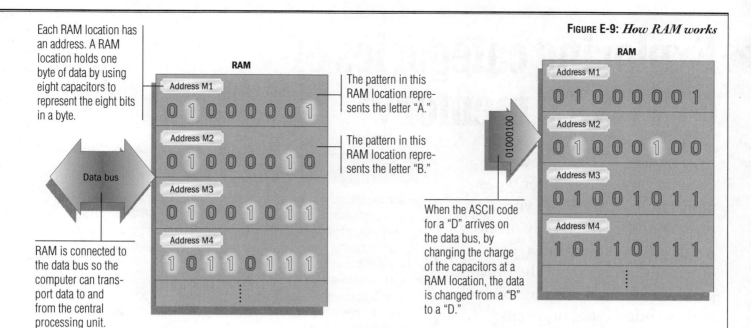

Each RAM location has an address. A RAM location holds one byte of data by using eight capacitors to represent the eight bits in a byte.

The pattern in this RAM location represents the letter "A."

The pattern in this RAM location represents the letter "B."

RAM is connected to the data bus so the computer can transport data to and from the central processing unit.

When the ASCII code for a "D" arrives on the data bus, by changing the charge of the capacitors at a RAM location, the data is changed from a "B" to a "D."

FIGURE E-10: *RAM avaliable for microcomputers*

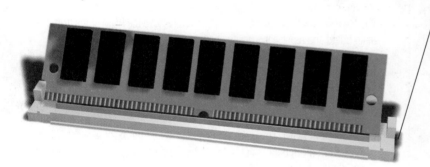

The edge of the SIMM circuit board plugs into a special SIMM slot in the main board.

How much RAM?

The amount of RAM a computer needs depends on the operating system and the applications software you plan to use. RAM requirements are usually specified on the outside of the software box. You can purchase RAM to expand the memory capacity of your computer. When you purchase additional RAM, you must make sure it is the correct type, size, and configuration for your computer system. Today, RAM costs about $10 per megabyte, so it isn't a major impact on the price of a computer system. To run many of today's software programs effectively, your computer should have at least 32 MB of RAM.

Exploring categories of computer memory

In addition to RAM, your computer uses three other types of memory to hold data: virtual memory, ROM (read-only memory), and CMOS. These other types of memory supplement the functions provided by RAM. This lesson looks at these other types of memory.

⌐ **Virtual memory** is the ability of a computer to use disk storage to simulate RAM. Virtual memory allows computers without enough RAM to run large programs, manipulate large data files, and run more than one program at a time. In the context of computing, *virtual* usually means simulated. Figure E-11 explains how virtual memory works.

One disadvantage of virtual memory is reduced performance. With most of today's operating systems the computer uses space on your computer's hard drive as an extension of RAM. It takes longer to retrieve data from virtual memory than from RAM because the disk is a mechanical device so access time is slower.

A disk access time of 10 milliseconds is quite a bit slower than a RAM access speed of 60 nanoseconds. Like RAM, data in virtual memory becomes inaccessible if the power goes off.

⌐ **Read-Only Memory**, or **ROM**, is a set of chips containing instructions that help a computer prepare for processing tasks. The instructions in ROM are permanent. You have no way to change them, unless you remove the ROM chips from the main board and replace them with another set.

ROM contains a small set of instructions called the **ROM BIOS (Basic Input Output System)**. The BIOS is a small but critical part of the operating system that tells the computer how to access the disk drives and look for the operating system. When you turn on your computer, remember RAM is empty. The central processing unit performs a series of steps by following the instructions stored in ROM. This series of steps is called the *boot process*, which is discussed in more detail later in this unit. Some steps in the boot process are permanently stored in ROM.

⌐ **CMOS memory** (pronounced "SEE moss") makes it possible for some boot instructions not to be permanent. CMOS is the acronym for **Complementary Metal Oxide Semiconductor**. CMOS uses battery power to retain vital data about your computer system configuration such as hard disk drive specifications and the date and time—even when your computer is turned off.

If information about the hard disk was permanently stored in ROM, you would never be able to replace your hard disk drive with a larger one. The computer could not access the new hard disk using information about the old disk. CMOS provides your computer with a type of memory more permanent than RAM, but less permanent than ROM.

When your system configuration changes, the data in the CMOS memory must be updated. See Figure E-12. To change the CMOS data, you usually run a CMOS setup program. Some operating systems have special utilities that help you update the CMOS settings so that hardware can be changed on any computer system. For example, the **plug and play** feature of most of today's computers helps you update CMOS if you install a new peripheral device.

1. Your computer is running a word-processing program that takes up most of the program area in RAM, but you want to run a spreadsheet program at the same time.

3. The spreadsheet program can now be loaded into the RAM vacated by the least-used segment of the word-processing program.

2. The operating system moves the least-used segment of the word-processing program into virtual memory on disk.

4. If the least-used segment of the word-processing program is needed in RAM, it is copied from virtual memory back into RAM. To make room, some other infrequently used segment of one of the programs will be transferred into virtual memory.

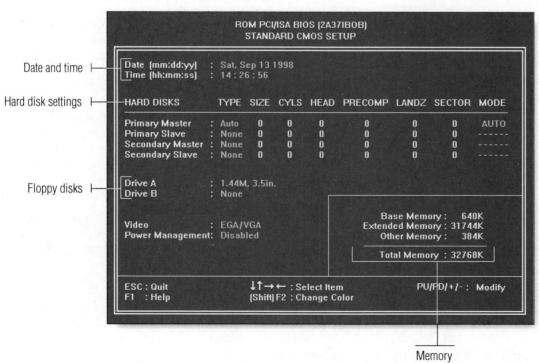

FIGURE E-12: *CMOS configuration*

Date and time ⊢

Hard disk settings ⊢

Floppy disks ⊢

```
                    ROM PCI/ISA BIOS (2A37IBOB)
                        STANDARD CMOS SETUP

 Date  (mm:dd:yy)    :  Sat, Sep 13 1998
 Time  (hh:mm:ss)    :  14 : 26 : 56


 HARD DISKS        TYPE  SIZE  CYLS  HEAD  PRECOMP  LANDZ  SECTOR  MODE

 Primary Master  : Auto   0     0     0       0       0      0     AUTO
 Primary Slave   : None   0     0     0       0       0      0    ------
 Secondary Master: None   0     0     0       0       0      0    ------
 Secondary Slave : None   0     0     0       0       0      0    ------


 Drive A         : 1.44M, 3.5in.
 Drive B         : None

                                          Base Memory :    640K
 Video           : EGA/VGA                Extended Memory : 31744K
 Power Management: Disabled               Other Memory :    384K

                                          Total Memory : 32768K

 ESC : Quit          ↓↑→← : Select Item        PU/PD/+/- :  Modify
 F1  : Help          (Shift) F2 : Change Color
```

Memory

The difference between memory types: RAM is temporary; virtual memory is disk-based; ROM is permanent; CMOS is battery powered and more permanent than RAM but less permanent than ROM.

Defining the central processing unit (CPU)

So far in this unit you have learned that data can be held in memory or transported over the data bus. But a computer does more than store and transport data. A computer processes data, performs arithmetic, sorts lists, formats documents, and so on. The computer processes data in the central processing unit (CPU).

Which Chip?

○── The **central processing unit (CPU)** is the circuitry in a computer that performs arithmetic and logic operations and executes instructions. The CPU receives instructions from RAM, and then uses the data in RAM for processing.

○── The central processing unit consists of one or more integrated circuits. A **microprocessor** is a single integrated circuit. In a microcomputer the central processing unit is a microprocessor. Figure E-13 shows a microprocessor that is probably similar to the one in the computer you use.

○── Most of today's microcomputers are designed around a microprocessor from one of two product families: x86 or PowerPC. See Figure E-14.

   The original IBM PC used the Intel 8088 microprocessor, one of the first models in the **x86 family** of microprocessors. Today's PCs still contain x86 processors, such as the Pentium. Most of these processors are manufactured by Intel, but companies such as Cyrix and AMD have produced what are called "work-alike" processors. Computers with "work-alike" processors are generally less expensive than an equivalent computer with an Intel processor.

○── If you would rather run Macintosh software, select a computer with a 68000-series or PowerPC microprocessor. Until 1994, Macintosh computers contained a **68000-series microprocessor** manufactured by Motorola. More recent models called "Power Macs" contain a **PowerPC microprocessor** that implements RISC architecture to provide relatively fast performance at a low cost.

○── The x86 chip family descended from Intel's 8086 microprocessor. The 80286, 80386, and 80486 models that followed were usually referred to by the last three digits, 286, 386, and 486. For the next generation, however, Intel broke with tradition. Initially, the 80586 chip was dubbed the P5, until it was officially named the **Pentium** in 1993. In 1995, Intel produced the P6 generation of processors called the **Pentium Pro**.

   In 1997, Intel launched two new processors. The **Pentium with MMX technology** was a jazzed-up version of the original Pentium chip and contained circuitry to speed the execution of multimedia applications. A second chip, the **Pentium II**, added MMX technology to the Pentium Pro chip.

Moore's Law			
	Integrated circuit technology is the basic building block of CPUs in today's micro, mini, mainframe, and supercomputers. Remarkable advances in this technology have produced exponential increases in computer speed and power. In 1965, Gordon Moore, cofounder of chip-production giant, Intel	Corporation, predicted that the number of transistors on a chip would double every 18 to 24 months. Much to the surprise of engineers and Moore himself, Moore's Law accurately predicted 30 years of chip development. In 1958, the first integrated circuit contained two transistors. The Pentium II processor,	introduced in 1997, has 7.5 million transistors.

The central processing unit of a microcomputer is a microprocessor. The microprocessor plugs into the main board and connects to the data bus.

The arithmetic logic unit is the circuitry that performs arithmetic and logical operations.

The control unit is the circuitry that coordinates the activities of the microprocessor.

The I/O circuitry provides a smooth path for data that travels to and from the microprocessor on the data bus.

The cache speeds up processing by holding data that has not been requested by the processor but is likely to be needed soon.

It is the microprocessor that truly defines the computer. A microprocessor is not the same as a microcomputer. A microprocessor is the CPU chip found on the main board of a microcomputer.

FIGURE E-14: *Microprocessor genealogy*

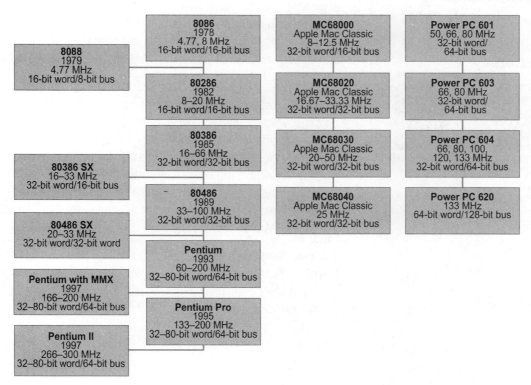

Understanding CPU architecture

THE CENTRAL PROCESSING UNIT (CPU) has two main parts: the arithmetic logic unit and the control unit. Each of these units performs specific tasks to process data.

A computer accomplishes a complex task by performing a series of very simple steps, referred to as instructions. An **instruction** tells the computer to perform a specific arithmetic, logical, or control operation. Each instruction tells the computer how to perform a single operation. Many instructions are required to accomplish a task such as adding a column of numbers. This lesson looks at how the ALU and control unit work together in a computer instruction.

CPU Simulator

CPUs

Instruction Sets

IN MORE DETAIL

☞ The **control unit** is the circuitry that directs and coordinates processing. It retrieves each instruction in sequence from RAM and places it in a special **instruction register**. The control unit then interprets the instruction to find out what needs to be done. The control unit helps get data into the ALU and tells the ALU what operation to perform. According to its interpretation, the control unit sends signals to the data bus to fetch data from RAM and to the arithmetic logic unit to perform a process as shown in Figure E-15.

☞ The **arithmetic logic unit (ALU)** is the circuitry that performs arithmetic operations such as addition and subtraction. It also performs logical operations such as comparing two numbers to see if they are the same. The ALU uses **registers** to hold the data that is being processed. In the ALU the result of an arithmetic or logical operation is held temporarily in the **accumulator**. See Figure E-16.

☞ An **instruction set** is the list of instructions that a central processing unit can perform. Every task a computer performs must be described in terms of the limited list of instructions in the instruction set.

The term **instruction cycle** refers to the process in which a computer executes a single instruction. The instruction cycle is repeated each time the computer executes an instruction. The steps in this cycle are summarized in Figure E-17.

☞ A computer instruction has two parts: the op code and the operands. An **op code**, which is short for operation code, is a command word for an operation such as add, compare, or jump. The **operands** for an instruction specify the data or the address of the data for the operation. For example, a computer instruction might read: **JMP M1**.

In the instruction JMP M1, the op code is JMP and the operand is M1. The op code JMP means *jump* or go to a different instruction. The operand M1 is the RAM address of the instruction.

☞ You have all the pieces you need to understand the details of the instruction cycle. You know how the ALU performs arithmetic and logical operations, and how the control unit retrieves data from RAM and tells the ALU which operation to perform.

2. The RAM address of the instruction is kept in the **instruction pointer**. When the instruction has been executed, the address in the instruction pointer changes to indicate the RAM address of the next instruction to be executed.

1. The control unit retrieves an instruction from RAM and puts it in the **instruction register**.

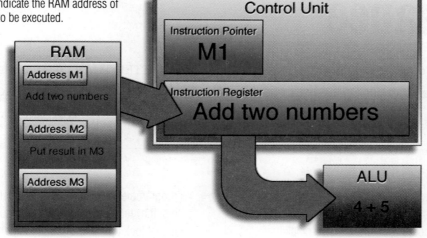

3. The control unit interpets the instruction in its instruction register.

4. Depending on the instruction, the control unit will get data from RAM, tell the ALU to perform an operation, or change the memory address in the instruction pointer.

FIGURE E-16: *How the ALU works*

1. The data to be processed arrives from RAM and is held in registers.

2. A signal from the control unit indicates which arithmetic or logical operation to perform.

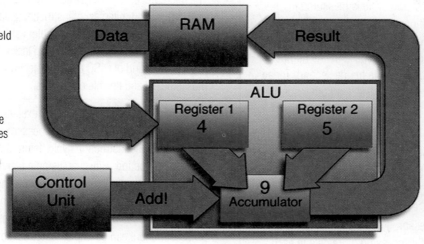

4. The results are usually sent to RAM so that they can be output or stored on disk.

3. The ALU performs the operation and places the result in the accumulator.

FIGURE E-17: *Instruction cycle*

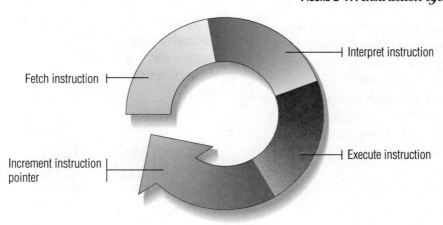

Like other data in the computer, instructions are stored as 1s and 0s. Using zeros and ones for instructions allows the computer to store and transport the instructions as a series of electrical signals.

Understanding CPU performance

ALL CPUS ARE NOT CREATED EQUAL; SOME PROCESS DATA FASTER THAN OTHERS. CPU SPEED IS influenced by several factors including clock rate, word size, cache, and instruction set size. This lesson looks at the factors that affect central processing unit performance.

IN MORE DETAIL

☞ A computer contains a **system clock** that emits pulses to establish the timing for all system operations. The system clock operates at a speed quite different from a clock that keeps track of the time of day. The system clock determines the speed at which the computer can execute an instruction, and therefore limits the number of instructions the computer can complete within a specific amount of time. The time to complete an instruction execution cycle is measured in **megahertz (MHz)**, or millions of cycles per second.

Although some instructions require multiple cycles to complete, you can think of processor speed as the number of instructions the processor can execute in one second. Today, microprocessor speeds exceed 300 MHz. If all other specifications are identical, higher megahertz ratings mean faster processing.

☞ **Word size** refers to the number of bits the central processing unit can manipulate at one time. Word size is based on the size of the registers in the CPU and the number of data lines in the bus. For example, a CPU with an 8-bit word size is referred to as an 8-bit processor; it has 8-bit registers and manipulates 8 bits at a time. Processing more data in each cycle contributes to increased performance. Today's faster computers use 32-bit or 64-bit microprocessors. All other factors being equal, larger word size means faster processing.

☞ **Cache** is special high-speed memory that gives the microprocessor more rapid access to data because a high-speed microprocessor can execute an instruction so quickly that it often waits for data to be delivered from RAM. Cache is sometimes called **RAM cache** or **cache memory**. The cache ensures that data is immediately available whenever the central processing unit requests it. All other factors being equal, more cache means faster processing.

☞ As programmers developed various instruction sets for computers, they tended to add more and more complex instructions that took up many bytes in memory and required several clock cycles for execution. A computer based on a central processing unit with a complex instruction set came to be known as a **complex instruction set computer**, or **CISC**.

☞ The microprocessor of a **reduced instruction set computer**, or **RISC**, has a limited set of instructions that it can perform very quickly. In theory, RISC computers should be faster than CISC computers for most processing tasks. However, that a balance or hybrid of CISC and RISC technologies produces the most efficient and flexible computers.

☞ Computers with a single processor execute one instruction at a time or "serially." Usually, the processor must complete all four steps in the instruction cycle before it begins to execute the next instruction. However, using a technology called **pipelining**, the processor begins executing an instruction before it completes the previous instruction. See Figure E-18. Pipelining speeds up processing in computers with a single processor and it can be implemented on computers with multiple processors.

☞ A computer that has more than one processor can execute multiple instructions at the same time. This method of executing instructions is called parallel processing. **Parallel processing** increases the amount of processing a computer can accomplish in a specific amount of time. Special software is required to take advantage of parallel processing. Figure E-19 explains the concept of parallel processing.

RISC

Parallel and Pipelining

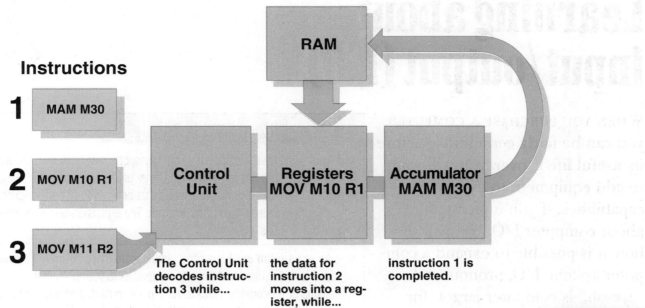

Instructions

1 MAM M30

2 MOV M10 R1

3 MOV M11 R2

The Control Unit decodes instruction 3 while...

the data for instruction 2 moves into a register, while...

instruction 1 is completed.

FIGURE E-19: *How parallel processing works*

Each processor completes its assigned instruction using data that has been transported from RAM into the CPU registers. Because the processors finish at different times, the results might not be in sequence.

The control unit sends an instruction to the next available processor.

Instructions are queued and waiting to enter the CPU.

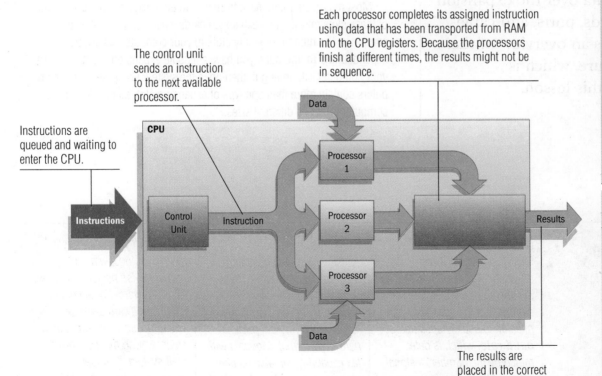

The results are placed in the correct sequence and sent out of the CPU.

A chain is only as strong as its weakest link. A computer system might also have weak links. Even with a high-performance processor, a computer system with a slow hard disk, no disk cache, and a small amount of RAM is likely to be slow at tasks such as starting programs, loading data files, printing, and scrolling through long documents.

Disk cache and RAM cache are not the same. Disk cache works with data between the disk and memory. RAM cache works with data between RAM and the central processing unit.

Learning about input/output (I/O)

WHEN YOU PURCHASE A COMPUTER, you can be fairly certain that before its useful life is over, you will want to add equipment to expand its capabilities. If you understand about computer I/O, you will see how it is possible to expand a computer system. I/O, pronounced "eye-oh," is computer jargon for input/output. I/O refers to collecting data for the microprocessor to manipulate and to transporting results to display, print, and storage devices. I/O between the central processing unit and peripheral devices often involves a long path that moves data over the expansion bus, slots, cards, ports, and cables. Figure E-20 is an overview of the I/O architecture, which is described in this lesson.

IN MORE DETAIL

○━ You already learned that a data bus transports data between RAM and the CPU. The data bus also extends to other parts of the computer. The segment of the data bus that transports data between RAM and peripheral devices is called the **expansion bus**. The expansion bus is an extension of the data bus.

○━ An **expansion card** is a small circuit board that can connect a device to your computer and that can add capabilities to your computer, such as sound or telecommunications. An expansion card, also referred to as an **expansion board** or a **controller card**, is plugged into an expansion slot. An expansion card provides the I/O circuitry for peripheral devices and sometimes contains an expansion device. Microcomputer users can select from a wide variety of expansion cards, such as those shown in Figure E-21.

○━ An **expansion slot** is a socket into which you can plug an expansion card. See Figure E-22. The expansion slots on mainframe, mini, and microcomputers provide a way to connect a large variety of peripheral devices.

 Most microcomputers have from four to eight expansion slots. Some of these slots may contain expansion cards when you purchase your computer. The number of empty slots in your computer determines its expandability. To find out if you have adequate expansion capability, turn your computer off, unplug it, then open the system unit case. Some computers contain more than one type of expansion slot, so the slots in your computer might be different sizes.

Modems

*Many computer systems include a modem. **Modems** are used to transmit and receive data over phone lines to other computers. The speed of transmission is usually specified by **baud rate**, which is determined by the number of signal changes that occur in one second during transmission. Faster baud rates mean faster data transmission. A fax-modem is a modem that can send a document that is in the memory of your computer to any standard fax machine where it prints in hard copy format. Modems with fax capability can also receive fax transmission from standard fax machines or other fax-modems. If your computer system includes a modem, it probably also has communications software. Some communications software packages allow you to set up your computer as an answering machine or voice-mail system. A modem is required for Internet access.*

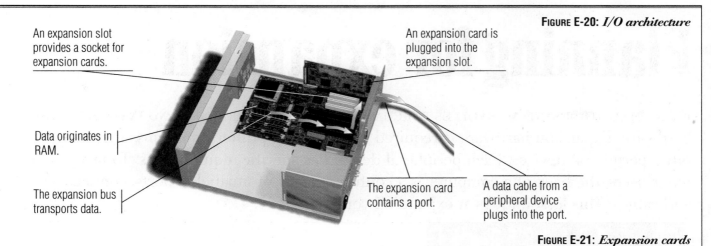

An expansion slot provides a socket for expansion cards.

Data originates in RAM.

The expansion bus transports data.

An expansion card is plugged into the expansion slot.

The expansion card contains a port.

A data cable from a peripheral device plugs into the port.

FIGURE E-21: *Expansion cards*

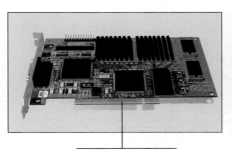 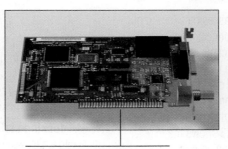 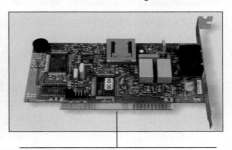

A **graphics card** connects your monitor and computer.

A **network card** connects your computer to the other computers on a local area network.

A **modem card** connects your computer to the telephone system so you can transport data from one computer to another.

FIGURE E-22: *Inserting an expansion card into a slot*

A microcomputer main board often features more than one type of expansion slot. The two slots shown are different types, as can be seen from their different lengths.

An **expansion slot** contains metallic contacts that connect to the expansion bus.

When the card is inserted into the slot, the metal card edge connectors contact the connectors in the slot to make a circuit for data transport.

An expansion card has a *card edge* connector with metal contacts that connect to the circuitry on the card.

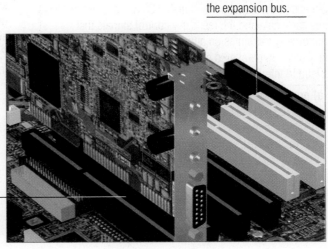

Expansion bus

Planning for expansion

EXPANDING YOUR SYSTEM INVOLVES PURCHASING EXPANSION HARDWARE AND INSTALLING THAT hardware. Expansion hardware is required when adding printers, modems, and many other peripheral devices. Each peripheral device has specific requirements. To many computer users, the back of a computer is a confusing array of unlabeled ports, connectors, and cables. This lesson looks at expanding your system.

IN MORE DETAIL

☞ An **expansion port** is a location that passes data in and out of a computer or peripheral device. To connect a peripheral device to an expansion card, you plug a cable from the device into the expansion port on the expansion card. An expansion port is often housed on an expansion card so that it is accessible through a hole in the back of the computer system unit, or it might also be connected directly to the main board, instead of an expansion card. Figure E-23 shows the shapes of the most frequently used expansion ports.

☞ A **parallel port** provides a connection for transmitting data eight bits at a time over a cable with eight separate data lines. Because all eight bits travel at the same time, parallel transmission is relatively fast. Parallel transmission is typically used to send data to a printer.

    In a microcomputer the parallel port is either built into the main board or mounted on an expansion card. The cable that connects two parallel ports contains 25 wires. Eight of the wires carry data and the rest carry control signals that maintain orderly transmission and reception. Since the wires that carry data run parallel to each other, the signals in the cables tend to interfere with each other over long distances.

☞ A **serial port** provides a connection for transmitting data one bit at a time. A serial port connects your computer to a device, such as a modem, which requires two-way data transmission, or to a device, such as a mouse, which requires only one-way data transmission. A serial cable contains one data line and an assortment of control lines. Because a serial cable requires fewer data lines, it is less susceptible to interference than a parallel cable.

☞ The system unit provides openings called **bays** for mounting disk, CD-ROM, and tape drives. An **external bay** provides an opening for installing a device that you need to access from the outside of the case, such as a floppy disk drive. An **internal bay** provides a mounting bracket for devices that don't need outside accessibility, such as a hard disk drive.

☞ A **docking station** is essentially an additional expansion bus into which you plug your notebook computer. It provides expansion slots for cards that would not fit into the notebook case.

☞ A **PCMCIA slot** (Personal Computer Memory Card International Association) is a special type of expansion slot developed for notebook computers, which do not have space in the case for full-size expansion slots and cards. A PCMCIA slot is a small, external slot into which you can insert a PCMCIA card. See Figure E-24. PCMCIA cards are credit-card sized circuit boards that incorporate an expansion card and a device. They can contain modems, memory expansion, or even hard disk drives. Unlike traditional expansion cards, PCMCIA devices can be plugged in or removed without turning the computer off.

PCMCIA

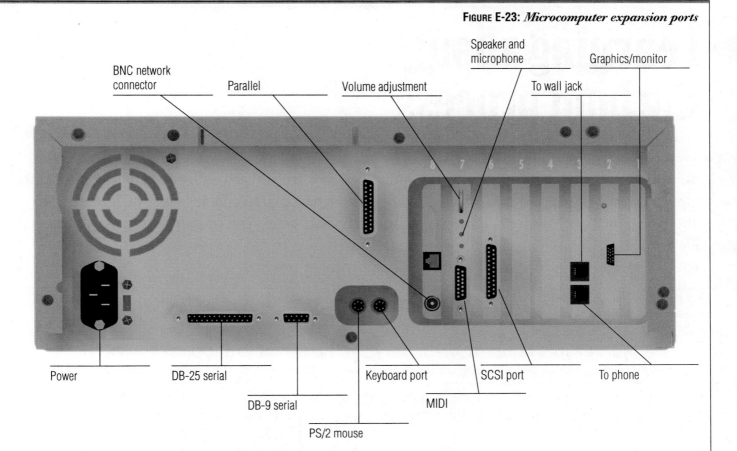

FIGURE E-23: *Microcomputer expansion ports*

BNC network connector

Parallel

Volume adjustment

Speaker and microphone

To wall jack

Graphics/monitor

Power

DB-25 serial

DB-9 serial

PS/2 mouse

Keyboard port

MIDI

SCSI port

To phone

FIGURE E-24: *Inserting a PCMCIA card*

▶ To add a modem, sound card, or a hard disk to a notebook computer, plug in a PCMCIA card.

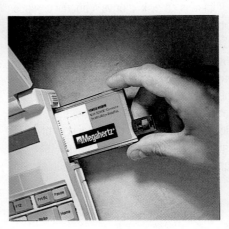

Learning about the boot process

THE SEQUENCE OF EVENTS THAT OCCUR BETWEEN THE TIME YOU TURN ON A COMPUTER AND the time it is ready for you to issue commands is referred to as the **boot process**. Micro, mini, and mainframe computers all require a boot process. In this lesson, you'll learn about the microcomputer boot process because that is the type of computer you are most likely to use. The main objective of the boot process is to get operating system files into RAM. Table E-1 summarizes the six steps in the boot process.

IN MORE DETAIL

☛ Power up: The first things that happen when you turn the power on are that the fan in the power supply begins to spin and the power light on the case of the computer comes on.

☛ Start boot program: When you turn on the computer, the microprocessor begins to execute the boot program stored in ROM.

☛ Power-on self test: The next step in the boot process is the **power-on self test (POST)** which diagnoses problems in the computer. See Figure E-25. The computer checks if the RAM, expansion cards, keyboard, and drives are functioning correctly.

☛ Load operating system: After successfully completing the POST, the computer continues to follow the instructions in ROM to load the operating system into RAM.

   If your computer has a hard disk, you generally want drive C to be the default drive, so it is best not to put disks in any of the floppy disk drives until the boot process is complete. The computer first checks drive A to see if it contains a disk. If there is a disk in this drive, then drive A becomes the **default drive**. If there is no disk in drive A but the computer has a drive C, the computer uses drive C as the default drive. The computer uses the default drive for the rest of the computing session unless you specify a different one.

   Next, the computer tries to locate and load operating system files from the default drive. If these files do not exist on the disk, the boot process stops, and the screen displays an error message such as "Non-system disk or disk error" or "Cannot load a file," or "Bad or missing command interpreter." If you encounter one of these messages, you should

turn off the computer and make sure drive A is empty; then turn the computer on again. If the error message reappears, you should check with a technical support person.

☛ Check configuration and customization: Early in the boot process, the computer checks CMOS to determine the amount of installed RAM and the types of available disk drives. Often, however, more configuration data is needed for the computer to properly access all available devices. In the next stage of the boot process, the computer searches the boot disk for configuration files.

   The computer also searches the default drive for customized startup instructions. On some computers these instructions are stored in a file called Autoexec.bat or a Windows startup group, which you can modify to customize your computing environment.

☛ Ready for commands and data: The boot process is complete when the computer is ready to accept your commands. Usually the computer displays the operating system main screen or prompt at the end of the boot process. If you are using Windows, you will see the Windows desktop. If you are using DOS, you will see the operating system prompt.

Troubleshooting

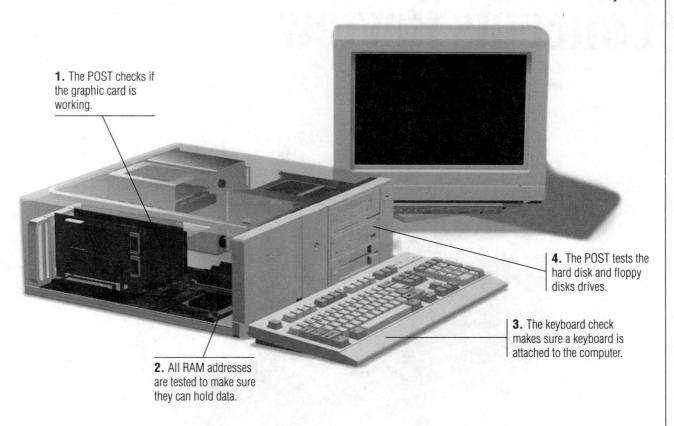

1. The POST checks if the graphic card is working.

4. The POST tests the hard disk and floppy disks drives.

3. The keyboard check makes sure a keyboard is attached to the computer.

2. All RAM addresses are tested to make sure they can hold data.

TABLE E-1: *The boot process*

STEP NUMBER	STEP	WHAT HAPPENS
1	Power up	When you turn on the power switch, the power light is illuminated, and power is distributed to the internal fan and main board
2	Start boot program	The microprocessor begins to execute the instructions stored in ROM
3	Power-on self test	The computer performs diagnostic tests of RAM, extension cards, keyboard, and disk drives
4	Load operating system	The operating system is copied from a disk to RAM
5	Check configuration and customization	The microprocessor reads configuration data and executes any customized startup routines specified by the user
6	Ready for commands and data	The computer is ready for you to enter commands and data

Problems may show up during the boot process. To find out how to troubleshoot problems related to the boot process, do the Troubleshooting Lab.

Concepts Review

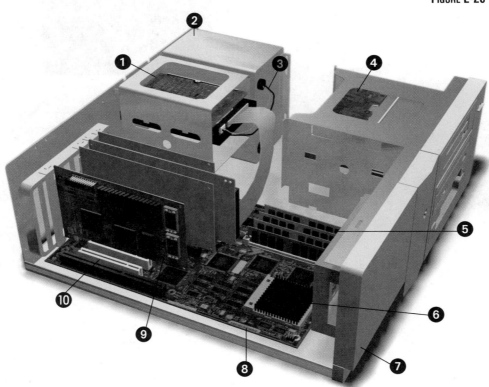

Label the microcomputer components shown in Figure E-26.

1. _____

2. _____

3. _____

4. _____

5. _____

6. _____

7. _____

8. _____

9. _____

10. _____

Place an X in the correct column to indicate which characteristic applies to each type of memory.

Characteristics	RAM	Virtual Memory	ROM	CMOS
11. Holds user data such as documents				
12. Holds program instructions such as word processor				
13. Holds boot program				
14. Holds configuration data for hard disk type				
15. Temporary				
16. Permanent				
17. Battery powered				
18. Disk-based				

Write a brief description of each type of memory: RAM, virtual memory, ROM, and CMOS.

RAM _____

_____

Virtual Memory _____

_____

ROM _____

_____

CMOS _____

_____

Match each statement with the term it describes:

19. ___ 166 HMz
20. ___ Byte
21. ___ External bay
22. ___ Binary number system
23. ___ ASCII
24. ___ 12 MB RAM
25. ___ Docking station
26. ___ ROM
27. ___ Microprocessor

a. Integrated circuit
b. Amount of temporary memory
c. Clock speed of a computer
d. Permanent memory for programs
e. Series of 8 bits
f. Used to represent symbols and numbers
g. Used by digital computers to represent numeric data
h. Used to mount a floppy disk drive
i. Expansion bus designed for notebook computers

Fill in the best answer:

28. A(n) _____ is a collection of microscopic circuit elements such as wires, transistors, capacitors, and resistors packed onto a very small square of silicon.

29. The _____ number system represents numeric data as a series of 0s and 1s.

30. Each _____ in a digital computer is either on or off.

31. Data travels from one location to another within a computer on a circuit called a(n) _____.

32. The smallest unit of information in a computer is a(n) _____.

33. A series of eight bits is referred to as a(n) _____.

34. A computer uses the _____ or _____ codes to represent character data.

35. Having a steady power source is important for a computer because RAM is _____.

36. RAM is measured in _____.

37. In RAM, microscopic electronic parts called _____ hold the electrical signals that represent data.

38. If your computer does not have enough RAM to run several programs at once, your computer operating system might simulate RAM with disk-based _____ memory.

39. The series of instructions that a computer performs when it is first turned on are permanently stored in _____.

40. System configuration information, such as the format of the hard disk drive, is stored in battery-backed _____ memory.

41. A microcomputer uses a(n) _____ chip as its CPU.

42. The _____ in the CPU performs arithmetic and logical operations such as adding or comparing two numbers.

43. The _____ in the CPU directs and coordinates the operation of the entire computer system.

44. A computer instruction has two parts: the _____ and the _____.

45. What are the four steps in the instruction cycle?

46. What factors affect the speed of a microprocessor?

47. A(n) _____ is an electronic path that transports data between RAM and expansion slots.

48. A(n) _____ is a small circuit board that plugs into an expansion slot.

49. An expansion _____ is located inside the system, whereas an expansion _____ is located on the exterior of the system unit.

50. Two types of expansion ports are _____ and _____.

INDEPENDENT CHALLENGE 1

It is important that you familiarize yourself with the type of computer you are working with. You may need to consult the computer resource person at your school or the manual that came with your computer to answer these questions.

To complete this independent challenge:

1. With the computer running, determine all the components of your computer.

    a. How much RAM does the computer have?

    b. What is the type of computer you are working with?

    c. Which microprocessor is inside your computer?

    d. What is the clock speed of your computer?

    e. Do you have a high-speed bus? If so, what kind?

    f. Is your system set up for cache memory? What kind and how much?

2. Turn the computer off.

    a. Draw a sketch and label each of the components you see.

    b. What kind of system unit case do you have?

    c. What devices are connected to external slots?

    d. Do you have any expansion slots?

    e. If you are using a notebook computer, do you have a PCMCIA slot?

    f. Do you have a docking station?

    g. How many bays does your computer have? Internal? External?

INDEPENDENT CHALLENGE 2

Computers would not be available to individuals today if not for the invention of the integrated circuit. Just four months apart in 1959, Jack Kilby and Robert Noyce independently created working models of the circuit that was to transform the computer industry. Jack Kilby worked at Texas Instruments, and you can find reproductions of his original research notes on the Web site **http://www.ti.com/corp/docs/history/kilby.htm**. Robert Noyce developed the integrated circuit while CEO of Fairchild Semiconductor. He left Fairchild to form Intel.

To complete this independent challenge:

Use your library and Internet resources to research the impact of the integrated circuit on the computer industry, and then do one of the following:

    a. Write a two- to three-page paper summarizing how the integrated circuit was used in the first five years after it was invented.

    b. Write two one-page biographical sketches: one of Jack Kilby and one of Robert Noyce.

    c. Create a diagram of the "family tree" of computer technologies that resulted from the development of the integrated circuit.

    d. Based on the facts you have gathered about the development of the computer industry, write a two- to three-page paper describing the computer industry today if the integrated circuit had not been invented.

INDEPENDENT CHALLENGE 3

Pretend you are a computer industry analyst preparing an article on computer memory for a popular computer magazine.

To complete this independent challenge:

Gather as much information as you can about RAM, including current pricing, the amount of RAM that comes installed in a typical computer, tips for adding RAM to computers, and so forth. If you have Internet access, you might find useful information at sites, such as **http://www.micron.com**. Use a word processor to write a one- to two-page article that would help your magazine's readers understand RAM.

INDEPENDENT CHALLENGE 4

In this unit, you learned about the microprocessor of a reduced instruction set computer (RISC).

To complete this independent challenge:

Write a one- to two-page paper about RISC technology. You can look at the use of RISC processors for the type of powerful workstation typically used for engineering and CAD applications. You might also research Apple's new PowerPC computer that uses the PowerPC RISC chip. If you have Internet access check one of IBM's sites: **http://www.ibm.com**, **www.rs6000.ibm.com/resource/interviews**, or **archi.snu.ac.kr/ course**. Scroll down and select "Instruction Set Architecture."

INDEPENDENT CHALLENGE 5

In this unit you learned about many computer components.

To complete this independent challenge:

Photocopy a full-page computer ad from a current issue of a computer magazine, such as *Computer Shopper*. On the copy of the ad use a colored pen and circle any of the key terms that were presented in this unit. Make sure you watch for abbreviations; they are frequently used in computer ads. On a separate sheet of paper, or using a word processor, make a list of each term you circled and write a definition of each.

Look in computer magazines to find advertisements for three peripheral devices that connect to a computer using different ports or buses. For example, you might find a modem that connects to the serial port. Photocopy each of these three ads. For each device, circle on the photocopy the device's brand name, model name and/or number, and the port or bus it uses. Also make sure you provide your instructor with the name and publication date of the magazine and the page number on which you found the information.

Complete the following steps to interview one of your friends who has a computer, and write a report that describes how your friend could expand his or her computer system.

To complete this independent challenge:

a. Find out as many technical details as you can about your friend's computer, including the type of computer, the type and speed of the microprocessor, the amount of memory, the configuration of disk drives, the capacity of the disk drives, the resolution of the monitor, and so on.

b. Find out how your friend might want to expand his or her computer system either now or sometime in the future. For example, your friend might want to add a printer, a sound card, CD-ROM drive, memory, or a monitor.

c. Look through computer magazines to find a solution for at least one of your friend's expansion plans. What would you recommend as a solution? If money was no object would your recommendation change? Why or why not?

d. Write a two-page report describing your friend's computer and his or her expansion needs. Then describe the solution(s) you found.

In 1994 Intel released the Pentium microprocessor. Within a matter of weeks, rumors began to circulate that the Pentium chip had a bug that caused errors in some calculations. As the rumors spread, corporate computer users became nervous about the numbers that appeared on spreadsheets calculated on computers with the Pentium processor.

To complete this independent challenge, write a short essay to answer these questions:

1. How can a computer make such mistakes? Are computers with Pentium processors destined for the dumpster? Is there any way users can save the money they have invested in their Pentium computers?

2. Suppose you own a computer store that sold many computers with the flawed Pentium microprocessor. Your customers are calling you to get the straight facts. Use your library and Internet resources to gather as much reliable information as you can about the Pentium flaw. Use this information to write a one-page information sheet for your customers. You might find the following resources useful:

- Intel's Internet site: **www.intel.com**

- "The Truth Behind the Pentium Bug," *Byte*, March 1995.

BINARY NUMBERS LAB

Computers process and store numbers using the binary number system. Understanding binary numbers helps you recognize how digital computers work by simply turning electricity on and off. In this Lab, you learn about the binary number system, and you learn how to convert numbers from binary to decimal and from decimal to binary.

1. Click the Steps button to learn about the binary number system. As you proceed through the Steps, answer all of the Quick Check questions that appear. After you complete the Steps, you will see a Quick Check Summary Report. Follow the instructions on the screen to print this report.

2. Click the Explore button, then click the Conversions button. Practice converting binary numbers into decimal numbers. For example, what is the decimal equivalent of 00010011? Calculate the decimal value on paper. To check your answer, enter the decimal number in the decimal box, and then click the binary boxes to show the 1s and 0s for the number you are converting. Click the Check It button to see if your conversion is correct.

Convert the following binary numbers into decimals:

   a. 00000101

   b. 00010111

   c. 01010101

   d. 10010010

   e. 11111110

3. In Explore, click the Conversions button. Practice converting decimal numbers into binary numbers. For example, what is the binary equivalent of 82? Do the conversion on paper. To check your answer, enter the decimal number in the decimal box, and then click the binary boxes to show the 1s and 0s of its binary equivalent. Click the Check It button to see if your conversion is correct.

Convert the following decimal numbers to binary numbers:

   a. 77

   b. 25

   c. 92

   d. 117

   e. 214

4. In Explore, click the Binary Number Quiz button. The quiz provides you ten numbers to convert. Make each conversion and type your answer in the box. Click the Check Answer button to see if you are correct. When you have completed all ten quiz questions, follow the instructions on the screen to print your quiz results.

CPU SIMULATOR LAB

In a computer central processing unit (CPU), the arithmetic logic unit (ALU) performs instructions orchestrated by the control unit. Processing proceeds at a lightning pace, but each instruction accomplishes only a small step in the entire process. In this Lab you work with an animated CPU simulation to learn how computers execute assembly language programs. In the Explore section of the Lab, you have an opportunity to interpret programs, find program errors, and write your own short assembly language programs.

1. Click the Steps button to learn how to work the simulated CPU. As you proceed through the Steps, answer all of the Quick Check questions that appear. After you complete the Steps, you will see a Quick Check Summary Report. Follow the instructions on the screen to print this report.

2. Click the Explore button. Use the File menu to open a program called ADD.CPU. Use the Fetch Instruction and Execute Instruction buttons to step through the program. Then answer the following questions:

   a. How many instructions does this program contain?

   b. Where is the instruction pointer after the program is loaded but before it executes?

   c. What does the INP 3 M1 instruction accomplish?

   d. What does the MMR M1 REG1 instruction accomplish?

   e. Which memory location holds the instruction that adds the two numbers in REG1 and REG2?

   f. What is in the accumulator when the program execution is complete?

   g. Which memory address holds the sum of the two numbers when program execution is completed?

3. In Explore, use the File menu to open a program called COUNT5.CPU. Use the Fetch Instruction and Execute Instruction buttons to step through the program. Then answer the following questions:

   a. What are the two input values for this program?

   b. What happens to the value in REG1 as the program executes?

   c. What happens when the program executes the JPZ 5 instruction?

   d. What are the final values in the accumulator and registers when program execution is complete?

4. In Explore, click File, then click New to make sure the CPU is empty. Write a program that follows these steps to add 8 and 6:

   a. Input 8 into memory address M3.

   b. Input 6 into memory address M5.

   c. Move the number in M3 to Register 1.

   d. Move the number in M5 to Register 2.

   e. Add the numbers in the registers.

   f. Move the value in the accumulator to memory address M1.

   g. Tell the program to halt.

Test your program to make sure it produces the answer 14 in address M1. When you are sure your program works, use the File menu to print your program.

5. In Explore, use the File menu to open a program called BAD1.CPU. This program is supposed to multiply two numbers together and put the result in memory location M3. However, the program contains an error.

   a. Which memory location holds the incorrect instruction?

   b. What instruction will make this program produce the correct result?

6. In Explore, use the CPU simulator to write a program to calculate the volume, in cubic feet, of the inside of a refrigerator. The answer should appear in the accumulator at the end of the program. The inside dimensions of the refrigerator are 5 feet, by 3 feet, by 2 feet. Make sure you test your program, then print it.

Computers sometimes malfunction, so it is useful to have some skill at diagnosing, if not fixing, some of the hardware problems you might encounter. In the Troubleshooting Lab, you use a simulated computer that has trouble booting. You learn to make and test hypotheses that help you diagnose the cause of boot problems.

1. Click the Steps button to learn how to make and test hypotheses about hardware malfunctions during the boot process. As you proceed through the Steps, answer all of the Quick Check questions that appear. After you complete the Steps, you will see a Quick Check Summary Report. Follow the instructions on the screen to print this report.

2. Click the Explore button. Use the File menu to load SYSTEM11.TRB. Click the Boot Computer button and watch what happens on the simulated computer (in this case, actually, what does not happen!). Make your hypothesis about why this computer does not boot. Use the Check menu to check the state of various cables and switches. When you think you know the cause of the problem, select it from the Diagnosis list. If you correctly diagnosed the problem, write it down. If your diagnosis was not correct, form another hypothesis and check it, until you have correctly diagnosed the problem.

3. Sometimes problems that appear very similar result from different causes. In Explore, use the File menu to load SYSTEM03.TRB, then diagnose the problem. Do the same for SYSTEM06.TRB. Describe the problems with these two systems. Then describe the similarities and differences in their symptoms.

4. In Explore, use the File menu to load System02 and System08. Both systems produce keyboard errors, but these errors have different causes. Describe what caused the problem in System02, and what caused the problem in System08. Once you have diagnosed these problems, what can you do about them?

5. In Explore, use the File menu to load Systems 04, 05, 07, 09, and 14. These systems produce similar symptoms on boot up. However, these systems have different problems. Diagnose the problem with each of these systems and indicate the key factor (the symptom or what you checked) that led to your diagnosis.

Computer Networks and the Internet

Unit F

THE IDEA THAT MICROCOMPUTER USERS COULD benefit by connecting their computers into a network became feasible about ten years ago with the introduction of reliable, reasonably priced software and hardware designed for microcomputer networks. The availability of this hardware and software ushered in a new era of computing, which increasingly provides ways for people to collaborate, communicate, and interact. The purpose of this unit is to help you understand how computer networks, electronic mail, and the Internet work. The unit begins with a tour of network resources, then presents practical information on network hardware and software including network applications such as groupware and electronic mail. The unit explores the Internet, commercial information services, and how to use Web browsers to create and manage Web sites. The unit concludes with practical discussions on how to take advantage of various Internet resources and how to access online information.

OBJECTIVES

Define computer networks

Administer computer networks

Use computer networks

Understand network components

Configure networks

Understand network software

Explore electronic mail (e-mail)

Introduce the Internet

Understand hosts, domains, and sites

Use Web browsers

Understand Internet multimedia

Interact online

Create Web sites

Communicate on the Internet

Defining computer networks

A COMPUTER NETWORK IS A collection of computers and other devices that communicate to share data, hardware, and software. A network that is located within a relatively limited area, such as a building or campus, is referred to as a **local area network** or **LAN**. A network that covers a large geographical area is referred to as a **wide area network** or **WAN**.

Worldwide there are an estimated 25 million computers connected to local area networks. LANs are found in most businesses, government offices, and educational institutions. Not all LANs are the same. Different types of networks provide different services, use different technology, have different resources, and require users to follow different procedures.

LANs

IN MORE DETAIL

- A computer that is not connected to a network is referred to as a **stand-alone computer**. When you physically connect your computer to a local area network, using a cable or other communications channel, your computer becomes a **workstation** on the network, and you become a "network user."

- Each device on a network, including workstations, servers, and printers, is referred to as a **node**. Figure F-1 illustrates the workstations, network server, and other network resources.

- Resources: Your workstation has all its usual resources, referred to as **local resources**, such as your hard drive, software, data, and printer. You also have access to **network resources**, which typically include application software, storage space for data files, and printers other than those on your local workstation.

- A **network server** is a computer that is connected to the network and that "serves," or distributes, resources to network users. On a network, application software and storage space for data files are typically provided by a network server.

- A **network printer** provides output capabilities to all the network users.

- Sharing resources: The main advantage of a computer network is that all the users can share resources, instead of users each maintaining their own. For example, a LAN permits many users to share a single printer. Most organizations with LANs are able to reduce the overall number of printers needed, reduce printer maintenance costs, and use the money saved to buy higher-quality printers.

Software licenses for networks

It would be very inexpensive for an organization to purchase a single copy of a software package, and then place it on the network for everyone to use. In an organization with 100 users, for example, word-processing software might cost $295 for a single copy, instead of $29,500 for 100 copies. However, using a single-user license for multiple users violates copyright law. Most single-user software licenses allow only one person to use the software at a time. Many software publishers also offer a **network license** that permits use by multiple people on a network. Typically, such a network license will cost more than a single-user license, but less than purchasing single-user licenses for all of the users. For example, a word-processing software package that costs $295 for a single-user license might have a $5,000 network license that allows up to 100 people to use the software.

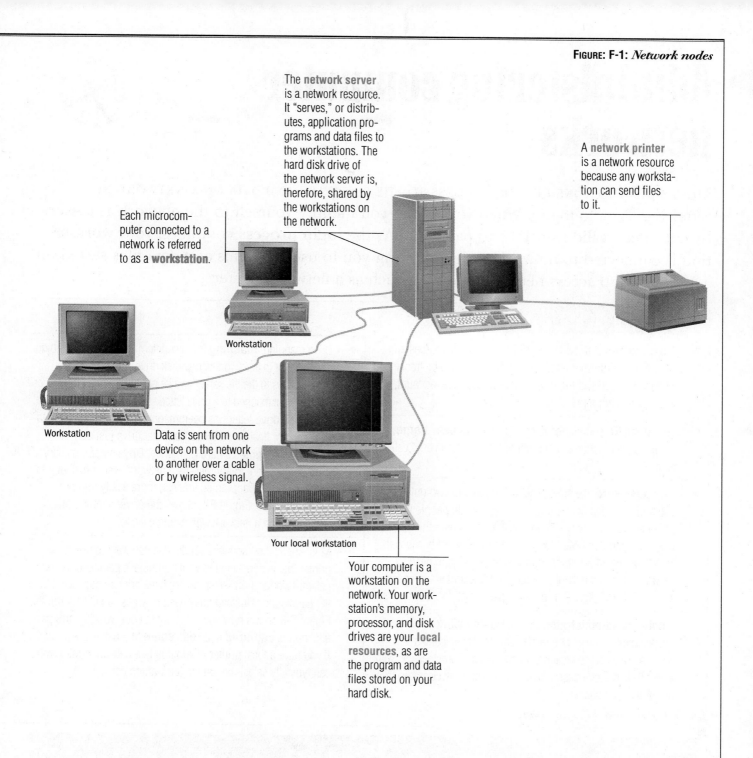

The **network server** is a network resource. It "serves," or distributes, application programs and data files to the workstations. The hard disk drive of the network server is, therefore, shared by the workstations on the network.

A **network printer** is a network resource because any workstation can send files to it.

Each microcomputer connected to a network is referred to as a **workstation**.

Workstation

Workstation

Data is sent from one device on the network to another over a cable or by wireless signal.

Your local workstation

Your computer is a workstation on the network. Your workstation's memory, processor, and disk drives are your **local resources**, as are the program and data files stored on your hard disk.

Most users and technical support people refer to local area networks simply as "networks."

Administering computer networks

MOST ORGANIZATIONS RESTRICT ACCESS TO THE SOFTWARE AND DATA ON A NETWORK BY requiring users to log in. When you **log in**, you identify yourself to the network as a user by entering a valid user ID and password. As the **login process** continues, your workstation is connected to network drives, allowing you to use programs and data files stored on a server and to access network resources such as a network printer.

IN MORE DETAIL

- A **user account** provides access to network resources and accumulates information about your network use by tracking when you log in and log out. To access your user account, you follow a login process.

- Your **user ID**, sometimes referred to as your **user name**, is a unique set of letters and numbers that serve as your "call sign" or "identification."

- Your **password** is a special set of symbols known only to you and the network administrator. You can let people know your user ID so they can send you messages over the network, but you don't want to reveal your password because it would violate your responsibility to help maintain network security. On most networks, users can select their own passwords. Refer to Table F-1 for some password do's and don'ts.

- A **network administrator**, also called a **network supervisor**, is the person responsible for maintaining a network. This person creates your account and provides you with a user ID and starter password giving you security clearance to use network resources.

- Drive mapping: **Mapping** is network terminology for assigning a drive letter to a network server disk drive. Your workstation gains access to the file server and its hard drive when the server hard drive is mapped to a drive letter.

  Once a drive letter has been mapped, you can access data files and application software from that drive just as you would from your local hard disk drive. Drive mappings vary from one network to another. As a network user, it is useful to know the drive mapping so you can more easily find programs and files. Figure F-2 shows the drive mapping of a workstation in a network with a single server.

- Most application software sends files you want to print to a printer that is connected to your computer's parallel port. But network workstations often do not have printers connected to the parallel port. Instead, they need to access a network printer. Figure F-3 shows how any data sent to your workstation's parallel port is **captured** and **redirected** to the network printer. If you have a local printer in addition to a network printer, you can typically select the printer you want to use.

TABLE F-1: *Password do's and don'ts*

DO	DON'T
Select a password that is at least six characters long and that you can remember.	Select a password that can be found in the dictionary.
Use numbers as well as letters in your password.	Use your name, nickname, Social Security number, birth date, or name of a close relative.
Consider making a password by combining two or more words or by using the first letters of the words in a poem or phrase.	Write your password where it is easy to find— under the keyboard is the first place a password thief will look.
Change your password periodically.	

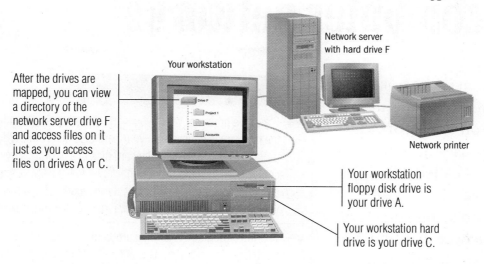

FIGURE F-2: *A typical workstation drive map*

Network server with hard drive F

Your workstation

After the drives are mapped, you can view a directory of the network server drive F and access files on it just as you access files on drives A or C.

Drive F
Project 1
Memos
Accounts

Network printer

Your workstation floppy disk drive is your drive A.

Your workstation hard drive is your drive C.

FIGURE F-3: *Capturing your workstation printer port*

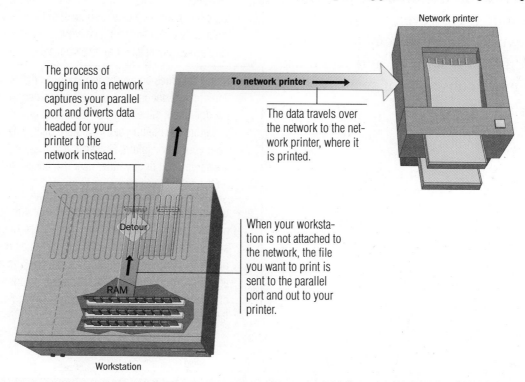

Network printer

The process of logging into a network captures your parallel port and diverts data headed for your printer to the network instead.

To network printer

The data travels over the network to the network printer, where it is printed.

Detour

RAM

When your workstation is not attached to the network, the file you want to print is sent to the parallel port and out to your printer.

Workstation

What is a print queue?

Most networks would not allow two files to travel simultaneously over the network. However, it is possible that before the printer has completed one printout, other files arrive to be printed. A **print job** is a file that has been sent to the printer. Files sent to a network printer are placed in a print queue. A **print queue** is a special holding area on a network server where files are stored until they are printed. When more than one user sends a file to the print queue, the files are added to the print queue and printed in the order in which they are received.

Using computer networks

ONE ADVANTAGE OF A NETWORK IS that with proper licensing more than one user on a network can simultaneously use the same program. This is called **sharing** a program.

When you use a computer network, you'll discover that finding, retrieving, and storing files on a network is not very different from the process you use on a stand-alone computer. However, when you use a network, you must remember to use additional resources, and you must be more conscious of security.

▫➙ Starting a program: When you start a program on a stand-alone computer, the program is copied from your hard disk into RAM. When you start the program that is stored on the hard disk of a network server, the program is copied from the hard drive of the server to the RAM of your workstation. Once the program is in memory, it runs just as if you had started it from your workstation hard disk drive. Figure F-4 shows how this works.

▫➙ Sharing a program: Sharing a program is effective for several reasons. First, less disk storage space is required because the program is stored only once on the server, instead of being stored on the hard disks of multiple stand-alone computers. Second, when a new version of the software is released, it is easier to update one copy of the program on the server than to update many copies stored on stand-alone computers. Third, purchasing a software license for a network can be less expensive than purchasing single-user licenses for all the workstations on the network.

▫➙ Using data files on a network: Suppose that while connected to a network, you create a document using a word-processing program. You can store the document either on your local hard disk or on the server hard disk. If you store the file on your local hard disk, you can access the file only from your workstation. However, if you store the file on the hard disk of the server, you or any other user can access the file from any workstation on the network, as shown in Figure F-5.

▫➙ Locking files: Although a *program* file on the file server can be accessed by more than one user at the same time, most of the *data* files on a network server can be opened by only one user at a time. When one user has a file open, it is **locked** to other users. File locking is a sensible precaution against losing valuable data. Groupware addresses the need for more than one person to work on a file at one time. You'll learn about groupware in a later lesson.

Why networks lock files

Suppose two users were allowed to make changes to the same file at the same time. Each user would open a copy of the original file and make changes to it. The first user to finish making changes would save the file on the server. So far so good—the first user has replaced the original version of the file with an edited version. Remember, however, that the second user has been making revisions to the original file, but has no idea of the first user's revisions. When the second user saves his/her revised version of the file, the changes made by the first user are overwritten by the second user's version. This would be counterproductive since one user's changes might contradict the other user's changes. Therefore, on a network, when one user has a data file open, it is locked to other users.

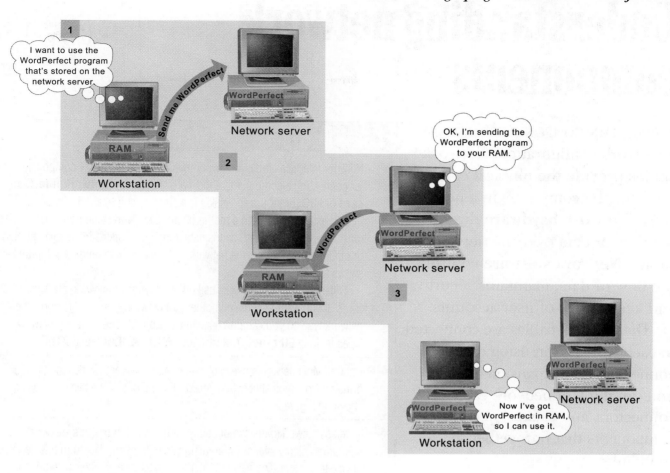

FIGURE F-4: *Starting a program that is stored on the file server*

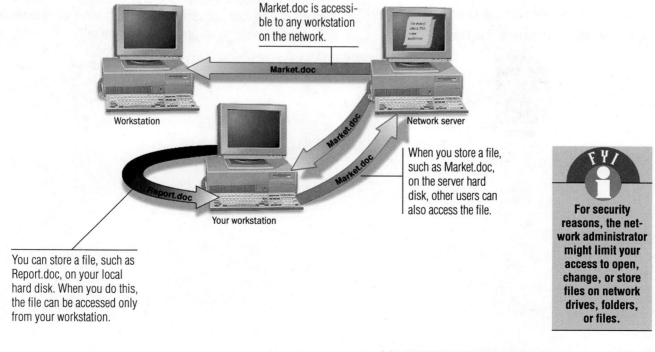

FIGURE F-5: *Network file access*

Understanding network components

THREE MAIN COMPONENTS MAKE UP a network configuration. **Network cables** provide the physical connections for the computers in a network. **Network hardware** directs the flow of data over the network cables. **Network software** controls the flow of data, maintains security, and keeps track of user accounts.

The network cables are connected to each workstation using cable connectors and expansion cards. You can think of network cables, connectors, and expansion cards as components that fit together to form links.

Knowing about network configuration will help you recognize if a computer is on a network, help you troubleshoot loose connections, or move and reconnect a computer on a network computer system.

Ethernet

IN MORE DETAIL

○━ Network interface cards: A network interface card is the key component for connecting a computer to a local area network. A **network interface card** or **NIC** (pronounced "nick") is a small circuit board designed to plug into an expansion slot on a motherboard. Each workstation on a network must have a NIC. The NIC sends data from your workstation, server, printer, or other device out over the network and collects incoming data. Figure F-6 shows two types of NICs.

Different types of networks use different types of network interface cards. If you want to add a computer to a network, you need to know the network type so you can purchase the appropriate NIC. Popular network types include **Ethernet**, **Token Ring**, **FDDI**, **ARCnet**, and **ATM**.

○━ Cables: Most networks use cables to connect servers, workstations, and printers. On a typical network, you would find one of the two cable types shown in Figure F-7.

○━ Wireless networks: Instead of using cables, some **wireless networks** use radio, microwave, or infrared signals to transmit data from one network device to another. The network interface cards on a wireless network contain the transmitting devices necessary to send data to other devices on the local area network. Wireless networks are handy in environments where wiring is difficult to install, such as in historical buildings. In addition, wireless networks provide mobility making it possible to carry a notebook or hand-held computer throughout a large warehouse to take inventory. Wireless networks are also useful for temporary installations, when drilling holes to install wiring is not practical or economical.

FIGURE F-6: *Desktop and notebook network interface cards*

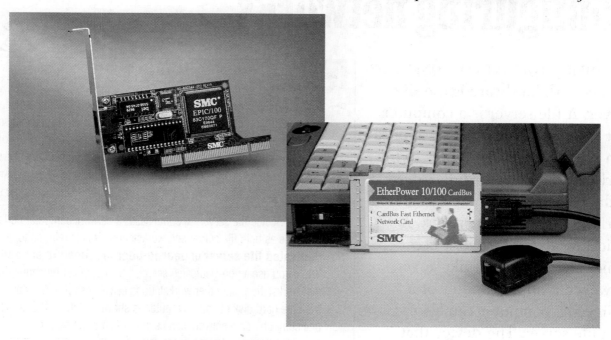

FIGURE F-7: *Network cables*

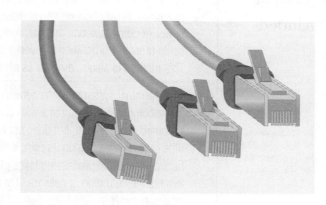

◄ A **twisted pair cable**, sometimes referred to as **UTP**, looks similiar to a telephone cable with a square plastic **RJ-45 connector** on either end.

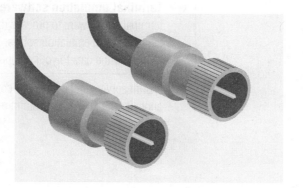

◄ A **coaxial cable** resembles a cable-TV cable with a round, silver **BNC connector** on either end.

Cable television is transmitted through coaxial cable.

COMPUTER NETWORKS AND THE INTERNET ◄ **F-9**

Configuring networks

ANOTHER IMPORTANT COMPONENT OF the network hardware is the **file server**. A file server is a computer that "serves," or distributes, application programs and data files to the workstations. The hard disk drive of the file server is shared by the workstations on the network. A typical local area network uses a microcomputer as a file server. However, a minicomputer or a mainframe computer can also be a file server. The device that processes your data when you are connected to a network depends on the types of servers included on your network.

Client/Server

IN MORE DETAIL

⌐☞ Dedicated file servers: A **dedicated file server** is devoted only to the task of delivering programs and data files to workstations. As you can see in Figure F-8, a dedicated file server does not process data or run programs for the workstations. Instead, programs run using the memory and processor of the workstation. A dedicated file server does not mean a network has only one server. Many networks have more than one dedicated file server.

⌐☞ Non-dedicated file server: In some cases a network computer performs a dual role as both file server and workstation. This is referred to as a **non-dedicated file server** or **peer-to-peer architecture capability**. When you use a non-dedicated server, your computer functions like a normal workstation, but other workstations can access programs and data files from the hard disk of your computer as shown in Figure F-9. More than one computer on a network can be a non-dedicated server.

⌐☞ Client/server: An **application server** is a computer that runs application software and forwards the results of processing to workstations as requested. An application server makes it possible to use the processing power of both the server and the workstation. Use of an application server splits processing between the workstation *client* and the network *server*. This method is also referred to as **client/server architecture**.

⌐☞ Host-terminal systems: Some networks include a **host computer**, usually a minicomputer or mainframe with attached terminals. A **terminal** has a keyboard and a screen, but does not have a local storage device and does little or no processing on its own. When you use a terminal connected to a host computer, all processing takes place on the host. Although this system fits the definition of network, it is more commonly called a **time-sharing system**. The terminals essentially share the host's processor by each being allocated to a fraction of each second of processing time.

⌐☞ **Terminal emulation software** makes a microcomputer function like a terminal. If you want to process data you receive from a host, instead of using terminal emulation software you must use communications software to transfer the data to your computer.

⌐☞ A print server can be the same computer as the file server, or it can be another micro, mini, or mainframe computer connected to the network.

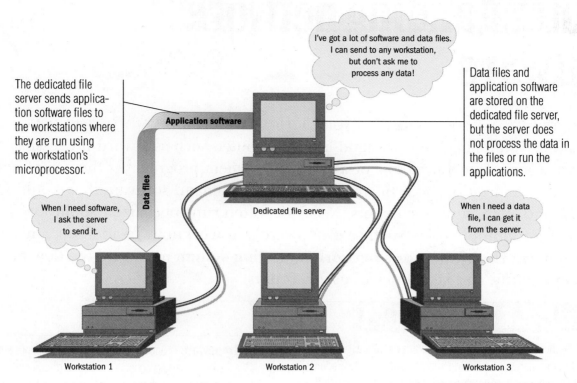

FIGURE F-9: *A non-dedicated file server*

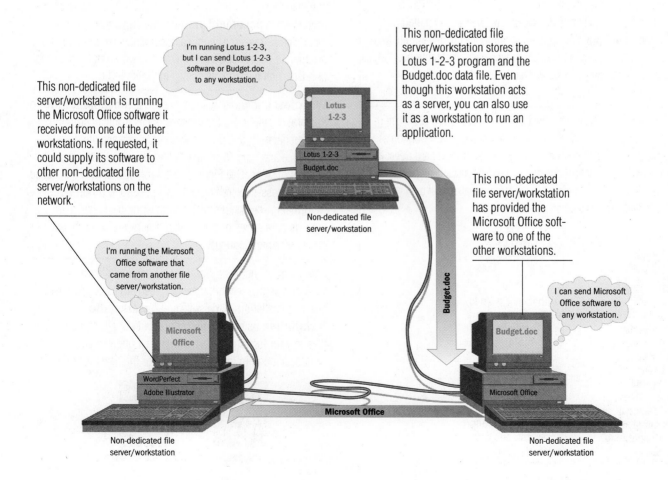

Understanding network software

THE SOFTWARE ON A LOCAL AREA NETWORK TYPICALLY INCLUDES MANY OF THE SAME applications you might use on a stand-alone computer, such as a word-processing program, a spreadsheet program, or a data management program. As the use of networks increased, organizations and businesses began to demand software that would facilitate the flow and sharing of documents. Networks often run specialized applications designed for multiple users such as groupware and workflow. In addition, a network requires **network software** or a **network operating system** to control the flow of data, maintain security, and keep track of user accounts.

IN MORE DETAIL

☞ Network operating systems: There are usually two components to a network operating system: server software and client software. **Network server software** is installed on a file server and controls file access from the server hard drive, manages the print queue, and tracks user data such as IDs and passwords. **Network client software** is installed on the local hard drive of each workstation and is essentially a device driver for the network interface card. It establishes the connection between your workstation and other devices on the network.

☞ Stand-alone applications: Most of your favorite word-processing, spreadsheet, graphics, and presentation software will work on a network just as if they were running from your local hard drive. In addition, some applications that you use on a stand-alone computer have built-in features for networking that appear only when the software is installed on a network.

☞ **Groupware** is application software that supports collaborative work by managing schedules, shared documents, and intragroup communications. Essentially, groupware manages a pool of documents and allows users to access those documents simultaneously, as shown in Figure F-10. A key feature of groupware is **document version management**, which maintains all revisions within a document when more than one group member revises a document. The workgroup can accept or reject each revision, as shown in Figure F-11.

☞ **Workflow software**, also referred to as **document routing software**, automates the process of electronically routing documents from one person to another in a specified sequence and time. Workflow software facilitates a process or a series of steps. See Figure F-12. Workflow software is based on a "process-centered model" as opposed to groupware's "information-centered model." With workflow software the focus is on a series of steps. With groupware software the documents are the focus.

☞ After a new Windows program has been installed on a network server, the network manager needs to complete a workstation installation of the software. A **workstation installation** usually copies some, but not all, of the program files to your local hard disk, and then it updates your Windows menu to include a listing for the new program.

Network operating systems include Novell NetWare, Banyan Vines, and LANtastic. Network software is sometimes included as a component of some computer operating systems.

Windows 3.1 does not include network software. Therefore, if your school uses the Windows 3.1 operating system, your school network also requires a network operating system, such as Novell NetWare.

Groupware

Workflow Software

FIGURE F-11: *A shared document*

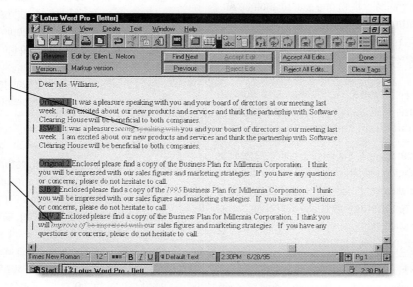

One user's revisions are shown in red.

The other user's revisions are shown in blue.

FIGURE F-12: *Workflow software facilitates a process*

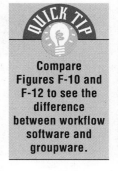

Compare Figures F-10 and F-12 to see the difference between workflow software and groupware.

Exploring electronic mail (e-mail)

ELECTRONIC MAIL, OR E-MAIL, IS CORRESPONDENCE CONDUCTED BETWEEN TWO OR MORE users on a network. E-mail is a more efficient means of communication than ground or air mail. Rather than waiting for a piece of paper to be physically transported, you can send an electronic version of a message directly to someone's electronic "mailbox."

IN MORE DETAIL

▸ How e-mail works: An **e-mail message** is essentially a letter or memo sent electronically from one user to another. An **electronic mail system** is the hardware and software that collects and delivers e-mail messages. Typically, a local area network provides electronic mail services to its users. The software on the network server that controls the flow of e-mail is called **mail server software**. The software on a workstation that helps each user read, compose, send, and delete messages is called **mail client software**.

▸ Store and forward technology: E-mail messages are *stored* on a server. When you want to read this mail, the server *forwards* the messages to your workstation. Hence e-mail is called a **store and forward technology**. Because the server stores the messages, your workstation does not need to be on when someone sends you e-mail. See Figure F-13.

▸ Getting e-mail: When someone sends you e-mail, the message is stored on a host or network server in an area you can think of as your **mailbox**. Refer to Figure F-14. When you log into the electronic mail system and check your mail, the message is listed as new mail. You can choose to display and read the mail on your computer screen, print it, delete it, reply to it, forward it, or save it on disk.

E-mail

E-mail

▸ Sending e-mail: To send e-mail, you type the recipient's mail address or select it from an address book that contains a list of e-mail addresses for the people you correspond with frequently. In the Subject area on the e-mail form, you specify the topic of the e-mail. When replying to an e-mail message, most e-mail software allows you to include the text of the message to which you are replying.

▸ Features: Some electronic mail systems offer features such as **priority mail**, which immediately alerts the recipient that an e-mail message has arrived; **return receipt**, which sends a message back to you when a recipient receives your message; **carbon copy**, which sends a copy of the message to another user; and **group addressing**, which allows you to send a copy of an e-mail message to all members of a group at the same time. In addition to these features, some e-mail systems allow you to send an **attachment**, which is a file such as a word-processing document, worksheet, or graphic that travels along with an electronic mail message. See Figure F-15.

▸ Sending e-mail out of network: Many e-mail systems are connected to other e-mail systems through electronic links called **gateways**. When you send an e-mail message to a user on another computer network, the message is transferred through the gateway to a larger e-mail system, which delivers the message to the recipient's network or host computer system.

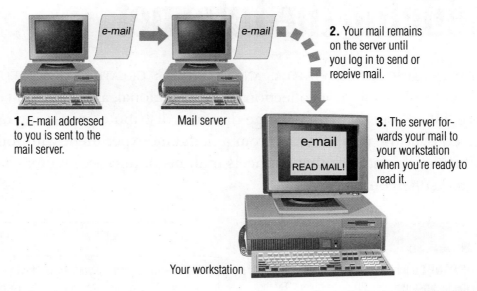

FIGURE F-13: *How e-mail works*

2. Your mail remains on the server until you log in to send or receive mail.

1. E-mail addressed to you is sent to the mail server.

Mail server

3. The server forwards your mail to your workstation when you're ready to read it.

e-mail
READ MAIL!

Your workstation

FIGURE F-14: *An e-mail mailbox*

Buttons at the top of the mail window help you reply to, forward, send, and delete messages.

Your inbox lists all the messages in your mailbox. An icon that looks like an unopened envelope indicates unread mail.

The text of the new message is displayed in the lower section of the window.

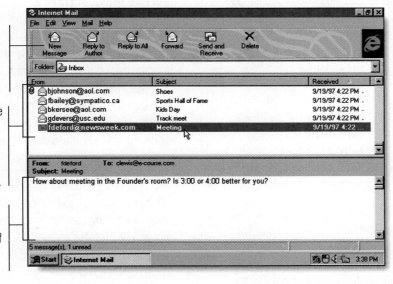

FIGURE F-15: *Sending an e-mail attachment*

1. Create a new message and address it to the person to whom you are sending the attachment.

2. Use the menus provided by your e-mail software to attach the file.

3. An icon indicates the name of the file you attached. Send the mail following your usual procedures. The recipient of the message can click the icon to see the attachment.

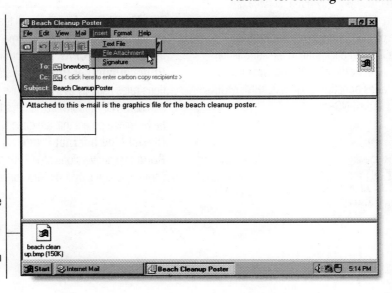

FYI

You can use stand-alone mail software such as Eudora or Pegasus; or you can use your browser to send e-mail over the Internet.

Introducing the Internet

AN INTERNETWORK, ALSO REFERRED TO AS AN INTERNET, IS CREATED BY CONNECTING TWO OR more networks. The Internet is a collection of local, regional, and national computer networks that are linked together to exchange data and distribute processing tasks. The Internet evolved over the past 30 years from a fledgling experiment with four computers into a vast information network that connects millions of microcomputers, minicomputers, mainframes, and supercomputers.

IN MORE DETAIL

- In 1969 the **ARPANET** connected computers at four universities. In 1980 the Internet included 200 computers. By the beginning of 1997, the Internet had mushroomed to include 1.7 million computers worldwide, not counting computers making temporary connections. Today the Internet is the largest and most widely used network in the world, serving an estimated 57 million people in 194 countries.

- **Internet traffic** is the number of bytes transmitted from one Internet host computer to another. By 1997 Internet traffic exceeded 100 terabytes a week. A **terabyte** is 1,000,000,000,000 bytes. An **exabyte** is a quintillion (10^{18}) bytes. Although there is no way to know for sure, the Internet, as large as it is, probably has a long way to go before it contains an exabyte of data.

- The cables, wires, and satellites that carry Internet data form an interlinked communications network. Data traveling from one Internet computer to another is transmitted from one link in the network to another, along the best possible route. If some links are overloaded or temporarily out of service, the data can be routed through different links. The major Internet communications links are called the **Internet backbone**. Figure F-16 illustrates the Internet backbone in the continental United States. In the U.S., nine **network service providers (NSPs)** each maintain a series of nationwide links. IBM, MCI, PSINet, and UUnet are the largest NSPs.

Internet History

- When you connect your computer to the Internet, you connect to an ISP that in turn connects to the backbone. An **Internet service provider (ISP)** is a company that charges you a monthly fee for providing Internet access to businesses, organizations, and individuals. The ISP provides you with communications software and a user account. You supply a modem that connects your computer to your phone line. Your computer dials the ISP's computer and establishes a connection over the phone line. Once you are connected, the ISP routes data between your computer and the Internet backbone. Figure F-17 illustrates the layers of communication that make it possible for your computer to access the Internet.

- A connection that uses a phone line to establish a temporary Internet connection is referred to as a **dial-up connection**. When your computer hangs up, the connection is broken. A phone line provides a very narrow pipe for transmitting data. Its typical capacity is only 28.8 thousand bits per second (bps). Using a phone line, the time to transfer the contents of a 680 megabyte CD-ROM would be over 53 hours.

- The efficient flow of data over all the communications links on the Internet requires a standard mechanism for routing data to its destination. **TCP/IP** is the acronym for **Transport Control Protocol/Internet Protocol**, a standard set of communications rules used by every computer that connects to the Internet. Standard TCP/IP software handles Internet communication between computers that are directly cabled to a network. **SLIP (Serial Line Internet Protocol)** and **PPP (Point-to-Point Protocol)** are versions of TCP/IP designed to handle Internet communications over dial-up connections.

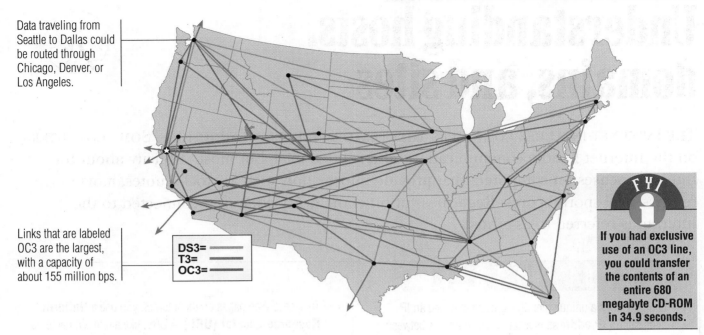

Data traveling from Seattle to Dallas could be routed through Chicago, Denver, or Los Angeles.

Links that are labeled OC3 are the largest, with a capacity of about 155 million bps.

DS3=
T3=
OC3=

If you had exclusive use of an OC3 line, you could transfer the contents of an entire 680 megabyte CD-ROM in 34.9 seconds.

FIGURE F-17: *Connecting to the Internet*

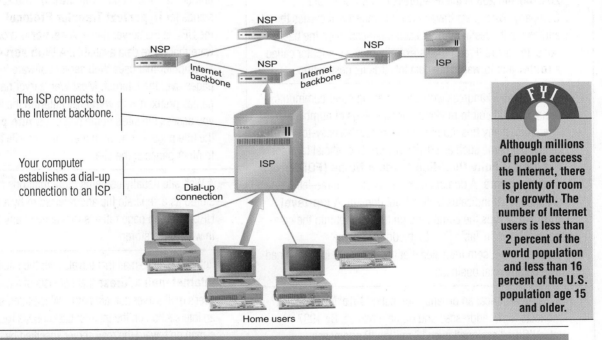

The ISP connects to the Internet backbone.

Your computer establishes a dial-up connection to an ISP.

NSP

NSP

NSP

NSP

NSP

ISP

Internet backbone

Internet backbone

ISP

Dial-up connection

Home users

Although millions of people access the Internet, there is plenty of room for growth. The number of Internet users is less than 2 percent of the world population and less than 16 percent of the U.S. population age 15 and older.

The history of the Internet

The history of the Internet begins in 1957 when the Soviet Union launched Sputnik, the first artificial satellite. In response to this display of Soviet technical expertise, the U.S. government resolved to improve its science and technical infrastructure. One of the resulting initiatives was the Advanced Research Projects Agency (ARPA), created by the Department of Defense. The plan was to construct a network of geographically dispersed computers that would continue to function even if one of the computers on the network was destroyed. In 1969 four computer networks were connected to each other and called ARPANET. Connecting two or more networks creates an **internetwork** or **internet**, so ARPANET was one of the first examples of an internet (with a lowercase i). Gradually, more and more networks were connected to the ARPANET, and it became known as the Internet (with an uppercase I).

Understanding hosts, domains, and sites

THE INTERNET INCLUDES COMPUTERS THAT PERFORM DIFFERENT FUNCTIONS. SOME COMPUTERS on the Internet handle communications and route e-mail, but most publicity about the Internet focuses on computers that provide information such as stock quotes, movie reviews, and sports scores. Regardless of function, every computer connected to the Internet is referred to as a **host**.

IN MORE DETAIL

☞ Each host has a unique identifying number called an IP address. An **IP address** is a set of four numbers between 0 and 255 that are separated by periods. For example, 204.146.144.253 is the IP address of the Coca Cola Company. When data travels over the Internet, it carries the IP address of its destination. At each intersection on the backbone, the data's IP address is examined by a computer called a **router** that forwards the data towards its destination.

☞ Although an IP address works for intercomputer communications, it is difficult to remember long strings of numbers. Therefore, many host computers also have an easy-to-remember name such as cocacola.com. The official term for this name is **Fully Qualified Domain Name (FQDN)**, or a **domain name**. A domain name ends with a three-letter extension that indicates its top-level domain. A **top-level domain** groups the computers on the Internet into the categories shown in Table F-2. In the domain name cocacola.com, com indicates that the computer is maintained by a commercial business.

☞ In North America, an organization called **InterNIC** handles requests for IP addresses and domain names. By 1997 InterNIC had assigned over 16 million IP addresses.

☞ Computers with domain names are popularly referred to as sites. A **site** is a metaphor for a virtual place that exists in cyberspace. **Cyberspace** is a term used to define a computer-generated mental image of a computer world. For example, a Web site provides a virtual location that you can visit to view information in the form of Web pages.

☞ To access Web pages on the Internet, you use a **Uniform Resource Locator (URL)**. A URL, like a domain name, is an Internet address. See Figure F-18. Each Web page has a unique URL that begins with **http://**. The acronym **HTTP** stands for **HyperText Transfer Protocol**. The next part of the URL is the server name. A **server** is a computer and software that make data available. A **Web server**, for example, is a computer that uses Web server software to transmit Web pages over the Internet. Most Web server names are domain names prefixed with **www**. By entering the Web server name, you access the site's home page. A **home page** is similar to the title page in a book. It identifies the site and contains links to other pages at the site.

☞ A Web site usually contains more than one page. Each page is stored as a separate file and referred to by a unique URL. The URL of a Web page reflects the name of any folder or folders in which it is stored.

☞ Internet mail: E-mail that travels over the Internet requires an **Internet mail address** that consists of a user ID and the user's mail server domain name. When Internet e-mail reaches an intersection on the Internet backbone, a router sends the e-mail on toward the mail server specified by the domain name. When the e-mail arrives at the mail server, it is held in a mailbox until the user next logs on to read mail. Figure F-19 illustrates the parts of an Internet mail address.

http://www.course.com/products/titlesites.html

Protocol | Web server name | Folder name | Document name and filename extension

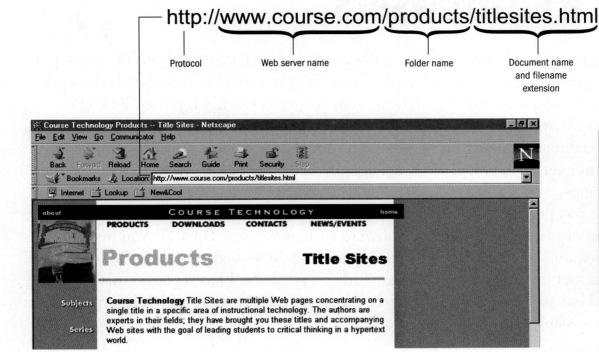

FIGURE F-19: *Components of an e-mail address*

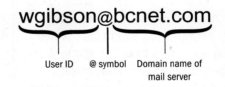

wgibson@bcnet.com

User ID | @ symbol | Domain name of mail server

TABLE F-2: *Top-level domains*

ORG	Professional and nonprofit organization
COM	Commercial businesses
EDU	Colleges and universities
NET	Internet administration
GOV	U.S. government agencies
MIL	U.S. military organizations
INT	Organizations established by international treaties

Using Web browsers

INTERNET HOST COMPUTERS FUNCTION AS SERVERS THAT LOCATE INFORMATION, TRANSFER DATA from one computer to another, and handle e-mail. If you want access to the services provided by a server, you need corresponding client software. On the Internet, **FTP** (File Transfer Protocol) **servers** maintain files that you can transfer to your own computer. **Web servers** maintain a collection of Web pages that you can view on your computer screen. A **Usenet server** handles the exchange of comments among members of Internet discussion groups.

In the past, you needed a separate client software program to access each type of server. For e-mail, you needed an e-mail client software such as Eudora. For FTP, you needed an FTP client software. Archie, WAIS, TelNet, Gopher, and Newsreader client software were all part of the Internet user's software toolbox. Today, a single tool has replaced this awkward collection of client software. A **Web browser** provides Internet users with all-purpose client software for accessing many types of servers.

IN MORE DETAIL

- The **World Wide Web** was created in 1990 as an easy-to-use, graphical source of information. The Web opened the Internet to millions of people interested in finding information rather than learning complex computer commands. Today, Web surfers (as Web users are sometimes called) can visit an estimated 80 million Web pages on over 1 million Web sites.

- The World Wide Web consists of documents, called **Web pages**, that contain information on a particular topic. A Web page might also include one or more **links** that point to other Web pages. Links make it easy to follow a thread of related information, even if the pages are stored on computers located in different countries. Figure F-20 shows a conceptual model of linked Web pages.

- **Web browsers** are used to view Web pages, transfer files between computers, access commercial information services, send e-mail, and interact with other Internet users. To request a Web page, you either type a URL or click a Web page link. The server sends the data for the Web page over the Internet to your computer. This data includes two things: the information you want to view and a set of instructions that tells your browser how to display it. The instructions include specifications for the color of the background, the size of the text, and the placement of graphics. Additional instructions tell your browser what to do when you click a link.

- The Web is a constantly changing environment as new Web sites come online and old sites close. As a result, links are not always valid. Sometimes when you click a link nothing happens, or you get an error message. If a Web server is offline for maintenance or busy from heavy traffic, you won't be able to get the Web pages you requested, or you might get them slowly.

- Your browser's **home page** is usually the first page you see displayed when your browser starts. You can always return to this page by clicking the **Home button**. Most browsers let you pick any Web page as the home page, so select one that you use often, such as your favorite search engine.

- Your browser's menu and tool bars help you navigate the Web as you follow links. The Back and Forward buttons trace and retrace your path through the links you've followed from one Web page to another. Your browser stores and can display a list of the pages you visit during each session. Your browser can also store a list of your favorite sites, often called **bookmarks**, so you can jump directly to them instead of entering a URL.

**The Internet:
World Wide Web**

1. Honolulu Community College (HCC) maintains an exhibit containing images, video clips, narration, and text about dinosaurs. Each image, video, and document is a separate **page**, stored as a file on the HCC computer. You can jump from one page to another at HCC. For example, you can begin at the introductory screen called a **home page**.

2. From the home page, you can jump to a page about iguanadons.

3. From the iguanadons page, you can jump to a page that contains a movie.

4. HCC also links to other Web sites with dinosaur information. You can jump to one of these sites by clicking the underlined text.

6. Another jump and you are in California at the University of California Museum of Paleontology where more Web pages on dinosaurs are stored.

5. A quick jump from Hawaii and you are at the Royal Tyrrell Museum of Paleontology in Alberta, Canada where additional Web pages on dinosaurs are stored.

The official description of the World Wide Web is a "wide-area hypermedia information retrieval initiative aiming to give universal access to a large universe of documents."

Understanding Internet multimedia

IN ADDITION TO TEXT, WEB PAGES INCLUDE MULTIMEDIA ELEMENTS, SUCH AS SOUND, ANIMATION, and video. A media element is stored on the Web server in a file. When you click a Web page to play a media element, the Web server sends a copy of the media file to your computer. Files can be sent to your computer in one of two ways, depending on how the Web server has been set up.

IN MORE DETAIL

☛ In one case, the Web server sends you the entire media file before starting to play it. For large video files, you might wait several minutes before the video begins to play. A newer technology, sometimes referred to as **streaming media**, sends a small segment of the media file to your computer and begins to play it. While this first segment plays, the Web server sends the next part of the file to your computer, and so on until the media segment ends. With streaming media technology, your computer plays a media file while receiving it.

☛ As you browse the Web, you'll find multimedia that is displayed "in place" and multimedia that "runs in a separate window." Of the two, in-place technology is more sophisticated. **In-place multimedia technology** plays a media element as a seamless part of a Web page. For example, an animated GIF, like the one in Figure F-21, uses in-place technology so it appears to play right on the Web page.

☛ **Multimedia overlay technology** adds a separate window to your screen in which multimedia elements appear. With some overlay technologies, you must manually close the window when the multimedia segment is finished. Figure F-22 illustrates a media window that overlays a Web page.

☛ A software program called a **media player** provides you with controls to start, stop, and rewind media segments. Many media players play only one type of media file such as sound files with .wav extensions or videos with .avi extensions. Before you can use a media element on the Web, your computer must have a corresponding media player. Your browser maintains a list of media players that have been installed on your computer.

☛ A software module that adds a specific feature to a system is called a **plug-in** or **viewer**. In the context of the Web, a plug-in adds a feature to your browser, such as the capability to play Web Theater videos. Popular plug-ins include Acrobat Reader, Shockwave, RealAudio, RealVideo, Vox Chat, and Cool Talk.

☛ The way most people use the Web is shaped by pull technology. With **pull technology** you use your browser to request Web pages and "pull" them into view on your computer screen. You only get those pages that you request, and a Web server will not send you information unless you request it.

☛ An alternative called **push technology** sends you information that you didn't directly request. To receive pushed information from a Web site, you first register and then download the push plug-in software. Each push technology requires its own plug-in. At most sites, the registration and the plug-in are free. Once you've registered, you receive pushed information whenever your computer is connected to the Internet. For example, if you register at a site that pushes stock information, then every time you connect to the Internet, your computer receives and displays current stock prices. Figure F-23 shows an example.

☛ A **webcast** uses push technology to broadcast a stream of continually changing information over the Web. A webcast can be used for special event coverage.

Plug-ins

Push

FIGURE F-21: *In-place multimedia technology*

An animated GIF runs in place as part of a Web page.

FIGURE F-22: *Multimedia overlay technology*

Some multimedia plays in a window that overlays the Web page.

FIGURE F-23: *Push technology*

A personalized newspaper includes a pushed ticker tape of headlines, temperatures, and sports scores.

QUICK TIP

Web servers usually give you an opportunity to download and install required media players that are not installed on your system.

Interacting online

YOUR BROWSER IS THE GATEWAY TO commercial information services as well as the free sites on the Internet. A **commercial information service** provides access to computer-based information for a fee. In 1997, approximately 17 million people subscribed to the top four commercial information services—America Online, CompuServe, Microsoft Network (see Figure F-24), and Prodigy. Most commercial information services are ISPs, offering dial-up Internet connections and e-mail, along with additional proprietary services.

Commercial Services

Games

IN MORE DETAIL

- Commercial information services typically charge a $20 per month fee to access basic services, but the number of hours you can spend on the Internet might be limited. You might be charged additional fees for additional Internet access or premium services. A **premium service** is information that has been designated as more valuable by the commercial information service. For example, many business-related services such as airline reservations, up-to-the-minute stock reports, and legal searches are often premium services.

- E-mail is one of the most popular ways to interact with people on the Internet. Another way is to join a **discussion group** in which participants share views on a specific issue or topic. The Internet has thousands of discussion groups on such diverse topics as snowboarding, urban policy, rave music, and William Gibson's cyberspace novels. Discussion groups take place **asynchronously**, meaning that the discussion participants are not online at the same time.

- If you would rather interact **synchronously** with people who are online at the same time, you can join a **chat group**. To participate in a chat group, you generally choose a nickname, and then enter a chat room. As chat participants type, their messages appear on your screen. You'll see the messages from everyone in the chat room. Chat groups are often less focused than discussion groups. However, chat groups can be an effective forum for professional interaction, such as when physicians in different locations use the Internet to collaborate on a diagnosis.

- **Online multiplayer gaming** is another aspect of Internet interaction. From simple competitive word games to massive adventure games, the world of Internet gaming has it all. See Figure F-25.
  Some multiplayer games are synchronous and others are asynchronous. As with chat groups, to participate in a synchronous game, you and the other players must be online at the same time. To participate in asynchronous games, you post each move to the game's referee, and then you can pick up the results and submit new moves the next time you are online. Many multiplayer games require a small fee to participate.

Chat group common sense

Recently chat groups have come under fire because of potential dangers to personal safety and privacy. Use common sense in your chat room interactions. Don't represent yourself as something you're not. Don't provide personal information such as your name or address. Internet society, like society as a whole, has its share of deviants and rip-off experts. Most chat groups, however, are fairly civilized, as shown in Figure F-26.

FIGURE F-24: *Microsoft Network*

Microsoft Network offers its own chat groups, games, and news services that are accessible only to subscribers.

FIGURE F-25: *Multiplayer games*

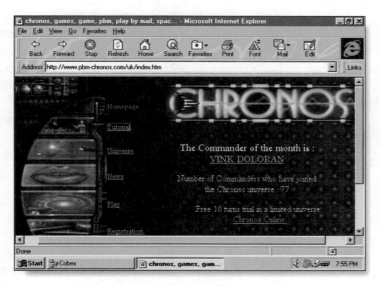

FIGURE F-26: *A sample chat session*

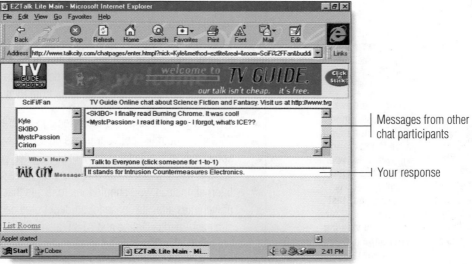

Messages from other chat participants

Your response

Creating Web sites

USING THE WEB AS A SOURCE FOR information and interaction is great, but at some time you might want to become a Web author and publish your own pages. You might become even more ambitious and decide to create and manage your own Web site. The Web provides opportunities for publishing tasks ranging from a single page to an entire Web site. Using today's software tools, Web authoring and publishing is not much more difficult than word-processing or desktop publishing.

Web Pages & HTML   **HTML**

IN MORE DETAIL

◦⊸ A single Web page is simple to create and can publish useful information such as your resume or a publicity flyer for a small business. Another use for a single Web page is to provide a list of links to sites with information on a particular topic. A series of **interlinked** Web pages is like a mini site, except that it does not have its own domain name.

◦⊸ Basic Web pages contain text, graphics, and links. More sophisticated Web pages include animation, sound, and video. Your pages can also include interactive elements such as questionnaires or surveys. To incorporate these sophisticated features in your Web pages, your Web server might require special server software.

◦⊸ Every Web page is stored as an HTML (HyperText Markup Language) document. See Figure F-27. An **HTML document** contains special instructions called **HTML tags** that tell a Web browser how to display the text, graphics, and background of a Web page. If you look at the text of a Web page before it is displayed by a browser, you'll see the HTML tags set off in angle brackets.

    A basic HTML document has two parts. The **head** of the document specifies a title that appears on the title bar of the Web browser when the Web page is displayed. The **body** of the document contains informational text, graphics, and links. Table F-3 contains a basic set of HTML tags that you can use to create HTML documents for Web pages.

◦⊸ Remembering the purpose of each HTML tag, typing the tags into a document, and revising them is a fairly tedious task. New HTML authoring tools make it much easier to create Web pages using word processor-style interfaces, predesigned templates, and Wizards. **Web authoring software** is designed specifically to create HTML documents that will be displayed as Web pages. The software automatically inserts HTML tags for each of the elements you've selected. Some of the top Web-authoring software titles include Microsoft FrontPage, Claris Home Page, Adobe Page Mill, and Corel Web Designer. Some browsers provide tools to create Web pages, too. For example, Netscape Communicator Professional Edition includes a module called Netscape Composer designed to make it easy to construct Web pages by selecting components from menus.

◦⊸ Whether you're publishing a single page, a series of pages, or an entire Web site, you must put your pages on a Web server. Although Web server software is available for your home computer, you'll probably not want to leave your computer on all the time with a live phone line link to the Internet. Instead, you should look for a site that will host your pages. Many universities allocate space for student home pages and resumes. ISPs, such as America Online and AT&T, also offer space for individual home pages. If you are setting up a site for your business, consider a Web hosting service that provides space on its Internet servers for a monthly fee.

TROUBLE?

Your hard drive is much faster than a dial-up connection, so the text and graphics for your Web page appear more quickly during your test than they will for someone viewing your page over the Internet.

QUICK TIP

Many Web authoring software packages also provide tools to manage an entire Web site.

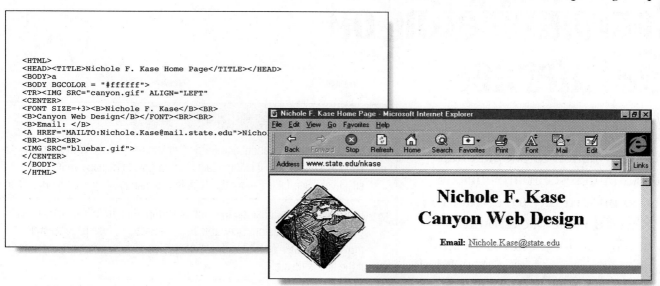

```
<HTML>
<HEAD><TITLE>Nichole F. Kase Home Page</TITLE></HEAD>
<BODY>a
<BODY BGCOLOR = "#ffffff">
<TR><IMG SRC="canyon.gif" ALIGN="LEFT"
<CENTER>
<FONT SIZE=+3><B>Nichole F. Kase</B><BR>
<B>Canyon Web Design</B></FONT><BR><BR>
<B>Email: </B>
<A HREF="MAILTO:Nichole.Kase@mail.state.edu">Nicho
<BR><BR><BR>
<IMG SRC="bluebar.gif">
</CENTER>
</BODY>
</HTML>
```

TABLE F-3: *Basic HTML tags*

HTML TAGS	MEANING AND LOCATION
<HTML></HTML>	States that the file is an HTML document. Opening tag begins the page; closing tag ends the page (required).
<HEAD></HEAD>	States that the enclosed text is the header of the page. Appears immediately after the opening HTML tag (required).
<TITLE></TITLE>	States that the enclosed text is the title of the page. Must appear within the opening and closing HEAD tags (required).
<BODY></BODY>	States that the enclosed material (all the text, images, and tags in the rest of the document) is the body of the document (required).
<H1></H1>	States that the enclosed text is a heading.
** **	Inserts a line break. Can be used to control line spacing and breaks in lines.
<UL></UL>, <OL></OL>	Indicates an unordered list (list items are preceded by bullets) or an ordered list (list items are preceded by numbers or letters).
<LI>	Indicates a list item. Precedes all items in unordered or ordered lists.
<CENTER></CENTER>	Indicates that the enclosed text should be centered on the width of the page.
<B></B>	Indicates that the enclosed text should appear boldface.
<I></I>	Indicates that the enclosed text should appear italic.
<A HREF=""></A>	Indicates that the enclosed text is a hypertext link. The URL of the linked material must appear within the quotation marks after the equal sign.
<IMG SCR="">	Inserts an in-line image into the document. The URL of the image appears within the quotation marks following the SCR="" attribute.
<HR>	Inserts a horizontal rule.

Communicating on the Internet

TODAY THE INTERNET CONNECTS computers all over the globe and supplies information to people of all ages and interests. It provides us with an opportunity to interact with people of diverse backgrounds, engage in life-long education, and enrich our knowledge of the global community. It is clear then that the Internet allows you to be in touch with a great many people. Therefore, when communicating on the Web via e-mail or Web pages, it is important to be sure your message is understood, and you follow proper netiquette. **Netiquette** are guidelines for communicating appropriately online. When Internet users follow proper Internet protocol, they help to ensure the quality of information published on the Internet. This lesson looks at e-mail protocol and Web page design.

Authoring Tips

IN MORE DETAIL

➤ E-mail accounts for about one-third of all Internet activity. With so many people using e-mail, it is important to know how to manage your e-mail effectively. See Table F-4 for tips to help you manage e-mail communication.

➤ If you decide to publish on the Web, it is important to follow basic rules for good Web page design. See Table F-5. Viewers will lose patience and move on to other Web sites if it takes too long for your pages to appear or if the text is illegible.

➤ A really great Web page is one that clearly communicates its purpose. However, it is not always easy to find the right balance of art and functionality to make a really great Web page. In addition to following the basic rules for Web page design, here are some other protocols you should follow when designing Web pages:

Plan your Web page so it fulfills its purpose: It is easier to communicate your Web page's message if you have a clear idea of what you want it to say.

Design a template to unify your pages: A design template is a set of specifications for the location and format of all the elements that you want to include on your Web pages.

Include navigation elements: A carefully selected set of navigational buttons or links makes it easier for people to jump from page to page in a logical order. Navigation elements should be clearly visible and easy to understand.

Respect copyright and intellectual property rights of other Web sites: Make sure you obtain permission before you use material from other Web sites and always give credit.

Identify your pages: Always include a title, a way for people to contact you, copyright information, and the latest updated information.

Test your links: Test the links on your pages, transfer your pages to your Web server, and then test all your links again.

E-mail privacy

E-mail Privacy

You should be aware that your e-mail might be read by someone other than the recipient. Although the U.S. justice system has not yet made a clear ruling, current legal interpretations indicate that e-mail is not legally protected from snooping. You cannot assume that the e-mail you send is private.

Therefore, you should not use e-mail to send any message that you want to keep confidential. Some employers read employee e-mail to discover if any illegal activities are taking place on the computer system. Many employers are genuinely concerned about such activities because they could, in some

cases, be held responsible for the actions of their employees. Also, the network administrator might see the contents of e-mail messages while performing system maintenance or when trying to recover from a system failure.

TABLE F-4: *Tips to help you manage e-mail*

Read your mail regularly.	When you use e-mail, your correspondents expect a quick response.
Delete messages after you read them.	Your e-mail is stored, along with everyone else's, on a file server where storage space is valuable. Leaving old messages in your mailbox takes up space that could be used more productively.
Don't reply to every e-mail message.	The purpose of some e-mail messages is to give you information. Don't reply unless there is a reason to respond, such as to answer a question.
If you receive mail addressed to a group, it might be better to reply only to one person in the group.	You might receive mail as a member of a mailing list. If you use the automatic reply feature of your e-mail system, your message will be sent to everyone on the list.
Think before you send e-mail.	It is easy to write a message in haste or in anger and send it off before you have time to think it through. If you're upset, write your message, but wait a day before you send it.
Don't write anything you want to remain confidential.	Remember that with e-mail it is easy to forward messages.
Don't get sloppy.	Your e-mail is a reflection of you, your school, and your employer. Use a spell checker if one is available; if not, proofread your message before you send it. Use standard grammar, punctuation, and capitalization. A message in all uppercase means you're shouting.

TABLE F-5: *Basic Web design rules*

Text	For readability, use black type for large sections of text.
	Maintain narrow line widths. Text that stretches across the entire width of the screen is more difficult to read than text in columns.
	Make sure you proofread your document for spelling errors.
Background	White or a very pale color makes a good background.
	Avoid drab gray and don't let your background color or graphic make it difficult to read the text.
Graphics	Try not to use graphics files that exceed 30 KB because larger files take too long to transfer, load, and appear on a Web page.
	Use graphics with .gif, not .bmp extensions.
	To include a large graphic, present it as a small "thumbnail" with a link to the larger version of the graphic.

Why a Web site?

Why would you want to publish on the Web? You might have information that you want to make available to the public, such as your resume or a calendar of events for your club. You might have services or products to offer that you would like people to easily obtain from any geographic location. You might want to collect information from people by using surveys or questionnaires. You might publish a series of Web pages as part of a corporate site to describe the products and services of your department. Freelance artists or programmers could use a series of Web pages to publish examples of their work. A university instructor might publish a series of Web pages containing the syllabus, study guide, and assignments for a course. Web publishing can help you get your message out as well as collect data.

Concepts Review

FIGURE F-28

http://www.course.com/products/titlesites.html

1.   2.   3.   4.

Identify each element shown in Figure F-28 and describe its function.

1. _____

2. _____

3. _____

4. _____

List three password do's and three password don'ts.

5. Do _____

6. Do _____

7. Do _____

8. Don't _____

9. Don't _____

10. Don't _____

Match each statement with the term it describes:

11. ___ Local area network (LAN)

12. ___ Network server

13. ___ Node

14. ___ Password

15. ___ Application server

a. Computer connected to the network that "serves," or distributes, resources to network users

b. Special set of symbols known only to you and the network administrator

c. Splits processing between the workstation *client* and the network *server*

d. Network that is located within a relatively limited area

e. Each device on a network, including workstations, servers, and printers

True or False?

16. Assuming proper licensing, while Jenny uses a spreadsheet program from the file server, Atkin who is working on the same network can also use this spreadsheet program at the same time at his workstation. True or False?

17. While Sandi is using the word-processing program stored on a network server, Karl must wait until she quits the program to use the same program at his terminal. True or False?

18. Client/server architecture takes advantage of the processing capabilities of both the workstations and the server. True or False?

19. If you want others who share your network to be able to access a word-processing document you are creating, you should save it to your local hard drive. True or False?

20. If you do not reply to every e-mail message that you receive, it is considered rude and improper e-mail netiquette. True or False?

21. Typically, you would connect your home computer directly to the Internet backbone using a T3 link. True or False?

22. Webcasting is pull technology that broadcasts information over the Web. True or False?

23. Most commercial information services are ISPs. True or False?

24. To participate in a chat group, you must be online at the same time as other participants. True or False?

25. On Web pages, links make it easy to follow a thread of related information even if the pages are stored on different computers in different countries. True or False?

26. The more traditional way to create HTML documents with word-processing software is being replaced by Web authoring software. True or False?

Fill in the best answer:

27. A network _____ is a computer connected to a network that distributes files to network users.

28. _____ is network terminology for assigning a drive letter to a file server disk drive.

29. When a network printer is assigned to your workstation, any data sent to the workstation's parallel port is _____ and _____ to the network printer.

30. Three reasons why sharing programs is effective for an organization are _____, _____, and _____.

31. The circuit board that connects a computer to a local area network is called a(n) _____.

32. If a network computer functions both as a file server and as a workstation, it is referred to as a(n) _____.

33. A(n) _____ is devoted to the task of delivering program and data files to workstations.

34. Novell NetWare would be classified as a(n) _____ software.

35. If an organization is planning to use software on a network, it should purchase a(n) _____ so multiple users can legally use the software.

36. If you are a team leader and you want your team members to collaborate on a project using the network to complete their contributions as a series of steps, you might try to find a(n) _____ product.

37. If you were the manager of a newspaper, you might request _____ so the network will automatically send news articles to each member of your department for editing.

38. The _____ is a collection of local, regional, and national computer networks that are linked together to exchange data and distribute processing tasks.

39. Internet traffic is measured in _____.

40. All the computers on the Internet use a standard set of communications rules called _____.

41. The address http://www.cyberspace.com is a(n) _____.

42. Your browser's _____ page is the first one you see when your browser starts.

43. A technology called _____ essentially plays a media file while your computer receives it.

44. A(n) _____ is a software module that adds a specific feature to your browser, such as the capability to play Web Theater videos.

45. Basic Web pages contain only _____, _____, and _____.

46. A basic HTML document has two parts: the head and the _____.

47. _____ software is specifically designed to create HTML documents that will be displayed as Web pages.

INDEPENDENT CHALLENGE 1

Creating passwords requires some thought and creativity. Based on the guidelines presented in this unit, help Latisha Simms to select a password for herself.

To complete this independent challenge:

1. Rank the following, listing the most secure password first:
   - XX32nsa (a totally random selection of letters and numbers)
   - LASIMMS (for Latisha Alexandra Simms)
   - RRRYBGDTS (the first letters of row, row, row your boat gently down the stream)
   - SMMIS (Latisha's last name spelled backwards)
   - Henry (Latisha's husband's name)

2. List five possible passwords for yourself if you were to go on a secure network.

3. List five bad examples of passwords for yourself.

INDEPENDENT CHALLENGE 2

Research your school network. Determine who is the network administrator at your school and prepare to interview him/her or to gain access to the system to find out about the network.

To complete this independent challenge, answer the following questions.

1. What is the network operating system?

2. What drives are mapped to a student workstation?

3. Is the file server a micro, mini, or mainframe computer?

4. Is the print server a different device than the file server?

INDEPENDENT CHALLENGE 3

Client/server architecture is becoming more and more popular in corporations.

To complete this independent challenge:

Find out more about client/server computing. Use library and Internet resources to look for case studies and articles about corporations that are using client/server applications. Write a one- or two-page description of an effective use of client/server computing. Be sure to include a list of references.

INDEPENDENT CHALLENGE 4

Understanding and knowing how to use the Internet will help you in many areas of your life.

To complete this independent challenge:

1. Draw a conceptual diagram that shows how the Internet connects computers. Include and label the following elements: backbone, dial-up connection, host computers, router, NSP computer, ISP computer, home computer.

2. Make a list of the steps you would take to connect your computer at home to the Internet.

3. Provide an example of an IP address, a domain name, a URL, and an e-mail address. Then, in your own words, describe the elements each contains.

4. On the Internet, you can interact with people in discussion groups, chat groups, and interactive games. Describe the difference between synchronous and asynchronous interactions, and explain how each relates to chats, discussion groups, and games.

INDEPENDENT CHALLENGE 5

The history of the Internet is fascinating. Although only 30 years old, it is rich in history. Use Internet or library resources to write a research paper about the Internet. In your paper be sure to answer, but do not limit yourself to, the following questions.

To complete this independent challenge:

1. What are the key events in the development of the Internet?

2. Include a timeline of these key events.
   a. What is the Internet's current status?
   b. What changes are likely to take place in the future?
   c. What ethical issues do you think are raised by the existence of the Internet?

3. The Internet, like most societies, has certain standards for behavior. What's generally acceptable online behavior in cyberspace culture?

4. Design a poster of netiquette rules. Decide what audience your poster targets: children, high school students, college students, business people, and so on. Try to use words and images that will appeal to your target audience.

INDEPENDENT CHALLENGE 6

Surfing the Web will take you to many interesting sites. As you visit each site, you can notice differences among the many Web pages. To some extent, good design is a matter of taste, and when it comes to Web page design, there are usually many possible solutions that provide a pleasing look and efficient navigational tools. On the other hand, there are some designs that just don't seem to work because they make the text difficult to read or navigate.

To complete this independent challenge:

1. Select a Web page that you think could use improvement. You may find the page by browsing on the Web or by looking in magazines for screen shots of Web pages.

2. Save and print the page or photocopy the magazine picture.

3. Use colored pencils or markers to sketch your plan for improving the page. Annotate your sketch by pointing out the features you have changed and why you think your makeover will be more effective than the original Web page.

INDEPENDENT CHALLENGE 7

Many people have their own home pages. It is a very personal statement of who you are and what your interests may be. You can design your own home page. Depending on the tools you have available, you might be able to create a real page and publish it on the Web. If these tools are not available, you will still be able to complete the initial design work. Your instructor will provide you with guidelines on which of the following steps to complete.

To complete this independent challenge:

1. Write a brief description of the purpose of your home page and your expected audience. For example, you might plan to use your home page to showcase your resume to prospective employers.

2. Make a list of the elements you plan to include on your home page. Briefly describe any graphics or media elements you want to include.

3. Create a document that contains the information you want to include for your home page.

4. Make a sketch of your home page showing the colors you plan to use and the navigation elements you plan to include. Annotate this sketch to describe how these elements follow effective Web page design guidelines.

5. If you have the tools to create the entire HTML document for your home page, do so. Make sure that you test the page locally using your browser. Use the Print option on the File menu of your browser to print your page.

6. If you have permission to publish your Web page on a Web server, do so. Provide your instructor with the URL for your page.

INDEPENDENT CHALLENGE 8

The URL for each Web page uniquely identifies each site. When selecting a URL, businesses try to include their name or their products in the URL in an effort to better promote themselves on the Internet. As being on the WWW becomes more common in our society, companies are including URLs in their print advertisements. As you encounter URLs, you need to be aware that sometimes they are not what they appear to be.

To complete this independent challenge:

1. Look through a local paper and list five local businesses in your area that advertise Web sites in their advertisements. Cut out the advertisement and circle the URL.

2. Find the URLs for five of the following businesses or organizations:

   Nike, Trek Bicycles, Burger King, McDonalds, *The New York Times*, *The Washington Post*, GM, IBM, Microsoft, the U.S. Congress, the U.S. Department of Agriculture, your college or university, the New York Yankees, the Chicago Bulls, your favorite baseball team, your favorite football team, your local town government, a hospital in your area.

3. Search the Web and list three URLs whose names don't clearly identify the business or product.

   - Then search the name that you think would have been a better choice.
   - Did you find the name used by another company? Why do you think the business could not use the name you might have selected?

4. The top-level domain makes a difference in a Web site. List the differences between the following sites, identifying each:

   - FCC.gov and FCC.com
   - FBI.com and FBI.gov
   - MIT.com and MIT.edu

E-MAIL LAB

E-mail that originates on a local area network with a mail gateway can travel all over the world. That's why it is so important to learn how to use it. In this Lab you use an e-mail simulator, so even if your school computers don't provide you with e-mail service, you will know the basics of reading, sending, and replying to electronic mail.

1. Click the Steps button to learn how to work with e-mail. As you proceed through the Steps, answer all of the Quick Check questions that appear. After you complete the Steps, you will see a Quick Check Summary Report. Follow the instructions on the screen to print this report.

2. Click the Explore button. Write a message to re@films.org. The subject of the message is "Picks and Pans." In the body of your message, describe a movie you have recently seen. Include the name of the movie, briefly summarize the plot, and give it a thumbs up or a thumbs down. Print the message before you send it.

3. In Explore, look in your In Box for a message from jb@music.org. Read the message, and then compose a reply indicating that you will attend. Carbon copy mciccone@music.org. Print your reply, including the text of JB's original message, before you send it.

4. In Explore, look in your In Box for a message from leo@sports.org. Reply to the message by adding your rating to the text of the original message as follows:

Equipment:	Your Rating:
Rollerblades	2
Skis	3
Bicycle	1
Scuba gear	4
Snowmobile	5

Print your reply before you send it.

THE INTERNET: WORLD WIDE WEB LAB

One of the most popular services on the Internet is the World Wide Web. This Lab is a Web simulator that teaches you how to use Web browser software to find information. You can use this Lab whether or not your school provides you with Internet access.

1. Click the Steps button to learn how to use Web browser software. As you proceed through the Steps, answer all of the Quick Check questions that appear. After you complete the Steps, you will see a Quick Check Summary Report. Follow the instructions on the screen to print this report.

2. Click the Explore button on the Welcome screen. Use the Web browser to locate a weather map of the Carribean Virgin Islands. What is its URL?

3. A SCUBA diver named Wadson Lachouffe has been searching for the fabled treasure of Greybeard the pirate. A link from the Adventure Travel Web site (**http://www.atour.com**) leads to a Wadson's Web page called "Hidden Treasure." In Explore, locate the Hidden Treasure page and answer the following questions:

   a. What was the name of Greybeard's ship?

   b. What was Greybeard's favorite food?

   c. What does Wadson think happened to Greybeard's ship?

4. In the Steps, you found a graphic of Jupiter from the photo archives of the Jet Propulsion Laboratory. In the Explore section of the Lab, you can also find a graphic of Saturn. Suppose one of your friends wanted a picture of Saturn for an astronomy report. Make a list of the blue, underlined links your friend must click to find the Saturn graphic. Assume that your friend will begin at the Web Trainer home page.

5. Enter the URL **http://www.atour.com** to jump to the Adventure Travel Web site. Write a one-page description of this site. In your paper include a description of the information at the site, the number of pages the site contains, and a diagram of the links it contains.

6. Chris Thomson is a student at UVI and has his own Web pages. In Explore, look at the information Chris has included on his pages. Suppose you could create your own Web page. What would you include? Use word-processing software to design your own Web pages. Make sure you indicate the graphics and links you would use.

WEB PAGES & HTML

It's easy to create your own Web pages. As you learned in this unit, there are many software tools to help you become a Web author. In this Lab you'll experiment with a Web authoring wizard that automates the process of creating a Web page. You'll also try your hand at working directly with HTML code.

1. Click the Steps button to activate the Web authoring wizard and learn how to create a basic Web page. As you proceed through the Steps, answer all of the Quick Check questions. After you complete the Steps, you will see a Quick Check summary Report. Follow the instructions on the screen to print this report.

2. In Explore, click the File menu, then click New to start working on a new Web page. Use the wizard to create a home page for a veterinarian who offers dog day care and boarding services. After you create the page, save it on drive A or C, and print the HTML code. Your site must have the following characteristics:

   a. Title: Dr. Dave's Dog Domain

   b. Background color: Gold

   c. Graphic: Dog.jpg

   d. Body text: Your dog will have the best care day and night at Dr. Dave's Dog Domain. Fine accommodations, good food, play time, and snacks are all provided. You can board your pet by the day or week. Grooming services also available.

   e. Text link: "Reasonable rates" links to www.cciw.com/np3/rates.htm

   f. E-mail link: "For more information:" links to **daveassist@drdave.com**

3. In Explore, use the File menu to open the HTML document called Politics.htm. After you use the HTML window (not the wizard) to make the following changes, save the revised page on drive A or C, and print the HTML code. Refer to Figure 8-19 of your textbook for a list of HTML tags you can use.

   a. Change the title to Politics 2000.

   b. Center the page heading.

   c. Change the background color to FFE7C6 and the text color to 000000.

   d. Add a line break before the sentence "What's next?"

   e. Add a bold tag to the "Additional links on this topic:" line.

   f. Add one more link to the "Additional links" list. The link should go to the site **http://www.elections.ca** and the clickable link should read "Elections Canada."

   g. Change the last graphic to display the image "next.gif."

4. In Explore use the Web authoring wizard and the HTML window to create a Home page about yourself. You should include at least a screenful of text, a graphic, an external link, and an e-mail link. Save the page on drive A, and then print the HTML code. Turn in your disk and printout.

Data Security and Control

IN THIS UNIT YOU WILL LEARN ABOUT HUMAN errors and equipment failures that cause lost or inaccurate data. You will learn about threats to the data stored on computer systems such as intentional acts of vandalism and computer crime in which data is tampered with or stolen. The lesson on risk management explains the steps you can take to protect your data. You can begin to assess your risk of losing important data, becoming the target of computer vandalism, or being affected by inaccurate data. The unit explores security on the Internet and the technology available to protect you as you download files and perform commercial transactions. On a practical level, you will learn how to disinfect disks that contain viruses, make backups, and design an effective backup plan for your data. You will find out why data backup is one of the most effective security measures for protecting your data.

OBJECTIVES

Know what can go wrong

Avoid disasters

Introduce computer viruses and vandalism

Explore viruses and vandalism

Avoid and detect viruses

Understand data security and risk management

Restrict access to data

Understand encryption

Explore Internet security

Provide redundancy

Create backups

Knowing what can go wrong

DATA STORED ON COMPUTERS IS VULNERABLE TO HUMAN ERROR AND POWER PROBLEMS. Today's computer users battle to avoid lost, stolen, and inaccurate data. **Lost data**, also referred to as **missing data**, is data that is inaccessible, usually because it was accidentally removed. **Stolen data** is not necessarily missing, but has been accessed or copied without authorization. **Inaccurate data** is data that is not accurate because it was entered incorrectly, was deliberately or accidentally altered, or was not edited to reflect current facts.

IN MORE DETAIL

☞ Human error: Despite all the sensational press coverage of computer criminals and viruses, the most common cause of lost data is human error, also known as operator error. **Operator error** refers to a mistake made by a computer user, such as entering the wrong data or deleting a file that is still needed. Everyone who has used a computer has probably made a mistake that resulted in lost or inaccurate data.

The number of operator errors can be reduced if users pay attention to what they're doing and establish habits that help them avoid mistakes. Many organizations have reduced the incidence of operator errors by using direct source input devices. A **direct source input device**, such as a bar code reader, collects data directly from a document or object.

Computer software designers can also help prevent operator error by designing products that anticipate mistakes users are likely to make and that provide features to help users avoid those mistakes. Figure G-1 shows a Windows 95 dialog box that asks for confirmation before a file is deleted.

☞ Computer software problems: Commercial software is complex, and, therefore, is sometimes released with program errors that can affect the integrity of your data. Although catastrophic loss of data due to errors in programming is rare, it is important to be aware of your data and to look for inaccuracies that may be caused by the program itself.

☞ Power problems: Since computers are powered by electricity, they are susceptible to power failures, spikes, and surges. A **power failure** is a complete loss of power to the computer system. Although you can lose power by bumping the on/off switch, a power failure is usually caused by something over which you have no control. Even a brief interruption in power, noticeable only as a flicker of the room lights, can force your computer to reboot and lose all the data in RAM.

An uninterruptible power supply is the best protection against power problems. An **uninterruptible power supply**, or **UPS**, is a device containing a battery and other circuitry that provides a continuous supply of power. A UPS is designed to provide enough power to keep your computer working through momentary power interruptions and to give you time to save your files and exit your programs in the event of a longer power outage. Figure G-2 shows a typical UPS.

Two other common power problems are spikes and surges. Both of these can damage sensitive computer components. A **power spike** is an increase in power that lasts only a short time—less than a millionth of a second. A **power surge** lasts a little longer. Spikes and surges are caused by malfunctions in the local generating plant and the power distribution network, and are potentially more damaging than a power failure. They can destroy the circuitry that operates your hard disk drive or damage your computer's motherboard.

The same UPS you use to provide a few minutes of power in the event of a power loss will also filter out power surges and spikes. As a low-cost alternative, you can plug your computer into a **surge protector** (also called a surge strip or surge supressor). Just remember that a surge protector does not protect the data in RAM if the power fails. Figure G-3 shows a surge protector.

UPS

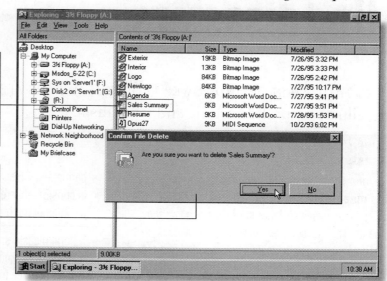

The user selects the file Sales Summary and presses [Delete] to initiate an operation that will, in effect, destroy the data in the selected file.

The Windows operating system displays a prompt asking the user to confirm the operation. The file is deleted only if the user clicks Yes.

FIGURE G-2: *An uninterruptible power supply (UPS)*

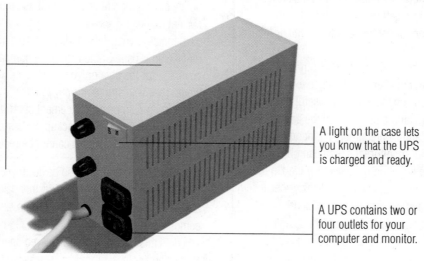

A UPS contains a battery that keeps your computer going for several minutes during a power failure. The battery does not supply indefinite power, so in the event of a power failure you should save your work and turn off your computer.

A light on the case lets you know that the UPS is charged and ready.

A UPS contains two or four outlets for your computer and monitor.

Lightning can cause a power surge. Many experts recommend that you unplug your computer equipment, including your modem, during electrical storms.

FIGURE G-3: *A surge protector*

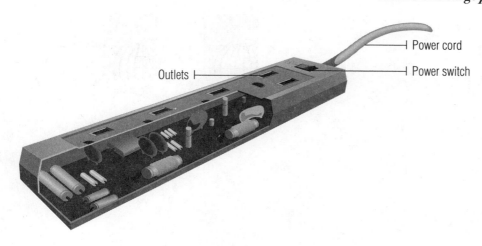

Power cord

Outlets

Power switch

Although a power failure results in lost data from RAM, it is unlikely to cause data loss from disks because magnetic storage does not require power to maintain data.

Avoiding disasters

In addition to human error and power problems, data is also vulnerable to hardware failure, natural disasters, and vandalism.

IN MORE DETAIL

- Hardware failure: The reliability of computer components is measured as **mean time between failures**, or **MTBF**. The MTBF is an estimate based on laboratory tests of a few sample components. The measurement is somewhat misleading to most consumers because the tests are conducted in a regulated laboratory environment where power problems, failure of other components, and regular wear and tear do not exist. For example, a 125,000 hour MTBF means that, *on average*, a hard disk drive is likely to function for 125,000 hours without failing. The fact remains, however, that your hard disk drive might work for only ten hours before it fails. With this in mind, it is important to plan for hardware failures, rather than hope they won't happen.

  Much of the equipment that fails does so within the first hours or days of operation, but after that it can be expected to work fairly reliably until it nears the end of its useful life.

  The effect of a hardware failure depends on the component that fails. Most hardware failures are simply an inconvenience. For example, if your monitor fails, you can obtain a replacement monitor, plug it in, and get back to work. On the other hand, a hard disk drive failure can be a disaster because you might lose all the data stored on the hard disk drive. While an experienced computer technician might be able to recover some of the files on the hard disk drive and transfer them to another hard disk, it is more often the case that all programs and data files stored on the hard disk are permanently lost. The impact of a hard disk drive failure is considerably reduced if you have complete, up-to-date backups of the programs and data files on your hard disk.

- Natural disasters: Computers are not immune to unexpected damage from smoke, fire, water, and breakage; therefore it is a good practice to carry insurance to cover your equipment. Under the terms of many standard household and business insurance policies, a computer is treated like any other appliance. You should make sure, however, that your insurance policy covers the full cost of purchasing a new computer at current market prices.

  Replacing your damaged computer equipment will not replace your data. Some insurance companies provide extra coverage for the data on your computer. This means that you would receive a sum of money to cover the time it takes to reload your data on a replacement computer. However, this assumes that you have a backup of your data. Without a backup, much of your data cannot be reconstructed.

- Vandalism: Your data can also be destroyed by vandalism; for example, computer viruses can destroy data. Computer vandals are people who, for thrills or illegal gain, attack the data of other computer users. Read the message in Figure G-4. What would you do if this message were displayed on your computer screen? Understanding how programs such as viruses work is the first line of defense against attacks and pranks. You will learn more about computer viruses and vandalism in the next lesson.

Computer Insurance

Virus Alert

It is possible for a virus to migrate to a file other than the one to which it was originally attached.

Viruses can replicate themselves and spread to other programs on hard or floppy disks.

Viruses can destroy the contents of your hard disk.

The first hint that the message is a fake: Experts have not been able to confirm the existence of any viruses that damage hardware.

The prank becomes obvious: Printing out all your files, then erasing them from computer storage is *definitely not* the way to deal with a virus attack!

Warning! A serious virus is on the loose. It is disguised as a program called AVBKGD2, however, the virus will remain on your system even after you have erased this file. The virus does the following:
1. Copies itself to other programs on hard and floppy disks.
2. Randomly scrambles the contents of your data files.
3. Sends an electrical signal to your printer that causes it to short circuit.
This virus is not detectable using any antivirus software. The only safe way to protect yourself against this virus is to print all your files, erase all the disks on your system, and type in all your data again.

What are disaster recovery centers?

Disaster recovery centers provide emergency computing facilities to businesses. A business can build its own or contract with a company for this service. When disaster strikes, businesses cannot afford to disrupt their operations. Disaster recovery facilities are ready to take over operations when disaster strikes and until the main systems can be restored. This facility is a remote location, which can have a complete backup of the hardware, software, and data for a company, or simply provide a building where computers can be brought in quickly.

QUICK TIP

A good insurance policy provides funds to replace computer equipment, but the only insurance for your data is an up-to-date backup tape or disk.

Introducing computer viruses and vandalism

DATA STORED ON MICRO, MINI, OR mainframe computers can be damaged, destroyed, or altered by vandalism. Computer vandals are called **hackers**, **crackers**, or **cyberpunks**. The programs these hackers create are colorfully referred to as malware, pest programs, vandalware, or punkware. More typically, though, these programs are referred to as *viruses*. The term *virus* technically refers to only one type of program created by hackers.

Macro Viruses

If your computer is attacked by a macro virus, you might have to manually extract the macros from each infected document. You'll find information on combating macro viruses at Microsoft's Web site and in recent editions of computer magazines.

A macro is essentially a miniature program that usually contains legitimate instructions to automate document production.

IN MORE DETAIL

- **Computer viruses:** A **computer virus** is a program that attaches itself to a file and reproduces itself to spread from one file to another. A virus can destroy data, display irritating messages, or disrupt other computer operations.

- **Computer jargon:** The jargon that describes a computer virus sounds similar to medical jargon. Your computer is a "host," and it can become "infected" with a virus. A virus can reproduce itself and spread from one computer to another. You can "inoculate" your computer against many viruses. If your computer has not been inoculated and becomes infected, you can use antivirus software to "disinfect" it.

- **Virus attacks:** A computer virus generally infects the executable files on your computer system, not the data files. Most viruses attach themselves to an executable file because these are the files that your computer runs. Each time your computer runs an infected program, your computer also runs the attached virus instructions to replicate or deliver its payload. Because a virus needs to be executed to spread, a data file can only be a carrier; it cannot deliver the payload.

- **Payload:** The term **payload** refers to the ultimate mission of a virus. For example, the payload of the "Stoned" virus is to display the message, "Your PC is now stoned" on your screen. Figure G-5 illustrates how a computer virus spreads and delivers its payload.

- **Boot sector virus:** **Boot sector viruses** are viruses that infect the system files your computer uses every time you turn it on. They can cause widespread damage and persistent problems.

- A **macro virus** infects documents such as those created with a word processor. Infected documents are stored with a list of instructions called a **macro**. A hacker can create a destructive macro, attach it to a document, and then distribute it over the Internet or on disk. When anyone views the document, the macro virus duplicates itself into the general macro pool where it is picked up by other documents. The two most common macro viruses are the Concept virus that attaches to Microsoft Word documents, and Laroux that attaches to Microsoft Excel spreadsheets.

    Experts say there are over 2,000 viruses. However, 90 percent of virus damage is caused by fewer than 10 viruses. Of the top viruses, macro viruses account for about 75 percent of the virus attacks, as shown in Figure G-6.

- **Symptoms of a virus:** The symptoms of a virus infection depend on the virus. Some symptoms indicating that your computer might have contracted a virus include the following: Your computer displays annoying messages. Your computer develops unusual visual or sound effects. You have difficulty saving files, files mysteriously disappear, or executable files unaccountably increase in size. Your computer suddenly seems to work very slowly or reboots unexpectedly. However, some of these symptoms can also be caused by other factors.

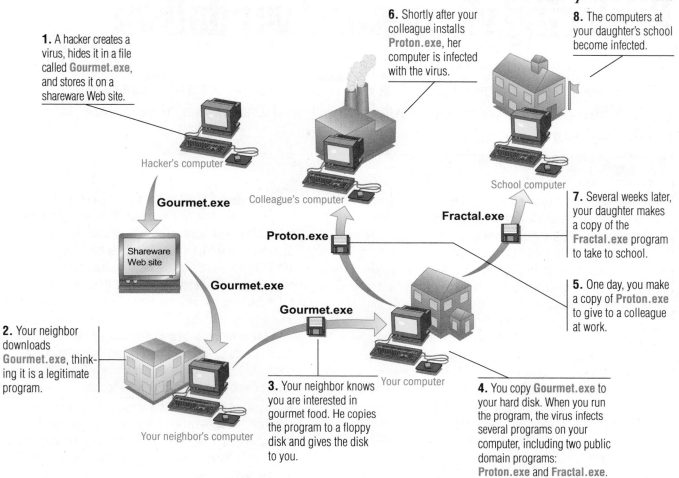

1. A hacker creates a virus, hides it in a file called **Gourmet.exe**, and stores it on a shareware Web site.

Hacker's computer

Gourmet.exe

Shareware Web site

Gourmet.exe

2. Your neighbor downloads **Gourmet.exe**, thinking it is a legitimate program.

Your neighbor's computer

Gourmet.exe

3. Your neighbor knows you are interested in gourmet food. He copies the program to a floppy disk and gives the disk to you.

Colleague's computer

Proton.exe

6. Shortly after your colleague installs **Proton.exe**, her computer is infected with the virus.

Your computer

4. You copy **Gourmet.exe** to your hard disk. When you run the program, the virus infects several programs on your computer, including two public domain programs: **Proton.exe** and **Fractal.exe**.

Fractal.exe

School computer

8. The computers at your daughter's school become infected.

7. Several weeks later, your daughter makes a copy of the **Fractal.exe** program to take to school.

5. One day, you make a copy of **Proton.exe** to give to a colleague at work.

FIGURE G-6: *Top viruses*

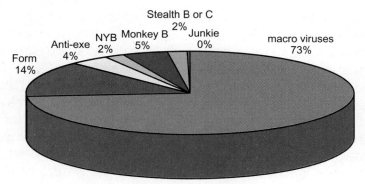

Stealth B or C 2%
NYB 2% Monkey B 5% Junkie 0%
Anti-exe 4%
Form 14%
macro viruses 73%

Data source: NCSA 1997 Virus Prevalence Survey

Computer crime and the law

"Old-fashioned" crimes that take a high tech twist because they involve a computer are often prosecuted using traditional laws. Most states have computer crime laws that specifically define computer data and software as personal property. These laws also define as a crime the unauthorized access, use, modification, or disabling of a computer system or data. Under most state laws, intentionally circulating a destructive virus is a crime. Laws are made to deter criminals, bring them to trial if they are caught, and punish them if they are convicted. But laws don't actually protect your data. That is something you need to do by making frequent backups and taking steps to prevent unauthorized access to data.

Exploring viruses and vandalism

VIRUSES ARE JUST ONE TYPE OF PROGRAM IN A LARGE CATEGORY OF SOFTWARE VANDALISM. Hackers also cause problems with programs such as Trojan horses, time bombs, logic bombs, and worms.

IN MORE DETAIL

☞ Trojan horse: A **Trojan horse** is a computer program that appears to perform one function while actually doing something else. A Trojan horse sometimes, but not always, harbors a virus. Think of a Trojan horse as a container that hides a secret program. That program might be a virus or a time bomb, or simply a program that, when run, carries out a nasty task such as formatting your hard disk. Figure G-7 shows how one type of Trojan horse program works.

It is easy to be fooled by Trojan horse programs because they are designed to be difficult to detect. For example, one popular Trojan horse looks just like the login screen on a network. Keep your ears open for information about the latest computer pranks circulating in your local area. Also, be suspicious of anything out of the ordinary on your computer system. For example, if your login screen looks a little different one day, check with your technical support person.

☞ Time bombs and logic bombs: Although a virus usually begins to replicate itself immediately, a virus or other unwelcome surprise can lurk in your computer system for days or months without discovery.

A **time bomb** is a computer program that stays in your system undetected until it is triggered by a certain event in time, such as when the computer system clock reaches a certain date. A time bomb is usually carried by a virus or Trojan horse. For example, the Michelangelo virus contains a time bomb, designed to damage files on your hard disk on March 6, the birthday of artist Michelangelo. March 6 is an odd date for a time bomb attack. Hackers seem to favor dates such as Halloween, Friday the 13th, and April Fool's day for time bomb attacks.

The year 2000 time bomb refers to a problem with software that does not require a four-digit date field (for example, 89

entered instead of 1989) written to save precious disk space and processing time. As it turns out, this decision has the potential to cause havoc when the year 2000 arrives. Why? Suppose a person born in 1984 applies for a driver's license in 1999. The computer uses the last two digits of the dates, subtracts 84 from 99, and determines that the applicant is 15 years old. If the same person applies for a license in the year 2000, the computer subtracts 84 from 00 and gets -84 years old!

A **logic bomb** is a computer program that is triggered by the appearance or disappearance of specific data. A logic bomb can be carried by a virus or Trojan horse. Alternatively, a logic bomb can be a stand-alone program.

☞ Worms: A software **worm** is a program designed to enter a computer system—usually a network—through security "holes." A lead story in *The Wall Street Journal* reported the now famous Internet worm that spread to more than 6,000 Internet host computers. Like a virus, a worm reproduces itself. Unlike a virus, a worm does not need to be attached to a document or executable program to reproduce.

The software worm that attacked the Internet entered each computer through security holes in the electronic mail system, and then used data stored on the computer to, in effect, mail itself to other computers. The worm spread rapidly, as shown in Figure G-8. The Internet worm was not designed to destroy data. Instead, it filled up storage space and dramatically slowed computer performance. The only way to eradicate the Internet worm was to shut down the electronic mail system on the Internet hosts, and then comb through hundreds of programs to find and destroy the worm, a process that took up to eight hours for each host.

Year 2000   Internet Worm

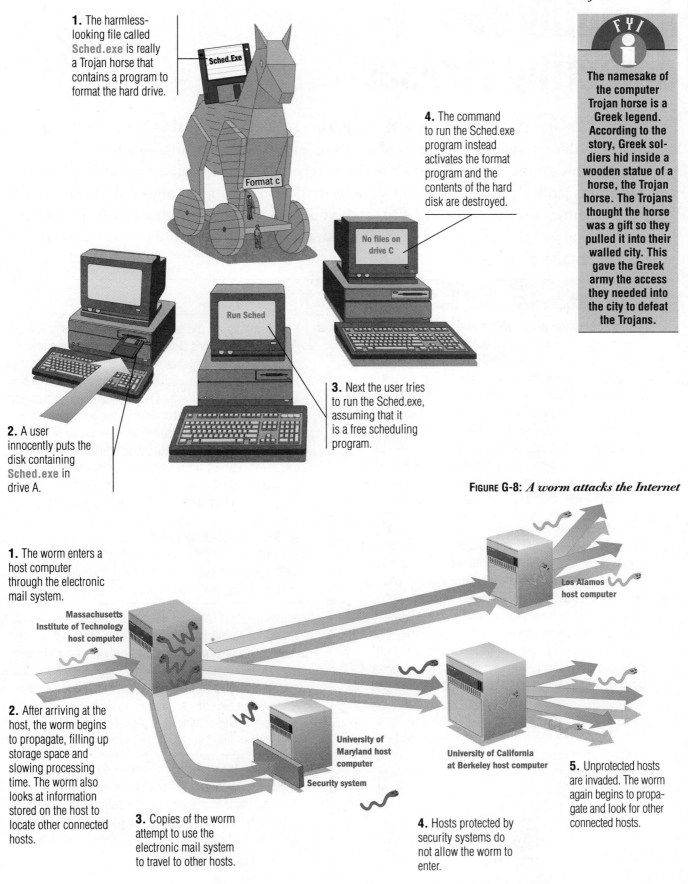

1. The harmless-looking file called **Sched.exe** is really a Trojan horse that contains a program to format the hard drive.

Sched.Exe

Format c

4. The command to run the Sched.exe program instead activates the format program and the contents of the hard disk are destroyed.

No files on drive C

Run Sched

3. Next the user tries to run the Sched.exe, assuming that it is a free scheduling program.

2. A user innocently puts the disk containing **Sched.exe** in drive A.

FYI

The namesake of the computer Trojan horse is a Greek legend. According to the story, Greek soldiers hid inside a wooden statue of a horse, the Trojan horse. The Trojans thought the horse was a gift so they pulled it into their walled city. This gave the Greek army the access they needed into the city to defeat the Trojans.

1. The worm enters a host computer through the electronic mail system.

Massachusetts Institute of Technology host computer

Los Alamos host computer

2. After arriving at the host, the worm begins to propagate, filling up storage space and slowing processing time. The worm also looks at information stored on the host to locate other connected hosts.

University of Maryland host computer

Security system

University of California at Berkeley host computer

3. Copies of the worm attempt to use the electronic mail system to travel to other hosts.

4. Hosts protected by security systems do not allow the worm to enter.

5. Unprotected hosts are invaded. The worm again begins to propagate and look for other connected hosts.

Avoiding and detecting viruses

COMPUTER VIRUSES AND OTHER TYPES OF MALICIOUS SOFTWARE TYPICALLY LURK ON DISKS containing public domain software or shareware, on disks containing illegal copies of computer programs downloaded from the Internet, and in e-mail attachments. Disks and programs from these sources should be regarded as having a "high risk" of infection. Figure G-9 shows tips for avoiding viruses. If you need to use a disk that you suspect might be infected, you can use a virus detection program to check for viruses before you run any programs from the disk.

IN MORE DETAIL

- A **virus detection program,** or **antivirus program**, examines the files stored on a disk to determine if they are infected with a virus and then disinfects the disk, if necessary. Virus detection programs use several techniques to detect viruses, which attach themselves to an existing program increasing the length of the original program. The earliest virus detection software simply examined the programs on your computer and recorded their length. A change in the length of a program from one computing session to the next indicated the possible presence of a virus. Table G-1 shows what to do if you detect a virus.

- Checksums: A **checksum** is a value that is calculated by combining all the bytes in a file. In response to early virus detection programs, hackers became more cunning. They created viruses that insert themselves into unused portions of a program file, but do not change its length. Of course, the people who designed virus detection programs fought back. They designed programs that examine the bytes in an uninfected application program and calculate a checksum. Each time you run the application program, the virus detection program recalculates the checksum and compares it to the original. If any byte in the application program has been changed, the checksum will be different, and the virus detection program assumes that a virus is present. The checksum approach requires that you start with a copy of the program that is not infected with a virus. If you start with an infected copy, the virus is included in the original checksum, and the virus detection program never detects it.

- Virus signature: Another technique used by virus detection programs is to search for a signature. A **virus signature** is a unique series of bytes that can be used to identify a known virus, much as a fingerprint is used to identify an individual. The signature is usually a section of the virus program, such as a unique series of instructions. Most of today's virus detection software scans for virus signatures and for this reason virus detection software is sometimes referred to as a "scanner." The signature search technique can identify only those viruses with a known signature. To detect new viruses, you must obtain regular updates for your virus detection program that include new virus signatures.

  Some viruses are specifically designed to avoid detection by one or more of the above virus detection methods. For this reason, the most sophisticated virus protection schemes combine elements from each of these methods.

- Reliability: Virus detection software finds and eradicates many viruses, but it is not 100 percent reliable. It will fail to detect viruses without a known signature, **polymorphic viruses** that change after they infect your computer, and viruses that use **stealth technology** to hide from virus detection programs. Virus detection software is generally successful in detecting and eradicating most widespread viruses, so it should be included in your software collection.

- Availability: There are many virus detection programs, produced by different software publishers. You can purchase these programs from your local computer dealer or by mail order. Shareware virus detection programs are available from Web sites, computer bulletin boards, and shareware dealers.

Antivirus Software

1. Install and use virus detection software.

 2. Keep your virus detection software up to date.

 3. Make frequent backups after you use virus detection software to scan your files for viruses.

 4. Download software only from sources that take steps to make sure files do not contain any viruses. Use a virus detection program to scan downloaded software before you use it.

 5. Be careful with disks that contain shareware. Scan them before you run or copy any files from these disks.

QUICK TIP

If viruses are a recurring problem in your computing environment, you might want to configure your virus detection software to continually monitor the behavior of your computer files and alert you if it spots signs of virus-like activity. The disadvantage to this strategy is that continually monitoring files slows down your computer operation.

TABLE **G-1**: *What to do if you detect a computer virus*

IN GENERAL	IF YOU ARE CONNECTED TO A COMPUTER NETWORK	IF YOU ARE USING YOUR OWN COMPUTER SYSTEM
Take immediate steps to stop the virus from spreading.	Alert the network administrator that you found a virus on your workstation.	Method 1: Use a virus detection program to remove the virus.
Test and remove the virus from every floppy disk and backup used on your computer system.	The network administrator can take action to prevent the virus from spreading throughout the network.	Follow Method 2 if you cannot successfully remove the virus without destroying the program.
Alert your colleagues and anyone with whom you have shared disks that a virus from your system might have traveled on those disks and infected their computer systems.		Method 2: • Erase the infected program. • Test the system to be sure the virus has been removed. • Reinstall the program from the original disks.
If you don't remove every copy of the virus, your system will become infected again the next time you use the infected disk.		In cases where the virus has infected most of the programs on your system, it is best to make a copy of your data files, reformat the hard drive, and then reinstall all the programs.
Use a virus detection program to remove the virus.		

Understanding data security and risk management

IT IS NOT PRACTICAL TO TOTALLY protect computer data from theft, viruses, and natural disasters. In most situations providing total data security is too time-consuming, too expensive, or too complex. **Data security** is the collection of techniques that provide protection for data. In order to determine the extent to which you practice data security, you must do risk management analysis. This lesson takes a closer look at policies and procedures.

INFOWEB

Risks

IN MORE DETAIL

☞ Risk management: **Risk management** is the process of weighing threats to computer data against the amount of data that is expendable and the cost of protecting crucial data. Table G-2 shows steps for a risk management strategy. Once you have completed your risk management analysis, you can establish policies and procedures to help you maintain data security.

☞ Policies: **Policies** are the rules and regulations that specify how a computer system should be used. Policies are most often determined by management and used by large organizations to stipulate who can access computer data. Policies also help an organization define appropriate uses for its computers and data. The advantages of policies are that they define how a computer system should be used, make users aware of limits and penalties, and provide a framework for legal or job action for individuals who do not follow policies. Policies are an inexpensive building block in the overall structure of data security. Policies do not require any special hardware or software. The cost of policies is the time it takes to compose, update, and publicize them. The disadvantage of policies for data security is that some users disregard policies.

☞ Procedures: Successful computer users develop habits that significantly reduce their chances of making mistakes. These habits, when formalized and adopted by an organization, are referred to as **procedures**. Procedures help reduce human errors that can erase or damage data. The major advantage of procedures is reducing operator error. Procedures have two disadvantages. First, they must be kept up-to-date as equipment and software change. Second, there is no way to make sure that people follow them. Figure G-10 lists some possible policies and procedures.

Why practice risk management?

The most popular data security techniques used to reduce the risk of data loss apply to micro, mini, and mainframe computer data. Risk management is important for you as an individual for three reasons. First, it is likely that you will work with computers within an organization when you graduate, so you will share the responsibility with your coworkers for that organization's data. Second, many organizations maintain data about you, such as your credit rating, educational record, and health records. You have a vested interest in the accuracy and the confidentiality of this data. Finally, you currently have data stored on disks that might be time-consuming to reconstruct. Consider using backup and virus detection to secure your own data.

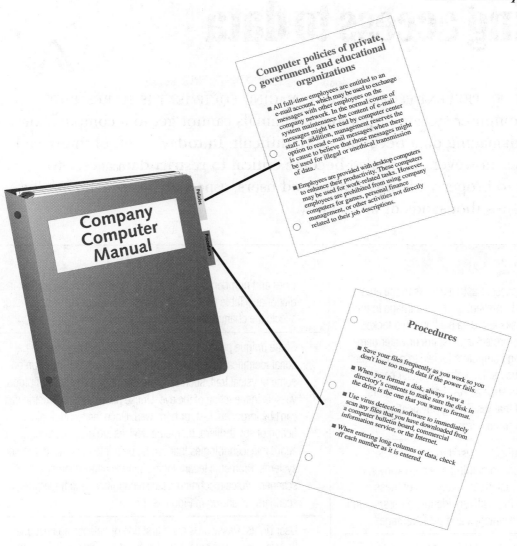

Computer policies of private, government, and educational organizations

■ All full-time employees are entitled to an e-mail account, which may be used to exchange messages with other employees on the company network. In the normal course of system maintenance the content of e-mail messages might be read by computer center staff. In addition, management reserves the option to read e-mail messages when there is cause to believe that those messages might be used for illegal or unethical transmission of data.

■ Employees are provided with desktop computers to enhance their productivity. These computers may be used for work-related tasks. However, employees are prohibited from using company computers for games, personal finance management, or other activities not directly related to their job descriptions.

Procedures

■ Save your files frequently as you work so you don't lose too much data if the power fails.
■ When you format a disk, always view a directory's contents to make sure the disk in the drive is the one that you want to format.
■ Use virus detection software to immediately scan any files that you have downloaded from a computer bulletin board, commercial information service, or the Internet.
■ When entering long columns of data, check off each number as it is entered.

Policies are rules and regulations that apply to computer use in a general way. Procedures describe steps or activities that are performed in conjunction with a specific task. Because procedures are more specific they generally take longer to write than policies, making them somewhat more costly for an organization to create and document.

TABLE G-2 *Planning a risk management strategy*

STEP	FOR THIS ASSESSMENT
1. Determine the likely threats to your computer data.	You must recognize hardware failure, human error, and vandalism as the major threats.
2. Assess the amount of data that is expendable.	You must ask yourself, "How much data will I have to re-enter if my hard drive is erased?" and "How much of my data would be lost forever because it could not be reconstructed?"
3. Determine the cost of protecting all of your data versus protecting some of your data.	You must define cost to include time as well as money.
4. Select the protective measures that meet your needs.	You must take into account which protective measures are affordable to you, effective against the threats you identified, and are easy for you to implement.

Restricting access to data

ONE OF THE BEST WAYS TO PREVENT PEOPLE FROM DAMAGING EQUIPMENT IS TO RESTRICT physical access to a computer system. If potential criminals cannot get to a computer or a terminal, stealing or damaging data becomes more difficult. In today's web of interlaced computer technologies, however, it has also become critical to restrict data access to authorized users and to properly identify authorized users, especially those who are logging in from remote sites thousands of miles away.

IN MORE DETAIL

☞ Ways to restrict physical access: Restrict access to the area surrounding the computer to prevent physical damage to the equipment. Keep floppy disks and data backups in a locked vault to prevent theft and to protect against fire or water damage. Keep offices containing computers locked to prevent theft and to deter unauthorized users. Lock the computer case to prevent theft of components such as RAM and processors.

    However, keep in mind that restricting physical access will not prevent a determined criminal from stealing data.

☞ Methods of personal identification used to restrict access: Something a person carries, something a person knows, or some unique physical characteristic—any one of these methods has the potential to positively identify a person, and each has a unique set of advantages and disadvantages.

☞ Something a person carries: An identity badge featuring a photo, or perhaps a fingerprint or bar code, is still a popular form of personal identification. Designers have created high-tech identity card readers, like the one in Figure G-11, that can be used from any off-site PC. However, because an identity badge can be easily lost, stolen, or duplicated, it works best on site where a security guard checks the face on the badge with the face of the person wearing the badge. Without visual verification, the use of identity badges from a remote site is not secure, unless combined with a password or PIN (personal identification number).

☞ A person knows: User IDs and passwords fall into this category of personal identification. When you work on a multiuser system or network, you generally must have a user ID and password. Data security on a computer system that is guarded by user IDs and passwords depends on password secrecy. If users give out their passwords, choose obvious passwords, or write them down in obvious places, hackers can break in. The brute force method of trying every word in an electronic dictionary to steal a password decreases if a password is based on two words, a

word and number, or a nonsense word that does not appear in a dictionary. Table G-3 shows how the composition of passwords affects the chance of unauthorized access.

☞ Some unique physical characteristic: This third method of personal identification called **biometrics**, bases identification on some physical trait, such as a fingerprint or the pattern of blood vessels in the retina of the eye. Unlike passwords, biometric data can't be forgotten, lost, or borrowed. Once the technological fiction of spy thrillers, biometric devices are today becoming affordable technologies that can be built into personal computer systems. Biometric technologies include hand-geometry scanners, voice recognition, face recognition, and fingerprint scanners, as shown in Figure G-12.

☞ User rights: Passwords are a first line of defense against unauthorized access. What if a hacker breaks in anyway? One way to limit the amount of damage from a break-in is to assign user rights. **User rights** limit the directories and files that each user can access. When you receive a user ID and password for a password-protected system, the system administrator gives you rights that allow you to only access particular directories and files on the host computer or file server. Assigning user rights helps prevent both accidental and deliberate damage to data. If users are granted limited rights, a hacker who steals someone's password has only the same access as the person from whom the password was stolen.

☞ Trap door: Hackers occasionally gain unauthorized access to computer systems through something called a trap door. A **trap door** is a special set of instructions that allows a user to bypass the normal security precautions and enter the system. Trap doors are often created during development and testing and should be removed before the system becomes operational.

A disk-shaped carrier allows a floppy disk drive to read an identity card.

FIGURE **G-12:** *Fingerprint scanner*

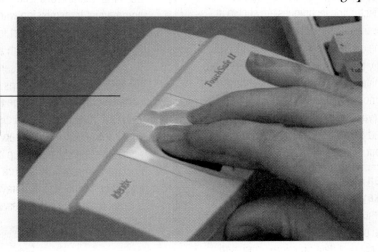

Fingerprint scanners can confirm your identity in less than two seconds, even from a pool of thousands of employees.

TABLE **G-3:** *How password length and composition affect the chances of unauthorized access*

PASSWORD RULE	EXAMPLE	NUMBER OF POSSIBILITIES	AVERAGE TIME TO DISCOVER
Any short or long name	Ed, Christine	2,000 (using a name dictionary)	5 hours
Any short or long word	it, electrocardiogram	60,000 (using the words in a spell checker)	7 days
Two words together	whiteknight	3,600,000,000	1,140 years
Mix of initials and numbers	JP2C2TP307	3,700,000,000,000,000	1,200,000,000 years
First line of a poem	onceuponamidnightdreary	10,000,000,000,000,000,000,000,000,000	3,000,000,000,000,000,000,000 years

Understanding encryption

THERE ARE SPECIAL SECURITY CONSIDERATIONS THAT APPLY TO DATA AND TRANSACTIONS ON THE Internet. When an unauthorized person reads data, the data is no longer confidential. The increasing popularity of online shopping has created some nervousness about the security of online transactions. Important data such as credit card accounts, bank records, and medical information must be encrypted to foil hackers who break into computers.

IN MORE DETAIL

- **Encryption** is the process of scrambling or hiding information so it cannot be understood until it is **decrypted**, or **deciphered**, to change it back to its original form. Encryption provides a last line of defense against the unauthorized use of data. Simple encryption and decryption techniques are shown in Figure G-13. When a computer encrypts data for storage, the program that encrypts the data also decrypts it. The encryption method or key needs only to be known by the encrypting computer. Encrypting transmitted data presents a different problem because the sender's computer that encrypts the data is not the same computer that decrypts the data on the recipients end of the transmission. Transmitted data must use an encryption key that is shared by everyone, but that cannot be decrypted by everyone.

- **Public key encryption** is an encryption method that uses a pair of keys, a **public key** known to everyone and a **private key** known only to the message recipient. The public key encrypts a message; the private key decrypts a message. Software is available to encrypt data on micro, mini, and mainframe computers. Encryption software is virtually a necessity for some businesses, such as financial institutions, that transmit and store funds electronically. Several public key encryption systems are currently available, including the popular and easy-to-use **Pretty Good Privacy (PGP)**.

- Secure e-commerce: The security of an Internet transaction is about the same as when you purchase merchandise by mail or by phone. However, current Internet security technology does not guarantee a secure transaction. Web servers encrypt commercial transmission with a security protocol such as SSL or S-HTTP. **SSL**, short for **Secure Sockets Layer**, uses encryption to establish a secure connection between your computer and a Web server. When you use an SSL page, the URL will begin with https: instead of http:, and you will generally receive a message that transactions are secured. **S-HTTP (Secure HTTP)** also encrypts data sent between your computer and a Web server, but does so one message at a time rather than by setting up an entire secure connection. Encrypted transactions ensure that your credit card number cannot be intercepted as it travels from your computer, through Internet routers, to a Web server. See Figure G-14.

Encryption

| 17 | 21 | 15 | 20 | 8 | 20 | 8 | 5 | 18 | 1 | 22 | 5 | 14 | 14 | 5 | 22 | 5 | 18 | 13 | 15 | 18 | 5 |

1. This is a message encrypted using a simple substitution technique in which the number of each letter's position in the alphabet represents the letter.

2. The key to this encryption looks like this. The 17 in the encrypted message is the letter "Q," the 21 is the letter "U," and so forth. This is a very simple encryption technique.

A	B	C	D	E	F	G	H	I	J	K	L	M	N	O	P	Q	R	S	T	U	V	W	X	Y	Z
1	2	3	4	5	6	7	8	9	10	11	12	13	14	15	16	17	18	19	20	21	22	23	24	25	26

3. Once you know the key, you can then decipher the message to see that it is the famous quote from Edgar Allan Poe's poem "The Raven."

Quoth the Raven Nevermore

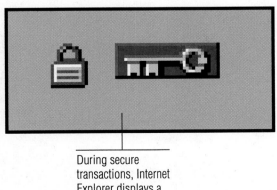

During secure transactions, Internet Explorer displays a lock icon and Netscape Navigator displays a key icon.

Exploring Internet security

SECURITY INCLUDES PROTECTING YOUR system from viruses. When you download a file from the Internet, you can use virus detection software to make sure the file is virus free before you run it, but some Web sites automatically send a program to your computer and run it before you even know it's there. Many security problems on the Internet are the result of two technologies: Java applets and ActiveX controls. This lesson looks at Internet security.

DETAILS

☞ **Java applets** are small programs that are intended to add processing and interactive capabilities to Web pages. When you access a Web page containing a Java applet, it is downloaded automatically to your computer and executed in a supposedly secure area of your computer. However, some hackers have been able to breach security and create hostile Java applets that damage or steal data.

☞ **ActiveX controls** are also downloaded automatically to your computer. They provide another way to add processing capabilities and interaction to Web pages. Unlike Java applets, ActiveX controls have full access to your entire computer system. It is possible for hackers to use ActiveX controls to cause havoc. A **digital signature** identifies the author of an ActiveX control. A programmer in effect signs a program by attaching his or her digital signature. Theoretically, a programmer would not sign a hostile program, so all programs with a digital signature should be safe. Your browser will warn you about programs that do not have a digital signature so you can decide whether or not to accept them, as shown in Figure G-15. The only way to entirely avoid dangerous Java applets and ActiveX controls is to tell your browser not to accept them. However, many Web pages include legitimate applets and controls. If your browser doesn't accept them, you might miss some valuable features and interactions. As an alternative, you might consider **personal firewall software** that protects your computer from hostile Java applets and ActiveX controls.

☞ A **cookie** is a message sent from a Web server to your browser and stored on your hard disk. These sites use a cookie to remember your name, the date of your last visit, your e-mail address, your last purchase, and the links you followed at the site. When you use a Web site that distributes cookies, this information is incorporated into the cookie that the Web server sends to your computer. The next time you connect to that Web site, your browser sends the cookie to the Web server.

Internet Security

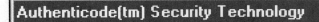

Authenticode(tm) Security Technology ? X

A Windows application is attempting to open or install the following software component:

http://www.esafe.com/delfile2.CAB

Please be aware that some files may contain viruses or otherwise harm your computer. This component has not been digitally "signed" by its publisher. Do you wish to continue?

Yes   No

Your browser will warn you before you accept an unsigned Java applet or ActiveX control.

Cookies are usually harmless, but some Web sites might ask for information that you would not want to make public. Try to use good sense when responding to requests for personal information.

File transfers

When viewed, a Web page is held temporarily in the RAM of your computer, but it is not stored as a file on disk. The process of transferring a copy of a file from a remote computer to your computer's disk drive is called **downloading**. Most Web browsers allow you to easily download Web page elements, such as pictures, sounds, animations, and videos. **Uploading** is the process of sending a copy of a file from your computer to a remote computer. Files can be uploaded to an **Internet FTP server**. Although most browsers allow you to download files, not all browsers allow you to upload. If your browser does not have upload capabilities, you can accomplish the task using FTP client software, such as WinFTP. Many FTP servers allow people to login and obtain downloads using "anonymous" as the user ID and their e-mail address as the password. For security reasons, however, most FTP servers provide upload capabilities only to people who have valid user accounts. To upload a file using your browser or FTP client software, you need to know the domain name for an FTP server and you must login using your user ID and password.

Providing redundancy

ACCIDENTS CAN DESTROY DATA AND EQUIPMENT. THE RESULT IS **DOWNTIME**, COMPUTER JARGON for the time a computer system is not functioning. The most dependable way to minimize downtime is to duplicate data and equipment.

IN MORE DETAIL

○—┬ Hardware redundancy: Duplicating equipment simply means maintaining equipment that duplicates the functions critical to computing activities. This is sometimes referred to as **hardware redundancy**. Figure G-16 shows some of the equipment that can be used to provide hardware redundancy.

Hardware redundancy reduces an organization's dependency on outside repair technicians. If it maintains a stock of duplicate parts, an organization can swap parts and be up and running before the manufacturer's repair technician arrives. Duplicate parts are expensive, however, and these costs must be weighed against lost revenue or productivity while repairs are underway.

○—┬ Software redundancy: A **backup** is a duplicate copy of a file or the contents of a disk drive. If the original file is lost or damaged, you can use the backup copy to restore the data to its original working condition.

Backup is probably the best all-around protection for your data. It provides good data protection from hardware failures, vandalism, operator error, and natural disasters. Although most people recognize that backups are important, they forget to make backups, or they tend to procrastinate. For effective backups, follow the recommendations in Table G-4.

○—┬ Software for backups: You must use software to tell the computer what to copy. There are three types of software you might use: a copy utility, a copy disk program, or backup software.

A **copy utility** is a program that copies one or more files. You can use a copy utility to copy files between a hard disk and a floppy disk, between two floppy disks of any size, from a CD-ROM to a hard disk, or from a CD-ROM to a floppy disk. A copy utility is usually included with a computer operating system.

A **copy disk utility** is a program that duplicates the contents of an entire floppy disk. You use a copy disk utility to copy all the files from one floppy disk to another floppy disk of the same size. You cannot use the copy disk utility for files on a hard disk drive.

Backup software is designed to manage hard disk backup to tapes or disks. When you use these software programs, you can select the files you want to back up. Many backup programs offer automated features which allow you to schedule automatic backups and to back up only those files that have changed since the last backup.

TABLE G-4: *Good backup habits*

WHAT YOU SHOULD DO	REASONS
Make frequent backups.	You can't restore data that you haven't backed up—if you wait a month between backups, you could lose a month's worth of data.
Scan for viruses before you back up.	Your backup will also be infected if your computer is infected with a virus when you back up.
Store your backup away from your computer.	Your backup could be damaged if it is next to your computer and your computer is damaged by flood, fire, or some other natural disaster.
Test your backup.	You depend on your backup to be able to restore data from your backup to your hard drive. You must be sure that your backup works properly—you would not want to discover when you go to use your backups that your backup files are blank because you had not followed the correct backup procedure.

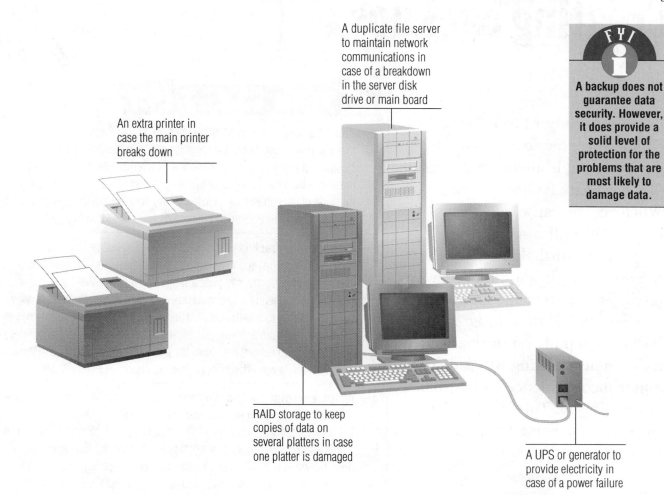

A duplicate file server to maintain network communications in case of a breakdown in the server disk drive or main board

An extra printer in case the main printer breaks down

RAID storage to keep copies of data on several platters in case one platter is damaged

A UPS or generator to provide electricity in case of a power failure

Backup equipment

Tape backups are the most popular microcomputer backup solution for small businesses and are gaining popularity with individuals as the price of tape drives decreases. Many microcomputer users back up their data onto floppy disks. This method is unrealistic for backing up the entire contents of today's high-capacity disk drives. However, it is not necessary to back up every file. Many users back up only those directories that contain data files. In the event of a hard disk failure, these users would need to reinstall all their software from original disks, and then copy their data files from the backups.

Creating backups

ONE OF THE MOST DISTRESSING computing experiences is to lose all your data. It might be the result of a hardware failure or a virus. Whatever the cause, most users experience only a moment of surprise and disbelief before the depressing realization that they might have to recreate all their data and reinstall all their programs. A backup can pull you through such trying times, making the data loss a minor inconvenience, rather than a major disaster. This lesson takes a closer look at some types of backups.

Data Backup

IN MORE DETAIL

○━ A **full backup** is a copy of all the files on a disk. A full backup ensures that you have a copy of every program and data file on the disk. Because a full backup includes a copy of every file on a disk, it can take a long time to make one for a hard disk. Some users consider it worth the time because this type of backup is easy to restore. You simply have the computer copy the files from your backup to the hard disk, as shown in Figure G-17.

○━ A **differential backup** is a copy of all the files that have changed since the last full backup. You maintain two sets of backups—a full backup that you make infrequently, say once a week, and a differential backup that you make more frequently, say once a day. It takes less time to make a differential backup than to make a full backup; however, it is a little more complex to restore data from a differential backup. To restore data using a differential backup, you restore data from the last full backup, and then restore the data from the latest differential backup, as shown in Figure G-18.

○━ An **incremental backup** is a copy of the files that have changed since the last backup. When you use incremental backups, you must have a full backup, and you must maintain a series of incremental backups. The incremental backup procedure sounds like the differential backup procedure, but there is a difference. With a differential backup, you maintain one full backup and one differential backup. The differential backup contains any files that were changed since the last full backup. With an incremental backup procedure, you maintain a full backup and a series of incremental backups. Each incremental backup contains only those files that have changed since the last incremental backup. To restore the data from a series of incremental backups, you restore the last full backup, and then sequentially restore each incremental backup, as shown in Figure G-19.

Incremental backups take the least time to make, and provide a little better protection from viruses than other backup methods because your backup contains a series of copies of your files. However, incremental backups are the most complex type of backup to restore.

○━ Backup schedule: Any data backup plan is a compromise between the level of protection and the amount of time devoted to backup. To be safe, you would need to back up your data every time you change the contents of a file, which would reduce the amount of work you could complete in a day. Realistically, however, you should make backups at regular intervals. The interval between backups will depend on the value of your data—what that data is worth to you.

Backup

Restore

Back up all files from the hard disk drive to a backup tape.

Suppose the hard drive fails. You must restore all the files from the backup tape to the hard disk drive.

FIGURE **G-18**: *Differential backup*

Make a full backup on Monday evening.

Backup

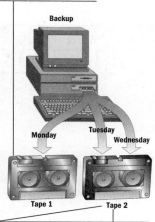

Monday

Tuesday

Wednesday

Tape 1   Tape 2

Restore

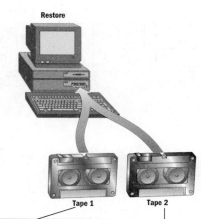

Tape 1   Tape 2

On Tuesday evening back up only the files that have been changed since the full backup. These are the files you changed or created on Tuesday. Put these files on another tape.

On Wednesday evening, back up only the files that have been changed since the full backup. These are the files you changed or created on Tuesday and Wednesday. Put these files on the same tape you used for Tuesday's backup.

Now suppose the hard disk fails. To restore, first load the full backup onto the hard disk drive. This step restores the files as they were on Monday evening.

Next load the data from the differential backup tape. This step restores the files you changed on Tuesday and Wednesday.

FIGURE **G-19**: *Incremental backup*

Backup

Restore

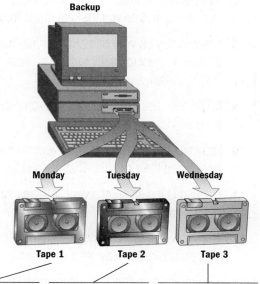

Monday   **Tuesday**   **Wednesday**

Tape 1   Tape 2   Tape 3

Tape 1   Tape 2   Tape 3

Make a full backup on Monday evening.

On Tuesday evening, back up only the files that have been changed or created on Tuesday.

On Wednesday evening, back up only the files that have been changed or created on Wednedsay.

Now suppose the hard disk fails. To begin the restore process, first load the data from the full backup.

Next load the data from Tuesday's incremental backup. This step restores the work you did on Tuesday.

Finally load the data from Wednesday's incremental backup. This step restores the work you did on Wednesday.

Concepts Review

FIGURE G-20

A	B	C	D	E	F	G	H	I	J	K	L	M	N	O	P	Q	R	S	T	U	V	W	X	Y	Z
1	2	3	4	5	6	7	8	9	10	11	12	13	14	15	16	17	18	19	20	21	22	23	24	25	26

Use Figure G-20 to decypher the following words and unscramble the message.

1. 25 15 21

   ___ ___ ___

2. 4 9 4

   ___ ___ ___

3. 1

   ___

4. 7 18 5 1 20

   ___ ___ ___ ___ ___

5. 10 15 2

   ___ ___ ___

6. 20 15 4 1 25

   ___ ___ ___ ___ ___

True or False?

7. As a result of a power failure your computer will lose all the data stored in RAM and the hard drive. True or False?

8. The circuitry on your computer circuit boards can be damaged by accidentally turning off your computer. True or False?

9. MTBF tells you how often an electronic device needs to be serviced. True or False?

10. You can eliminate a virus from your computer system by deleting the virus file. True or False?

11. Payload is the name of a very common virus. True or False?

12. A macro virus duplicates itself into the general macro pool where it is picked up by other documents. True or False?

13. Procedures help reduce human errors that can erase or damage data. True or False?

14. Public key encryption uses a pair of keys. True or False?

Complete the statement with the best answer:

15. The most common cause of lost data is _____.

16. A(n) _____ contains a battery that provides a continuous supply of power to your computer during a brief power failure.

17. A(n) _____ protects your computer from power spikes and surges but does not keep your computer operating if the power fails.

18. The failure of which computer component is potentially the most disastrous? _____

19. The best insurance for your data is _____.

20. A(n) _____ is a program that reproduces itself when the computer executes the file to which it is attached.

21. Suppose that your computer displays a weird message every time you type the word "digital." You might suspect that your computer has contracted a(n) _____.

22. Three symptoms of a computer virus infection are:

_____, _____, _____.

23. A(n) _____ is a software program that might contain a virus or time bomb.

24. A(n) _____ is a program that reproduces itself without being attached to an executable file.

25. Computer crime laws define _____ and _____ as personal property.

26. Two sources of disks that should be considered a "high risk" of virus infection are _____ and _____.

27. Many virus detection programs identify viruses by looking for a unique series of bytes called a(n) _____.

28. _____ is the process of weighing threats to computer data against the amount of data that is expendable and the cost of protecting crucial data.

29. A(n) _____ is a rule designed to prohibit employees from installing software that has not been preapproved by the information systems department.

30. If a network administrator assigns _____, users can only access certain programs and files.

31. Hackers sometimes gain unauthorized entry to computer systems through _____ that are not removed when development and testing are complete.

32. _____ is computer jargon that refers to the time a computer system is not functioning.

INDEPENDENT CHALLENGE 1

Describe a situation in which you or someone you know lost data stored on a computer.

To complete this independent challenge:

Write a brief essay that answers the following questions.

1. What caused the data loss?

2. What steps could have been taken to prevent the loss?

3. What steps could you or this other person have taken to recover the lost data?

INDEPENDENT CHALLENGE 2

Assess the risk to the programs and data files stored on the hard disk drive of your computer.

To complete this independent challenge:

Answer the following questions.

1. What threats are likely to cause your data to be lost, stolen, or damaged?

2. How many files of data do you have?

3. If you add up the size of all your files, how many megabytes of data do you have?

4. How many of these files are critical and would need to be replaced if you lost all your data?

5. What would you need to do to reconstruct the critical files if the hard disk drive failed and you did not have any backups?

6. What measures could you use to protect your data from the threats you identified in the first question? What is the cost of each of these measures?

7. Balancing the threats to your data, the importance of your data, and the cost of protective measures, what do you think is the best plan for the security of your own data?

INDEPENDENT CHALLENGE 3

Assume that your hard disk drive fails on a Friday afternoon.

To complete this independent challenge:

Explain how you would restore your data over the weekend if you had been using each of the following backup systems.

1. A full backup every Friday evening

2. A full backup every Friday evening with a differential backup on Wednesday night

3. A full backup every Friday evening with an incremental backup Monday through Thursday evenings

INDEPENDENT CHALLENGE 4

If you suspect your computer has become infected, it is prudent to immediately activate virus detection software to scan your files for a virus. With the continued spread of viruses, virus detection software has become an essential utility in today's computing environment. Many virus detection software packages are available in computer stores, on computer bulletin boards, and on the Internet.

To complete this independent challenge:

1. Find information about three virus detection software packages. Write a brief report on each one, compare and contrast the features and benefits of each.

2. Microsoft Word documents can harbor a macro virus. This type of virus is documented in many sources. Using library or Internet resources, find a list of symptoms for the Word macro virus that is currently circulating.

3. Use the latest version of your virus protection software to check the list of signatures in your virus software to see if it is listed.

4. Check your disks to see if you have the virus.

5. Write a one-page report describing what you learned about the Word macro virus and its presence on, or absence from, the documents you have on your disks.

INDEPENDENT CHALLENGE 5

The Internet worm created concern about the security of data on military and research computer systems, and it raised ethical questions about the rights and responsibilities of computer users.

To complete this independent challenge:

1. Select one of the following statements and write a two-page paper that argues for or against the statement. You might want to use the Internet or library resources to learn more about each viewpoint. Be sure you include the resources you used in a bibliography.

    a. People have the right to hone their computing skills by breaking into computers. As a computer scientist once said, "The right to hack is held higher than the right of someone to tell you not to. It's an inalienable right."

    b. If problems exist, it is acceptable to use any means to point them out. The computer science student who created the Internet virus was perfectly justified in claiming that he should not be convicted because he was just trying to point out that security holes exist in large computer networks.

    c. Computer crimes are no different from other crimes, and computer criminals should be held responsible for the damage they cause by paying for the time and cost of replacing or restoring data.

INDEPENDENT CHALLENGE 6

Obtain a copy of your school's student code or computer use policy.

To complete this independent challenge:

1. Write a brief paper that answers the following questions:

    a. To whom does the policy apply: students, faculty, staff, community members, others?

    b. What types of activities does the policy specifically prohibit?

    c. If a computer crime is committed, would the crime be dealt with by campus authorities or by state law enforcement agents?

    d. Does the policy state the penalties for computer crimes? If so, what are they?

Most Internet users have received panicked e-mail about the Good Times virus. It turns out that this virus does not exist—it is a hoax.

To complete this independent challenge:

1. How can you tell the difference between a real virus alert and a hoax? The best policy is to check a reliable site. You can easily locate sites that list hoaxes by entering "hoax" in any Internet search engine, such as Yahoo! Sites with reliable reports include **www.urbanlegends.com** and **ciac.llnl.gov/ciac/CIACHoaxes.html**.

2. Visit at least one of these sites and find the descriptions of five hoaxes. Write a one-page summary that includes the name and description of each hoax, how the hoax is spread, and why you think people believe the hoax.

DATA BACKUP LAB

The Data Backup Lab gives you an opportunity to make tape backups on a simulated computer system. Periodically the hard disk on the simulated computer will fail, which gives you a chance to assess the convenience and efficiency of different backup procedures.

1. Click the Steps button to learn how to use the simulation. As you work through the Steps, answer all of the Quick Check questions that appear. After you complete the Steps, you will see a Summary Report of your Quick Check answers. Follow the directions on the screen to print this report.

2. Click the Explore button. Create a full backup every Friday using only Tape 1. At some point in the simulation, an event will cause data loss on the simulated computer system. Use the simulation to restore as much data as you can. After you restore the data, print the Backup Audit Report.

3. In Explore, create a full backup every Friday on Tape 1 and a differential backup every Wednesday on Tape 2. At some point in the simulation, an event will cause data loss on the simulated computer system. Use the simulation to restore as much data as you can. Print the Backup Audit Report.

4. In Explore, create a full backup on Tape 1 every Monday. Make incremental backups on Tapes 2, 3, 4, and 5 each day for the rest of the week. Continue this cycle, reusing the same tapes each week. At some point in the simulation an event will cause data loss on the simulated computer system. Use the simulation to restore as much data as you can. Print the Backup Audit Report.

5. Photocopy a calendar for next month. On the calendar indicate your best plan for backing up data. In Explore, implement your plan. Print out the Backup Audit Report. Write a paragraph or two discussing the effectiveness of your plan.

Appendix: A Buyer's Guide

WHETHER YOU ARE A FIRST TIME BUYER OR upgrading, when the time comes to make your computer buying decision, you might find yourself overwhelmed by the information available to you. There are thousands of computer advertisements in magazines and newspapers featuring lists of technical specifications. To get the best deal on the computer that meets your needs, you need to understand what these technical specifications mean and how they will affect your computing power. This guide also includes information to help you get connected to the Internet.

This Buyer's Guide will help you to organize your purchasing decisions. At the end of this guide is a worksheet that you can use to summarize the specifications for a computer.

OBJECTIVES

Decide on a basic computer system

Determine your computer's architecture

Review notebook computers

Select peripheral devices

Set up for multimedia computing

Buy system and application software

Find purchasing and user support

Understand market tiers

Understand market channels

Connect to the Internet

Work in the computer industry

Compare computers: Buyer's Specification Worksheet

Organize your findings: Buyer's Guide Summary

Deciding on a basic computer system

Buying a Computer

THE FIRST DECISION YOU SHOULD MAKE IS DETERMINING THE BASIC CONFIGURATION FOR YOUR new computer system. The first step is to establish the budget for your computer system. You will exclude from your choices many system configurations because they are too costly.

IN MORE DETAIL

☛ **Desktop or notebook?** Will you be working from a single location or taking your computer with you to many locations? Choose a notebook if you plan to take your computer with you; however, notebooks cost more than a similarly configured desktop, so you will pay for portability.

☛ **Network or stand-alone?** Are you going to be working as part of a network or alone? Do you plan to tie into a network and take advantage of a central file server and microprocessor using your computer as a workstation? If you are setting up for a network, you need to purchase the network components, such as network interface cards (NICs) and cables.

☛ **Platform: Macintosh or IBM-compatible PC?** Evaluate the software available on both platforms to decide which better suits your needs. If you will be working closely with other people, decide if you need to work on the same platform.

☛ **Case type:** If you choose to buy a desktop, how much space is available for the computer? Towers can fit under a desk on the floor. The case provides openings, or "bays," for mounting disk, CD-ROM, and tape drives. A case with more bays provides you with greater expansion capability.

☛ **Display device:** The quality of the computer display depends on the features of the video display adapter and the capability of the monitor. Monitors are rated by their resolution capability as well as the size of the display screen. A typical desktop monitor is 15"; you might want to choose a 17" monitor if you are working with detailed graphics.

☛ **Floppy disk drives:** Most microcomputers today are config-ured with a single 3½" high-density floppy disk drive. Older com-puters often included an additional 5¼" drive. These two disk drive sizes were useful during the transition from the earlier 5¼" disks to newer 3½" disks. Today, most software is shipped on 3½" disks or on CD-ROMS, so a 5¼" disk drive is unnecessary.

☛ **Hard disk drives:** The factors that influence hard drive performance and price include storage capacity, access time, and controller type. When you compare computer systems,

the hard drive capacity is a significant factor. Most computers today are shipped with at least 5 GB of hard disk storage.

Computer ads usually specify hard disk access time as an indication of drive performance. Access times of 9, 10, or 11 ms are typical for today's microcomputer hard drives. A hard drive mechanism includes a circuit board called a **controller card** that positions the disk and read-write heads to locate data. Disk drives are categorized according to the type of controller cards they have. An **EIDE (Enhanced Integrated Device Electronics)** drive features high storage capacity and fast data transfer. **SCSI (Small Computer System Interface)** drives provide a slight performance advantage over EIDE drives and are recommended for high-performance microcomputer sys-tems and minicomputers.

☛ **CD-ROM drives:** A CD-ROM drive is a worthwhile invest-ment that lets you use multimedia, game, educational, and ref-erence applications that are available only on CD-ROM disks.

Today, most microcomputers are configured with a CD-ROM drive. Compared to a floppy disk drive, a CD-ROM drive delivers data at a faster rate and provides better performance, especially with multimedia applications. You should purchase the fastest CD-ROM drive that you can afford.

The access time of today's CD-ROM drives is 100 to 200 ms, ten times slower than a hard disk drive. In ads, however, the speed of a CD-ROM drive is measured by comparing its data transfer rate to the rate of the original CD-ROM drive tech-nology. For example, the original CD-ROM drives had a data transfer rate of 150 KB per second. Dual speed or 2X CD-ROM drives have a data transfer rate of 300 KB per second.

Today's 12X CD-ROM drives have a data transfer rate of 1.8 MB per second. As a point of reference, the data transfer rate of a hard drive is about 3 MB per second. A CD-ROM drive specified as "16X variable" means that the data transfer rate of the CD-ROM drive varies between a minimum transfer rate of 1.8 MB per second (12X) and a maximum speed of 2.4 MB per second (16X). Alternative terminology for 16X vari-able includes 12–16X and 16X max.

Determining your computer's architecture

ONCE YOU HAVE ESTABLISHED THE BASIC CONFIGURATION OF YOUR COMPUTER SYSTEM, YOU NEED to think about the computer architecture. These technical specifications will ultimately determine your computing power.

IN MORE DETAIL

☞ **Selecting a microprocessor:** The microprocessor is the core component in a computer. Computer ads typically indicate the type of microprocessor, which company manufactured the microprocessor, and its speed. Most of today's microcomputers are designed around a microprocessor from one of two product families: x86 or PowerPC. Today's PCs contain x86 processors such as the Pentium. Most of these processors are manufactured by Intel. Companies such as Cyrix and AMD have produced what are called "work-alike" processors that are generally less expensive than an equivalent computer with an Intel processor. If you want to run Windows software, choose a computer with an x86 processor.

☞ If you want to run Macintosh software, select a computer with a 68000-series or PowerPC microprocessor. Until 1994, Macintosh computers contained a 68000-series microprocessor manufactured by Motorola. More recent models, called "Power Macs" contain a PowerPC microprocessor that implements RISC architecture to provide relatively fast performance at a low cost.

☞ **Choosing between Pentiums:** Intel introduced the Pentium processor in 1993, which packed an impressive 3.3 million transistors on a chip .36-inch square. Using dual-pipeline architecture, the chip could execute two instructions at a time. In 1995, Intel produced the P6 generation of processors called the Pentium Pro. With five execution pipelines and 5.5 million transistors, the Pentium Pro was optimized for the 32-bit instruction set that Microsoft had used to develop the Windows NT operating system. A Level 2 cache contributes to the speed of this chip and is often referred to in computer ads. A **Level 2 cache (L2 cache)** is memory circuitry housed off the processor on a separate chip. The cache chip connects to the main processor by a dedicated high-speed bus. Level 2 cache is much faster than RAM and almost as fast as cache built into the processor chip.

In 1997, Intel launched two new processors. The Pentium with MMX technology was a jazzed-up version of the original Pentium chip and contained circuitry to speed the execution of multimedia applications. A second chip, the Pentium II, added MMX technology to the Pentium Pro chip. The Pentium with MMX technology is less expensive than the Pentium Pro but has similar performance levels on tests such as SYSmark32. **SYSmark32** is a standard benchmark test that measures computer speed for word-processing, graphics, spreadsheet, and database tasks. If cost is not a factor, the Pentium II is a more expensive chip but will provide you with the highest level of performance. The chart in Table BG-1 on page BG-5 summarizes features and performance factors for each of the Pentium processors.

☞ **RAM—requirements and cost:** The amount of RAM a computer needs depends on the operating system and application software you plan to use. Today, RAM costs about $10 per megabyte, so it doesn't have a major impact on the price of a computer system; therefore, your computer should have at least 32 MB of RAM, but additional memory modules can be added up to a maximum of 128 MB. Most consumer advocates recommend that you get as much RAM as you can afford with your initial purchase. If a computer features EDO (extended data out) RAM technology, you can expect better performance from it than from computers with standard memory technology.

Reviewing notebook computers

IF YOU DECIDE TO BUY A NOTEBOOK COMPUTER, THERE ARE ADDITIONAL DECISIONS YOU must make.

IN MORE DETAIL

Notebook displays: Notebook computers do not use monitors that are big, heavy, and require too much electrical power to run on batteries. Instead, notebooks have a flat panel liquid crystal display. A **liquid crystal display (LCD)** uses a technically sophisticated method of passing light through a thin layer of liquid crystal cells to produce an image. The resulting flat panel screen is lightweight and compact.

Many older notebooks have a **passive matrix screen**, sometimes referred to as dual-scan. A passive matrix screen relies on timing to make sure the liquid crystal cells are illuminated. As a result, the process of updating the screen image does not always keep up with moving images, and the display can appear blurred. Passive matrix technology is not suitable for multimedia applications that include animations and videos.

An **active matrix screen**, referred to as **TFT (thin film transistor)**, updates more rapidly and provides image quality similar to that of a monitor. Active matrix screens are essential for a crisp display of animation and video. However, active matrix screens are difficult to manufacture and add significantly to the price of a notebook computer.

External monitor port: Most notebook computers have a port to connect an external monitor. The advantage of an external monitor is the high-quality display. The disadvantage is that you need to disconnect the external monitor when you transport the computer.

A **PCMCIA slot (Personal Computer Memory Card International Association)** is a special type of expansion slot developed for notebook computers that do not have space in the case for full-size expansion slots and cards. A PCMCIA slot is a small, external slot into which you can insert a PCMCIA card.

PCMCIA cards, also called PC cards, are credit-card-sized circuit boards that incorporate an expansion card and device. Some PCMCIA cards contain a modem, others contain memory expansion, and others contain a hard disk drive. You can plug in and remove PCMCIA devices without turning the computer off, unlike desktop computer expansion cards. In this way, you can switch from one PCMCIA device to another without disrupting your work.

PCMCIA slots are categorized by size. Type I slots accept only the thinnest PCMCIA cards such as memory expansion cards. Type II slots accept most of the popular PCMCIA cards—those that contain modems, sound cards, and network cards. Type III slots accept the thickest PCMCIA cards, which contain devices such as hard disk drives. Many notebooks provide a multipurpose PCMCIA slot that will accept two Type I cards, two Type II cards, or one Type III card.

Docking station: A **docking station** is an additional expansion bus into which you plug your notebook computer. Notebook computer expansion devices tend to be more expensive than those for desktop computers, but it is possible to use desktop peripherals with notebook computers if you have a docking station or a port replicator. The notebook provides the processor and RAM. The docking station provides expansion slots for cards that would not fit into the notebook case. It allows you to purchase inexpensive expansion cards and peripherals designed for desktops, instead of the more expensive devices designed specifically for notebooks. When you use a docking station, you sacrifice portability since you probably won't carry your docking station and external CD-ROM drive with you. However, you gain the use of low-cost, powerful desktop peripherals.

Port replicator: A **port replicator** is an inexpensive device that connects to a notebook computer by a bus connector plug; it contains a duplicate of the notebook computer's ports and makes it more convenient to connect and disconnect your notebook computer from devices, such as an external monitor, mouse, and keyboard. Port replicators do not include expansion slots and typically cannot be used to add a sound card or CD-ROM drive to your notebook computer.

Pointing device: Although a mouse is the standard pointing device used with desktop computers, it can be inconvenient to carry and use while traveling. Most notebook computers include an alternative pointing device. The three most popular options are built-in track ball, track point, and touch pad.

Notebook power sources: Most notebook computers operate on power from either rechargeable batteries or a wall outlet. Because notebooks are designed for portability, the computing time provided by batteries is important. Fast processors, active matrix LCDs, and additional peripheral devices demand significant power from notebook computer batteries. On battery power, notebook computers typically provide two to four hours of operating time before the batteries need to be recharged. Most notebook computers use one of three types of batteries: **NiCad** (nickel cadmium), **NiMH** (nickel metal hydride), or **lithium ion**. NiCad batteries typically store less power than NiMH or lithium ion batteries of equivalent size and weight. Therefore, NiCad batteries provide the shortest operating times. Most ads for notebook computers indicate the battery type and estimated computing times.

Notebook manufacturers attempt to reduce power consumption by building power-saving features into their computers. These features automatically switch off the hard disk drive, LCD display, or the processor if you do not interact with the computer after a short time. These devices are reactivated when you press a key or move the mouse.

Most notebook computers require an **external AC adapter** to plug into a wall outlet or to recharge the batteries. Some notebook computers have eliminated the external adapter and require only a power cable to plug into a wall outlet. It is a good idea to use AC power whenever possible.

Weight: Notebook computers can weigh as little as 4 pounds or as much as 10 pounds or more. Consider how much you will be carrying your computer around to determine if weight is a factor.

Case to carry: Consider how you will carry your notebook computer and purchase a case that is well designed. The case should be well padded to protect the computer as well as provide the necessary compartments to store extra devices, power cords and cables, and any papers or notes you may carry.

Whether you purchase a desktop or notebook computer, the microprocessor is critical to the computer's performance. Table BG-1 summarizes features and performance factors for each of the Pentium processors.

TABLE **BG-1**: *Pentium feature summary*

	PENTIUM	PENTIUM PRO	PENTIUM with MMX technology	PENTIUM II
Speed	75–200 MHz	166–200 MHz	166–233 MHz	233–300 MHz
SySmark32	175	214	203	249
MMX	No	No	Yes	Yes
On-chip cache	16 K	16 K	32 K	32 K
L2 cache	No	Yes	No	Yes
Transistors	3.3 million	5.5 million	4.5 million	7.5 million
Execution pipelines	2	5	2	5
Chip package	PGA single chip	PGA dual chip	PGA single chip	SEC cartridge

Selecting peripheral devices

PERIPHERAL DEVICES ADD FUNCTIONALITY TO YOUR COMPUTER SYSTEM BY GIVING YOU different options for input, output, and storage. If your budget is limited, you do not have to include all of these devices when you buy your computer system. You can add any of them to your computer system as your needs and budget permit.

IN MORE DETAIL

Pointing device: The computer mouse is the standard pointing device for desktop computers. There are several types to choose from. The serial mouse, connects to your serial port, the bus mouse connects directly to a bus port if available on the motherboard or peripheral card. Also available is an infrared mouse which does not connect to your computer with a cable. Infrared is used to transmit the movements and clicks to a receiver that plugs into the port on your computer. Most desktop computers include a standard keyboard and a mouse, but you might want to consider alternative input devices. Cases of carpal tunnel syndrome, a stress-related wrist injury, are on the rise. Intensive keyboard and mouse use is the suspected culprit. Ergonomically designed keyboards may prevent computer-related injuries.

Printer: Printers are characterized as dot matrix, ink-jet, or laser. Occasionally a computer vendor offers a hardware bundle that includes a computer, printer, and software. More often, however, printers are sold separately so consumers can choose the quality, features, and price they want. Ink-jet and personal laser printers are most popular with today's consumers because they provide high-quality print on plain paper. Color printers are available in each category but color ink-jet printers offer the best price-performance because of the high price of color laser printers and the poor quality of color dot-matrix printers.

Computer display system: A computer display system consists of a monitor and a **graphics card**, also called a **video display adapter** or **video card**. A graphics card is an expansion card that controls the signals that the computer sends to the monitor. The clarity of a computer display depends on the quality of the monitor and the capability of the graphics card. Most graphics cards use special graphics chips to boost performance. These **accelerated graphics cards** can greatly increase the speed at which images are displayed. An accelerated graphics card connected to a fast **PCI bus** can move data between the microprocessor and the graphics card as fast as the microprocessor can process it. As a consumer, your goal is to buy the best display system that fits your budget.

Scanner: A scanner reads images from a page and converts them to digital representation. It is a fast way to convert images on paper to data that can be manipulated.

Modem: Many computer systems include a modem that transmits and receives data over phone lines to other computers. **Baud rate** identifies the transmission speed. Faster baud rates mean faster transmission; new systems should come with a minimum 33 Kbps (kilobits per second) modem but are better served with a 56.6 baud modem.

Fax modems: A fax modem is a modem that includes fax capability. This means that it can send a document that is in the memory of your computer to any standard fax machine, where it appears in hard copy format, or to another fax modem to be printed later. Fax modems can also receive fax transmissions from standard fax machines or other fax modems.

Backup system: Depending on how much and how often you want to backup the data from your hard disk, you may consider adding a tape backup system to your computer. Special high-capacity drives, such as Zip or Jaz drives, provide removable storage.

Surge protector: A surge protector protects your computer system against sudden fluctuations in power. A UPS, uninterruptible power supply, will protect your data if the power fails for a short time.

Game accessories: If you are planning to use your computer to play games that require motion input, you might want to purchase a joy stick, flight yoke, or steering wheel depending on your application.

INFOWEB

Modems

Setting up for multimedia computing

WITH THE PROLIFERATION OF multimedia applications, a sound system has become an essential part of a computer system. A basic computer sound system includes a sound card and a set of small speakers; but, if you want your computer-generated tunes to blow you away, you will want to invest in a more sophisticated sound system.

Sound Systems

IN MORE DETAIL

Selecting a sound card: A sound card converts the digital data in a sound file into analog signals for instrumental, vocal, and spoken sounds. In addition, a sound card lets you make your own recordings by converting analog sounds into digitized sound files that you can store on disk. To record your own sounds, you'll need to add a good quality microphone to your sound system. A more compact alternative to digitized sound is to store music as MIDI sound. A sound card generally supports one of two MIDI (Musical Instrument Digital Interface) standards. FM synthesis provides instructions for the computer to synthesize sounds by simulating the sounds of real musical instruments. Wave table synthesis creates music by playing digitized sound samples of actual instruments. Wave table synthesis provides better quality sound, but at a higher price than FM synthesis.

Most multimedia software specifies the type of sound required. A basic sound card with FM synthesis is usually sufficient for most reference software and educational software. Some games require Sound Blaster compatible sound. If you own such software, make sure your sound card is described as "Sound Blaster compatible."

Speakers: A sound card outputs sound to speakers or earphones. As with any audio system, higher quality speakers provide richer sound and enhanced volume. If you're really serious about sound, consider a subwoofer for big bass sound. For example, an Altec Lansing sound system with Dolby Surround Sound uses only two speakers but envelops you in a 3-D sound-scape for a price of about $300.

Storage: Digitized sound files require lots of storage space. Ten seconds of digitized stereo sound can consume up to 5 MB of disk space. Be sure you have the storage capacity to support these files.

Buying system and application software

WHAT WILL YOU BE USING YOUR COMPUTER FOR? ALTHOUGH YOU CAN BUILD YOUR SOFTWARE library over time, the operating system you choose determines what software will be available to you. You should also be aware of the software market and how to get the best deals.

IN MORE DETAIL

- **Operating system:** The platform you choose (Macintosh or IBM-compatible) will drive your choices of operating system. Vendors typically include the operating system with the computer, so if you purchase an IBM-compatible computer, you can expect that the latest version of DOS and Windows will be preinstalled on the hard drive. If you purchase a Macintosh computer, you can expect the latest version of Mac OS to be installed.

- **Software bundles:** Many vendors also include application software such as a word processor or basic games with a computer system. Multimedia computer systems usually include several CD-ROMs, such as encyclopedias, fact books, and games. All other factors being equal, a system with bundled software will cost slightly more than a system without bundled software. However, if the software meets your needs, the slight increase in price is generally less than you would pay if you bought the software separately.

- Companies that produce computer software are referred to as **software publishers**.

  A new software product can be an entirely new product, a new **version** (also called a release) with significant enhancements, or a **revision** designed to add minor enhancements and eliminate problems found in the current version. Before you buy software, you should be aware of the current version or any revisions for that product.

- **Price:** A variety of discounts and special offers make it worth while to shop around. You can purchase a $495 software package for less than $100 if you're a smart shopper. When a new software product first becomes available, the publisher often offers a special introductory price to entice customers. Several software products that now carry a list price of $495 were introduced at a special $99 price. Even after the introductory price expires, most vendors offer sizable discounts. The average discounted price is referred to as the street price. Expect software with a list price of $495 to be offered for a street price of $299.

  If you own an earlier version of a software package, you are probably eligible for the **version upgrade price**. By supplying the vendor with proof that you own the earlier version, you can get the new version at a discount. A **competitive upgrade** is a special price offered to consumers who switch from one company's software product to the new version of a competitor's product.

- **Obsolescence:** Unlike computer hardware products, older versions of software do not remain in the vendor's product line. Soon after a new version of a software product is released, the software publisher usually stops selling earlier versions. When a publisher offers a new version of the software you are using, it is a good idea to upgrade, but you can wait for several months until the initial rush for technical support on the new product decreases. If you don't upgrade, you might find that the software publisher offers minimal technical support for older versions of the program. Also, if you let several versions go by without upgrading, you might have to purchase the software at full price when you eventually decide to upgrade.

Finding purchasing and user support

AS WITH ANY MAJOR PURCHASE, YOU NEED RELIABLE SUPPORT *BEFORE* AND *AFTER* YOU PURCHASE your computer system. You need support before you buy in order to keep up with changes in technology and in the computer industry itself. For example, the announcement of a new operating system or a news article of a computer company downsizing could affect your purchasing decisions. After you make your purchase, you continue to need service and support. The level of service and support provided by the vendor or manufacturer should be a major consideration in your buying decision.

IN MORE DETAIL

Computer publications: Computer publications provide information on computers, computing, and the computer industry.

Computer magazines generally target users of both personal and business computers. Articles focus on product evaluations, product comparisons, and practical tips for installing hardware and using software. These magazines are full of product advertisements that are useful if you want to keep informed about the latest products available for your computer.

Computer industry trade journals target computer professionals, rather than consumers. Computer trade journals, such as *InfoWorld* and *Computer Reseller News*, focus on company profiles, product announcements, and sales techniques.

Computing journals offer an academic perspective on computers and computing issues. Such journals focus on research in computing. Academic journals rarely advertise hardware and software products because it might appear that advertisers could influence the content of articles. An article in a computing journal is usually "refereed," which means that it is evaluated by a committee of experts who determine if the article is original and based on sound research techniques. The best place to find computing journals is in a university library.

Internet sites: Internet sites are an excellent source of information about the computer industry and computer products. Several computer magazines and trade journals as well as many computer companies have Internet sites. Here you can usually find product specifications, product announcements, sales literature, technical support forums, and pricing information.

Computer TV: Television shows about computers provide hardware and software reviews, tips, and computer industry news for new and experienced users. The PCTV network, CNET, Jones Cable Network, Mind Extension University, CNN

Financial Network, and ZDTV produce a variety of shows that are carried on cable TV. Check your cable listings for airtimes of such shows as *The Internet Cafe*, *The Web*, and *Digital Jam*.

Vendor and manufacturer support: As part of your purchasing decision, you want to know what support and service you can expect from the vendor and from the manufacturer. You want to look specifically at the guarantee, the availability of telephone support, and local repair options.

Guarantee. Computer systems are major investments. Does the manufacturer provide reasonable guarantees on the equipment? Does the manufacturer or the vendor guarantee the system? Do you get a labor and parts warranty? Consider the reputation of the manufacturer and vendor.

Telephone support. If you have a problem and need to call the manufacturer or vendor, do they have a local or toll-free number? You don't want to add significant costs in phone expenses to your computer system. What is the typical waiting time for a technical support person? Your time is valuable too.

Local repair. If you need a component repaired, will the system be repaired locally? Do you have to send it out? Who pays shipping? These costs can be significant. Do you get a replacement while you wait for the system or part to be repaired? Some manufacturers have an instant exchange program for components giving you a refurbished unit in exchange for yours. This policy keeps you from having any downtime.

InfoWeb
Publications   **Web Resources**

Understanding market tiers

SINCE 1981, HUNDREDS OF COMPANIES HAVE PRODUCED PERSONAL COMPUTERS. INDUSTRY analysts often refer to three **tiers**, or **categories** of microcomputer companies, although not all analysts agree on which companies belong in each tier. Knowing the manufacturer of your computer will help you understand what accounts for price differences for computers with the same specifications from different vendors.

IN MORE DETAIL

Market tiers: The top tier consists of large companies that have been in the computer business for more than ten years and have an identifiable percentage of total computer sales— companies such as IBM, Apple, Compaq, and Hewlett-Packard. The second tier includes newer companies with high sales volume, but with somewhat less financial resources than companies in the first tier. Most analysts place companies such as Gateway, Dell, and Packard Bell in the second tier. The third tier consists of smaller startup companies that sell primarily through mail order.

The first tier: Computers from the top-tier vendors generally are more expensive than computers offered by second-tier or third-tier vendors. First-tier companies often have higher overhead costs, management is often paid higher salaries, and substantial financial resources are devoted to research and development. The first-tier companies are responsible for many of the innovations that have made computers faster, more powerful, and more convenient. Also, many consumers believe that computers sold by first-tier companies are better quality, and are a safer purchasing decision because there is less risk that computers from first-tier companies will quickly become obsolete or that the vendor will go out of business.

The second tier: Computers from second-tier companies are generally less expensive than those from the first tier, although the quality can be just as good. Most PCs are constructed from off-the-shelf circuit boards, cables, cases, and chips. The components in the computers sold by second-tier companies are often the same as those in computers sold by the first tier. The quality of the off-the-shelf parts, however, is not uniform; it is difficult for the consumer to determine the quality of parts.

Second-tier companies often maintain their low prices by minimizing operating costs. These companies have a limited research and development budget, and maintain a relatively small work force by contracting with another company to provide repair and warranty work.

The third tier: Computers from third-tier companies often appear to be much less expensive than those in other tiers. Sometimes this reflects the low overhead costs of a small company, but other times it reflects poor-quality components. A consumer who is knowledgeable about the market and has technical expertise can often get a bargain on a good-quality computer from a third-tier company. But some consumers think it's risky to purchase computers from third-tier companies. Third-tier companies are smaller and perhaps more likely to go out of business, leaving their customers without technical support.

Understanding market channels

UNDERSTANDING MARKET CHANNELS WILL HELP YOU GET THE BEST DEAL ON YOUR COMPUTER. Computer hardware and software are sold by marketing outlets or "channels." Market channels include retail stores, mail-order suppliers, value-added resellers, and manufacturer direct sales.

IN MORE DETAIL

Computer retail stores are either small local shops or nationwide chains that specialize in the sale of microcomputer software and hardware. They purchase computer products from a manufacturer or distribution center and then sell the products to consumers. Employees are often knowledgeable about a variety of computer products and can help you select a hardware or software product to fit your needs. Many computer retail stores also offer classes and training sessions, answer questions, provide technical support, and repair hardware products. A computer retail store is often the best source of supply for buyers who are likely to need assistance after the sale, such as beginning computer users or those with complex computer systems, such as networks. But computer retail stores can be a fairly expensive channel for hardware and software. Their prices reflect the cost of purchasing merchandise from a distributor, maintaining a retail storefront, and hiring technically qualified staff.

Mail-order suppliers take orders by mail or telephone and ship the product directly to consumers. Mail-order suppliers generally offer low prices but provide limited service and support. A mail-order supplier is often the best source of products for buyers who are unlikely to need support or who can troubleshoot problems with the help of a technical support person on the telephone. Experienced computer users who can install components, set up their software, and do their own troubleshooting are often happy with mail-order suppliers.

Value-added resellers (VARs) combine commercially available products with specialty hardware or software to create a computer system designed to meet the needs of a specific industry. Although VARs charge for their expertise, they are often the only source for a system that really meets the needs of a specific industry.

Manufacturer direct refers to hardware manufacturers that sell their products directly to consumers using a sales force or mail order to distribute directly to individual consumers. The sales force usually targets large corporate or educational customers where large volume sales can cover costs and commissions. They can sell their products directly to consumers for a lower price than when they sell them through retailers, but they cannot generally offer the same level of support and assistance as a local retailer. In an effort to improve customer support, some manufacturers have established customer support lines and some provide repair services at the customer's home or place of business.

Connecting to the Internet

IF YOUR SCHOOL HAS INTERNET ACCESS, YOUR ACADEMIC COMPUTING department has installed the hardware and software you need to access the Internet from your school lab, and possibly from your dorm room. To access the Internet from your home computer, you must set up the necessary computer equipment, locate an Internet service provider, install the appropriate software on your computer, then dial in.

INFOWEB

ISPs

IN MORE DETAIL

☞ **Set up equipment:** The basic equipment for setting up online communications is a computer, a modem, and a telephone line. The equipment you use does not change the activities you can do online, but it can affect the speed at which you can accomplish these activities. PCs and Macintosh computers can both connect to online services. A fast computer such as a 200 MHz Pentium speeds up some activities such as viewing graphics online. However, the overall speed of online activities is limited by the speed of the server, the speed of your modem, and the speed of your communications link.

A fast modem speeds the process of sending and receiving data. For example, a 33.6 Kbps (33,600 bits per second) modem provides you with faster online response than a 28.8 Kbps (28,800 bits per second) modem. Be careful when choosing a modem; some require special phone lines. Follow the instructions included with your modem to set it up, as shown in Figure BG-1.

☞ The telephone line that you use for voice communication is suitable for most online activities. Corporations sometimes use faster communications links such as ISDN or T1 lines. Your telephone line, though not the speediest communications link, is certainly the least expensive. When you are using your telephone line for online activities, you can't simultaneously use it for voice calls; while you are online, people who call you will get a busy signal. If you pick up the telephone receiver to make an outgoing call while you are online, your online connection might terminate.

☞ **Locate an Internet service provider:** An **Internet service provider (ISP)** supplies you with a user account on a host computer that has access to the Internet. When you connect your personal computer to the host computer using a modem and the appropriate software, you gain access to the Internet. Your school might provide Internet access for students and faculty who want to use the Internet from off campus. An

Internet connection provided by an educational institution is typically free. Many commercial information services such as CompuServe, Prodigy, Microsoft Network, and America Online provide Internet access. Internet connections are also offered by some telephone companies, cable TV companies, and independent telecommunications firms. These firms charge between $20 and $30 per month for Internet access. Unlike commercial information services, they usually do not maintain their own online information, discussion groups, or downloadable software.

☞ **Install software:** Many ISPs provide subscribers with a complete software package that includes a browser and Internet communications software. Internet communications software allows your computer to transmit and receive data using the Internet **TCP/IP communications protocol**. Standard TCP/IP software handles Internet communication between computers that are directly cabled to a network. **SLIP (Serial Line Internet Protocol)** and **PPP (Point-to-Point Protocol)** are versions of TCP/IP designed to handle Internet communications over dial-up connections. When you want to access the Internet from a computer using a modem, you must use PPP, SLIP, or other similar communications software.

☞ **Establishing successful computer communications:** Today, the software supplied by most Internet service providers is self-configuring; in other words, the first time you run the software, it examines your computer system and automatically selects the appropriate software settings. You have to deal with technical specifications only if your computer equipment, modem, or telephone line are not standard.

☞ **Dial in:** Most Internet communications software is represented by an icon on your computer's desktop or Start menu. You start the software by clicking this icon, and it automatically establishes a connection to the Internet. Figure BG-2 shows what happens when you dial in.

FIGURE BG-1: *Connecting your computer*

FIGURE BG-1: *Connecting your computer*

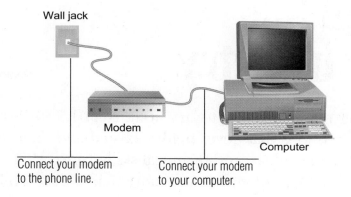

Wall jack

Modem

Computer

Connect your modem to the phone line.

Connect your modem to your computer.

FIGURE BG-2: *Dialing into the Internet*

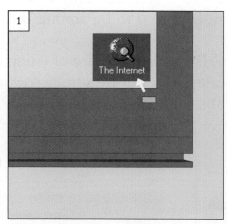

Click the Internet icon supplied by your Internet service provider.

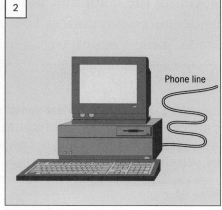

Phone line

By clicking the Internet icon, you tell the computer to load your Internet communications client software. Your communications client will probably use SLIP or PPP to handle the TCP/IP protocols as your computer transmits and receives data through your modem.

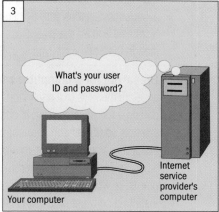

What's your user ID and password?

Internet service provider's computer

Your computer

Your communications client dials the Internet service provider. Usually, your communications client has stored the telephone number, so you do not need to enter it each time you want to connect.

OK, you can now access the Internet

To Internet

Internet service provider's computer

Your computer

If your communications client has stored your user ID and password, it will automatically log you in. Some people prefer to enter their password manually for better security.

APPENDIX: A BUYER'S GUIDE ◀ 13

Working in the computer industry

THE $290 BILLION COMPUTER INDUSTRY EMPLOYS MORE THAN 1.5 MILLION PEOPLE. OVER THE past 50 years, it has created jobs that never before existed and financial opportunities for those with motivation, creative ideas, and technical skills. Since 1970, high-tech business has produced more than 7,000 millionaires and more than a dozen billionaires. According to the U.S. Bureau of Labor Statistics, computer and data-processing services are projected to be the third fastest growing industry; systems analysts, computer engineers, and data-processing equipment repairers are expected to be among the 30 fastest growing occupations between now and 2005. However, not everyone who uses a computer is employed in the computer industry. For a clear picture of computer jobs, it is useful to consider three categories. These categories can be somewhat loosely defined as computer-specific jobs, computer-related jobs, and computer-use jobs.

IN MORE DETAIL

▭▸ **Computer industry categories: Computer-specific jobs**—such as computer programming, chip design, and Webmaster—would not exist without computers. **Computer-related jobs**, on the other hand, are variations of more generic jobs that you might find in any industry. For example, jobs in computer sales, high-tech recruiting and graphics design are similar to sales, recruiting, and design jobs in the automobile or medical industries. **Computer-use jobs** require the use of computers to accomplish tasks in fields other than computing. Writers, reporters, accountants, retail clerks, medical technicians, auto mechanics, and many others use computers in the course of everyday job activities. Of the three categories, computer-specific jobs require the most preparation and will appeal to those who like working with, learning about, and thinking about computers.

▭▸ **Educational requirements for computer-specific jobs:** Jobs for people who design and develop computer hardware and software require a high degree of training and skill. A college degree is required for virtually any of these jobs, and many require a master's degree or doctorate. Most colleges offer degrees in computer engineering, computer science, and information systems that provide good qualifications for computer-specific jobs.

▭▸ **Working conditions for computer-specific jobs:** Graduates with computer engineering, computer science, and information systems degrees generally work in a comfortable office or laboratory environment. Many high-tech companies offer employee-friendly working conditions that include child-care, flexible hours, and the opportunity to telecommute. As in any industry, the exact nature of a job depends on the company and the particular projects that are in the works.

▭▸ **Salary for computer-specific jobs:** In the computer industry, as in most industries, management positions command the highest salaries and salary levels increase with experience. Salaries vary by geographic location. In the Northeast and on the West Coast salaries tend to be higher than in the Southeast, Midwest, Southwest, and Canada.

▭▸ **Preparing for a computer career:** Education and experience are the keys to a challenging computer job with good potential for advancement. In addition to a degree in computer science, computer engineering, or information systems, think about how you can get on-the-job experience through internships, military service, government-sponsored training programs, or work-study programs. Owning your own computer, installing software, and troubleshooting provide good basic experience and familiarity with mass-market computing standards. You might pick up additional experience from projects sponsored by clubs and organizations. The three largest computer organizations in North America are the Association for Computing Machinery (ACM), the Association of Information Technology Professionals (AITP), and Institute of Electrical and Electronics Engineers–Computer Society (IEEE-CS).

Certification training: The Institute for Certification of Computing Professionals (ICCP) has a regular schedule of comprehensive exams for computer jobs, such as computer programming, systems analysis, and network management. If you are considering a career in computer network management, it might be worthwhile to complete the test for Novell NetWare or Microsoft NT certification. Certification for application software such as Microsoft Word, Excel, PowerPoint, and Access is also available.

Use technology to find a job: The first step in a job search is to realistically assess your qualifications and needs. Several excellent books and Web sites provide information to help your assessment. Your qualifications include your computer skills, educational background, previous work experience, communications skills, and personality. By comparing your qualifications to the requirements for a job, you can assess your chances of being hired. Your needs include your preferred geographical location, working conditions, corporate lifestyle, and salary. By comparing your needs to the information you discover about a prospective employer, you can assess your chances of enjoying a job once you've been hired.

Researching the job market on the Internet: In 1997, an estimated one out of every five employers in North America used the Internet for recruiting. Popular Web-based "want ads" post descriptions of job openings. Usually the employers pay for these postings, so access is free to prospective employees. Web sites include general information about jobs, employment outlook, and salaries in computer-industry jobs. Because the salaries for most jobs are vaguely stated as "commensurate with experience," it is useful to discover what you're worth by studying Web-based salary reports.

Preparing a resume: You will need to prepare a resume with your career goal, experience, skills, and education. Some career counselors suggest that high-tech candidates should not follow many of the rules delineated in traditional resume guidebooks. Your resume should demonstrate technical savvy without appearing overly "packaged." For example, dot-matrix printing is hard to read and old fashioned. By contrast, unless you're applying for a job as a Web site or graphical designer, you don't want your resume to look like an advertisement in a magazine. Remember that corporate cultures differ, so use your word processor to tailor your resume to the corporate culture of each prospective employer.

Contact prospective employers: The standard procedure for mailing letters of application and resumes remains valid even in this age of high technology. However, many companies will accept resumes by fax or e-mail to reduce the time it takes to process applicants. Include your e-mail address on your application materials. You can post your resume on a placement Web site where it can be viewed by corporate recruiters. Some of these Web sites charge a small fee for posting resumes; others are free. You can also post your resume along with your personal Web page, if you have one. This is particularly effective if you design these pages to showcase technical skills that are applicable to the job you're seeking.

College Connection

Organizations

Certification

Career Resources

Comparing Computers: Buyer's Specification Worksheet

BEFORE YOU MAKE A DECISION, SHOP AROUND TO COLLECT INFORMATION ON PRICING, features, and support. Although you might be tempted to buy the computer with the lowest price and best features, don't forget to consider the warranty and the quality of the support you are likely to get from the vendor. This worksheet will help you gather facts about pricing, features, and support.

Computer brand, model and manufacturer: _____

Processor type: _____

Processor speed: _____ MHz

MMX technology? ❑ Yes   ❑ No

RAM capacity: _____ MB

Number and size of floppy disk drives: _____

Capacity of hard disk drive: _____ GB

Speed of CD-ROM drive: _____

Capacity of tape drive: _____

Amount of cache memory: _____ KB

Monitor screen size: _____ vis or inches

Maximum monitor resolution: _____

Amount of memory on graphics card: _____ MB

Modem speed: _____ bps

Number of expansion slots: _____

Upgrade path for new processor? ❑ Yes   ❑ No

Operating system: _____

Mouse included? ❑ Yes   ❑ No

Sound card and speakers included? ❑ Yes   ❑ No

Value of bundled software: $_____

Service and Support

What is the warranty period? _____ years

Does the warranty cover parts and labor? ❑ Yes   ❑ No

Does the vendor have a good reputation for service? ❑ Yes   ❑ No

Are technical support hours adequate? ❑ Yes   ❑ No

Free 800 number for technical support? ❑ Yes   ❑ No

Can I contact technical support without waiting on hold for a long time? ❑ Yes   ❑ No

Are technical support people knowledgeable? ❑ Yes   ❑ No

Can I get my computer fixed in an acceptable time period? ❑ Yes   ❑ No

Are the costs and procedures for fixing the computer acceptable? ❑ Yes   ❑ No

Are other users satisfied with this brand and model of computer? ❑ Yes   ❑ No

Is the vendor likely to stay in business? ❑ Yes   ❑ No

Are the computer parts and components standard? ❑ Yes   ❑ No

Price: $_____

INFOWEB

Consumer Info

A Buyer's Guide Summary

CONSIDERATIONS	UNIT/FIGURE/TABLE	NOTES
Basic computer system		
Desktop or notebook?	Units A and D, Figures A-1, A-3, and A-4, Figure D-2	
Platform: Macintosh or IBM-compatible PC?	Unit A and Appendix, Figure A-3	
Case type: tower, desktop?	Unit D and Appendix, Figure D-2	
Display device	Unit A, Figures A-1, A-3, A-8, and A-12	
Computer architecture		
Network or stand-alone?	Units E and F, Figures F-1, F-2, and F-3	
Which microprocessor?	Unit E and Appendix, Figures E-13 and E-14, Table BG-1	
What clock speed?	Unit E	
How much RAM?	Unit E, Figure E-10	
Include RAM cache?	Unit E	
Expansion cards	Unit E, Figure E-21	
Special considerations for notebook computers		
LCD display	Units A, E, and Appendix	
External monitor	Units A, E, and Appendix	
PCMCIA slot	Units D and E, Figure E-23	
Weight	Appendix	
Power source/battery type	Appendix	
Mouse type	Unit A, Figure A-10	
Docking station	Unit E and Appendix	
Carrying case	Appendix	
Peripheral devices		
Pointing device	Unit A, Figures A-8 and A-13	
Printer	Unit A, Figures A-8 and A-13	
Scanner	Unit A, Figure A-8	
Modem	Units A and E, Figure A-8, Figure E-21	
Fax modem	Appendix	
Backup system	Units D and G, Figures D-6, D-10, and D-11, Figures G-16, G-17, G-18, and G-19	
Surge protector/UPS	Unit G, Figures G-2, G-3, and G-16	
Multimedia computing		
CD-ROM drive	Units A, B, and D, Figure A-1, Figure B-18, and Figure D-13	
Sound Card/Speakers	Units A and B, Figure A-8 and Figure B-18	
System and application software and storage		
Operating system	Units A and B, Figures B-4 and B-6	
Software bundles	Units A, B, and C, Tables B-1 and B-2	
Hard disk	Unit D, Figures D-2 and D-8	
Floppy disk drives	Unit D, Figures D-2, D-3, D-5, D-6, and D-7	
Zip disk drives	Unit D, Figure D-6	
Internet Service		
Connecting to the Internet	Unit F and Appendix	
Web Browsers	Unit F	

Glossary

68000-series microprocessor ► A type of microprocessor used in Macintosh computers until 1994

Absolute reference ► In a spreadsheet formula, a reference that never changes when the user inserts rows or columns or copies or moves formulas in the spreadsheet

Accelerated graphics cards ► Graphics cards that use special graphics chips to boost performance

Access time ► The average time it takes a computer to locate data on the storage medium and read it

Accumulator ► In the arithmetic logic unit, the component that temporarily holds the result of an arithmetic or logical operation

Active matrix screen ► On a notebook computer, a display screen that utilizes thin film transistor technology to improve update speed and image quality

ActiveX controls ► Software that adds processing and interactive capabilities to Web pages

Address ► In spreadsheet terminology, the location of a cell, derived from its column and row location

Address lines ► In data transport terminology, the components of the data bus that carry the location of the data being transported, to help the computer find the data that it needs to process

Analog device ► A device in which continuously varying data is processed as a continuous stream of varying information

Antivirus program ► *See* Virus detection program

Application server ► A computer that runs application software and forwards the results of processing to workstations, as requested

Application software ► Computer programs that help the user carry out a specific type of task (word processing, database management, etc.)

Archiving ► The process of moving data off a primary storage device onto a secondary storage device (such as a backup tape), for permanent storage

Arithmetic logic unit (ALU) ► The part of the central processing unit that performs arithmetic and logical operations

ASCII ► American Standard Code for Information Interchange, the data representation code most commonly used on microcomputers

Asynchronous discussion ► In Internet terminology, a discussion in which participants are not online at the same time

Attachment ► A file that is sent through an e-mail system along with an e-mail message

Auditing ► In spreadsheet terminology, testing in order to verify the accuracy of data and formulas

Autoexec.bat ► A batch file that runs automatically when the system is started up

Backup ► The process of making duplicate copies of data

Backup software ► Computer programs designed to manage hard disk backup to tapes or disks

Batch file ► A series of operating system commands used to automate tasks

Bays ► Openings in the computer system unit case that allow for the installation of peripherals

Binary number system ► Number system used by digital computers to represent data using two digits, 0 and 1 (base 2)

Biometrics ► A method of personal identification that bases identification on a unique physical characteristic, such as a fingerprint

Bit ► The smallest unit of information in a computer system, consisting of a 1 or a 0 that represents data (abbreviation of binary digit)

Bitmap display ► Also called graphics display. A form of display in which the monitor screen is divided into a matrix of small dots called pixels

Bitmapped image ► An image that is displayed and stored as a collection of individual pixels

Boilerplate ► Standard paragraphs used to create a new document

Bookmarks ► Frequently visited sites on the Web stored as a list on a user's computer, by means of Web browser software

Boot process ► The sequence of events that occurs within the computer system between the time the user starts the computer and the time it is ready to process commands

Boot sector viruses ► Computer viruses that infect the system files a user's computer relies on every time it is started up

Bus ► The component of a microcomputer motherboard that transports data between other components on the board

Business software ► Computer programs that help organizations to efficiently accomplish routine professional and clerical tasks

Button ► An area of the screen containing a three-dimensional image (usually square or rectangular) that can be pressed with the mouse pointer to activate a function

Byte ► An eight-bit unit of information, usually representing one character (a letter, punctuation mark, space, or numeral)

Cache ► Special high-speed memory that gives the CPU more rapid access to data (also called RAM cache or cache memory)

Capacitor ► Electronic circuit component that stores an electrical charge; in binary code, a charged capacitor represents an "on" bit, and a discharged one represents an "off" bit

CD-R (compact disc recordable) ► Compact discs on which the user can write data

CD-ROM (compact disc read-only memory) ► A high-capacity, optical storage medium

CD-ROM drive ► A storage device that uses laser technology to read data from a CD-ROM

Cell ► In spreadsheet terminology, the intersection of a column and a row

Cell reference ► A letter/number combination that indicates the position of a cell in a spreadsheet

Central processing unit (CPU) ► The main control unit in a computer, consisting of circuitry that executes instructions to process data

Character ► A letter, numeral, space, punctuation mark, or other symbol, consisting of one byte of information

Character data ► Letters, symbols, or numerals that will not be used in arithmetic operations (name, social security number, etc.)

Character-based display ► Method of display in which the monitor screen is divided into a grid of rectangles, each of which can display a single character from the standard character set

Chat group ► A discussion in which a group of people communicate online simultaneously

Chip ► *See* Integrated circuit

Client/server architecture ► A network architecture in which processing is split between workstations (clients) and the server

Cluster ► A group of sectors on a storage disk

CMOS memory (complementary metal oxide semiconductor) ► A type of semiconductor that holds data and requires very little power to retain its contents

Coaxial cable ► A type of cable in which a center wire is surrounded by a grounded shield of braided wire. Used in connecting nodes on a network with silver BNC connectors on both ends

Columns ► In document production terminology, newspaper-style layout of paragraphs of text; in spreadsheet terminology, a vertical arrangement of items within a grid

Command ► An instruction that the user inputs into the computer to tell it to carry out a task

Command-line user interface ► An interface that requires the user to type in commands

Commercial information service ► A company that provides access to computer-based information, for a fee

Communications software ► Computer programs that interact with a computer's modem to dial up and establish a connection with a remote computer

Compatible ► In computer terminology, able to operate using the same format, commands, or languages

Complex instruction set computer (CISC) ► A computer based on a CPU with a lengthy, intricate set of instructions that take several clock cycles to execute

Computer ► A device that accepts input, processes data, and produces output

Computer network ► A collection of computers and related devices, connected in a way that allows them to share data, hardware, and software

Computer program ► A set of detailed, step-by-step instructions that tells a computer how to solve a problem or carry out a task

Computer programming language ► A standardized set of specific English-like phrases or predefined instructions used for writing computer programs

Computer virus ► A program designed to attach itself to a file, reproduce, and spread from one file to another, destroying data, displaying an irritating message, or otherwise disrupting computer operations

Concurrent-use license ► Legal permission for an organization to use a certain number of copies of a software program at the same time

Connectivity software ► Computer programs that connect a computer to a local computer network or to the Internet and provide the user with tools to access the information it offers

Control unit ► The part of the ALU that directs and coordinates processing

Controller ► A circuit board in a hard drive that positions the disk and read-write heads to locate data

Controller card ► A circuit board that plugs into an expansion slot in the computer and provides the I/O circuitry for a peripheral device

Cookie ► A message sent from a Web server to a browser and stored on a user's hard disk

Copy Disk ► A utility program that duplicates an entire floppy disk

Copy utility ► A program that copies one or more files

Copyright ► A form of legal protection that grants certain exclusive rights to the author of a program or the owner of the copyright

CPU ► *See* Central processing unit

Cursor ► A symbol that marks the user's place on the screen and shows where typing will appear

Cyberspace ► A term coined in 1984 by writer William Gibson to describe a computer-generated conceptual environment shared among computers. It has come to refer to the interconnected communication networks across the Web.

Cylinder ► A vertical stack of tracks on a hard disk

DASD (direct access storage device) ► On a mainframe computer, a device that can directly access data

Data ► Symbols that describe people, events, things and ideas

Data access software ► The interface used to search for information in a database

Data bus ► An electronic pathway or circuit by means of which data travels from one location to another within a computer

Data file ► A file containing words, numbers, and/or pictures that the user can view, edit, save, send, and/or print

Data lines ► The wires in the data bus that carry the signals that represent data

Data management software ► Computer programs that help the user store, find, update, organize, and report information

Data security ► Techniques that provide protection for data

Database ► A collection of information stored on one or more computers

Database software ► Computer programs that provide tools for manipulating information stored in a database (also called database management software)

Dedicated file server ► A file server devoted solely to the task of distributing resources to workstations

Default drive ► The drive that a computer system will attempt to read from or write to unless an alternate drive is specified

Defragmentation utility ► A tool used to rearrange the files on a disk so that they are stored in contiguous clusters

Desktop metaphor ► A graphical interface in which the icons resemble items commonly found in an office

Desktop microcomputer ► A computer that is built around a single microprocessor chip and is small enough to fit on a desk

Desktop publishing software ► Computer programs that combine graphics and word-processing tools to allow the user to create documents

Device driver ► The software that provides the computer with the means to control a peripheral device

Dialog box ► A type of on-screen display, in the form of a window, that provides options associated with a command

Dial-up connection ► A connection that uses a phone line to establish a temporary Internet connection

Differential backup ► A copy of all the files that have changed since the last full backup of a disk

Digital certificate ► A security method that identifies the author of an ActiveX control

Digital device ► A device that works with discrete numbers or digits

Digitized sound files ► Sound recordings that have been converted into a form that can be stored on a computer disk

Digitizing ► The process of converting videos or continuous sound or images into a format that can be stored on a computer disk

Direct access ► The ability of a drive to move to any sector of a disk (also called random access)

Directory ► A list of files contained on a computer disk

Discussion group ► Online communications involving multiple participants sharing views on a specific issue or topic

Disk cache ► Part of RAM used to temporarily hold information read from a disk, speeding up processing

Disk density ► The size of the magnetic particles on the disk surface

Distribution disks ► Disks on which computer software is supplied to users

Docking station ► An expansion bus into which the user can plug a notebook computer

Document production software ► Computer programs that assist the user in composing, editing, designing, and printing documents

Document-centric model ► A method of using files in which the user chooses the document, and the computer automatically starts the appropriate application program

Domain name ► An identifying name by which host computers on the Internet are familiarly known (for example, cocacola.com)

DOS ► Disk Operating System

DOS prompt ► A symbol indicating that DOS is ready to accept a command

Dot matrix printer ► A printer that creates characters and graphics by striking an inked ribbon with small wires called "pins," generating a fine pattern of dots

Dot pitch ► A measure of image clarity

Double-click ► To click the mouse button twice in rapid succession

Double-density (DD) disk ► A type of floppy disk that increased the density of data that could be stored to 360 KB, which was twice the density of the previous generation of disks (*See also* high-density disk)

Double-sided disk (DS) ► A floppy disk that stores data on both the top and bottom sides of the disk

Downloading ► The process of transferring a copy of a file from a remote computer to another computer's disk drive

Downwardly compatible ► In reference to operating systems, able to use application software designed for earlier versions of the operating system, but not those designed for later versions

Drag, Dragging ► Placing the mouse pointer over an object, holding down the mouse button, moving the mouse pointer to a new location, and releasing the mouse button, in order to move an object to a new location

Drive hub ► The component of the floppy disk that the disk drive engages in order to rotate the disk

Drive spindle ► The component of the hard drive that supports one or more hard disk platters

Drop-down list ► A list of options that is displayed when the user clicks an arrow button

Dual-pipeline architecture ► A type of microprocessor chip design in which the chip can execute two instructions at one time

---

EBCDIC (extended binary coded decimal interchange code) ► A method by which digital computers represent character data

Education and training software ► Computer programs that help the user learn and perfect new skills

Edutainment software ► Computer programs that combine elements of game software and education software

EIDE (enhanced integrated device electronics) ► A type of drive that features high storage capacity and fast data transfer

Electronic mail (e-mail) ► Correspondence sent from one person to another electronically

Electronic mail system ► The hardware and software that collect and deliver e-mail messages

Electronic publishing ► The manipulation, storage, and transmission of electronic documents by means of electronic media or telecommunications services

e-mail software ► Computer programs that manage the user's computer mailbox

Encryption ► The process of scrambling or hiding information so that it cannot be understood without a key

Error message ► A statement that appears on the computer screen, indicating that the user has made a mistake

Exabyte ► A quintillion (10^{18}) bytes.

Executable file ► A file that contains the instructions that tell a computer how to perform a specific task

Expansion board ► *See* Controller card

Expansion bus ► The segment of the data bus that transports data between RAM and peripheral devices

Expansion card ► *See* Controller card

Expansion port ► A socket on the expansion card into which the user plugs a cable from a peripheral device, allowing data to pass between the computer and the peripheral device

Expansion slot ► A socket into which the user can plug a small circuit board called an expansion card

External bay ► An opening in the computer case that allows the user to install a device that must be accessed from outside the case

---

FAT (file allocation table) ► The file structure used by DOS to store information on disks.

File ► A named collection of program instructions that exists on a storage medium such as a hard disk, floppy disk, or CD-ROM

File management software ► Computer programs that help the user organize records, find records that match specific criteria, and print lists based on the information contained in records

File specification ► A combination of the drive letter, subdirectory, and filename and extension that identifies a file

Filename ► A unique set of letters and numbers that identifies a file

Filename extension ► A set of three letters and/or numbers added to the end of a filename, to assist in identifying the nature of the file

Filenaming conventions ► Specific rules followed in establishing a filename (for example, file.doc to indicate that a file is a document)

Floppy disk ► A portable magnetic storage medium

Floppy disk drive ► A storage device that writes data on, and reads data from, floppy disks

Folder ► A subdirectory (a subdivision of a directory)

Font ► A typeface or style of lettering

Footer ► Text that appears in the bottom margin of each page of a document

Formula ► A combination of numbers and symbols that tells the computer how to use the contents of cells in calculations

Fragmented ► When data in a file is stored in noncontiguous clusters

Frame ► An outline or boundary, frequently defining a box; a predefined area into which text or graphics may be placed

Free-form database ► A loosely structured collection of information, usually stored as documents rather than as records

FTP (File Transfer Protocol) server ► A computer that maintains a collection of data that can be transferred over the Internet

---

FTP client software ► Special software that allows a user to upload files

Full backup ► A copy of all the files on a disk

Function keys ► The keys numbered F1 through F12, located at the top of the computer keyboard, that activate program-specific commands

Gateway ► An electronic link that connects one e-mail system to other e-mail systems

GB ► *See* Gigabyte

Generic filename extension ► A filename extension that indicates the type of data that a file contains, but does not tell the user which software application was used to create the file

Gigabyte (GB) ► Approximately one billion bytes

Graphical object ► A small picture on the computer screen that the user can manipulate, using a mouse or other input device

Graphical user interface ► (GUI) Images on the screen that provide the user with a means of accessing program features and functions, by means of a mouse or other input device

Graphics ► Visual images such as pictures and illustrations

Graphics card ► An expansion card used to connect a monitor and a computer, to allow the computer to send visual information to the monitor (also called a video display adapter or video card)

Graphics software ► Computer programs that help the user create, edit, and manipulate images

Graphing software ► Computer programs that transform complex data into a visual format.

Groupware Software that provides ways for multiple users to collaborate on a project, usually through a pool of data that can be shared by members of the workgroup

Hackers ► (Also called crackers or cyberpunks) Vandals who damage, destroy, alter, and/or steal data

Hard disk ► One or more hard disk platters and their associated read-write heads (often used synonymously with hard disk drive)

Hard disk drive ► An electronic storage device containing a nonremovable disk platter

Hard disk platter ► The component of the hard disk drive on which data is stored, a flat, rigid disk made of aluminum or glass and coated with a magnetic oxide

Hardware ► The electric, electronic, and mechanical devices used for processing data. *See also* specific hardware

Hardware redundancy ► Maintaining equipment that duplicates the functions of equipment critical to computing activities

Head ► The part of an HTML document that specifies the title that appears on the title bar of a Web browser when a Web page is displayed

Head crash ► A collision between the read-write head and the surface of the hard disk platter, resulting in damage to some of the data on the disk

Header ► Text that appears in the top margin of each page of a document

Header label ► An initial component of a record stored on magnetic tape, which signals the beginning of a file

High-capacity fixed disk drive ► A mainframe storage technology similar to a microcomputer hard disk drive with platters and read-write heads, but with higher storage capacity

High-density (HD) disk ► A floppy disk that can store more data than a double-density disk

Home page ► The first page that comes up when a Web site is accessed. It identifies the site and contains links to other pages at the site

Horizontal market software ► Any computer program that can be used by many different kinds of businesses

Host computer ► A central minicomputer or mainframe to which multiple terminals are attached. All processing takes place on the host computer. In Internet terminology, any computer connected to the Internet

HTML (Hypertext Markup Language) document ► An electronic document that contains special instructions that tell a Web browser how to display the text, graphics, and background of a Web page

HTML authoring tools ► Software that facilitates the creation of Web pages by means of word-processor style interfaces

HTML tags ► The instructions used by an HTML document to display information to a Web browser

HTTP (HyperText Transfer Protocol) ► An identifier that appears at the beginning of each Web page URL

Hypermedia ► A type of multimedia hypertext that involves graphics, sound, and video, as well as text

Hypertext ► In multimedia computer applications, a component in which documents are linked to each other

Hypertext index ► A screen-based menu that allows the user to access information in specific categories by clicking a hypertext link

I/O (Input/Output) ► The collection of data for the microprocessor to manipulate, and the transportation of the results to display, print, or storage devices

IC ► *See* Integrated circuit

Icon ► A small picture on a computer screen that represents an object

Importing ► The process by which a program reads and translates data from another source

Incremental backup ► A copy of the files that have changed since the last backup

Information ► The words, numbers, and graphics used as the basis for human actions and decisions

---

Information and reference software ► Computer programs that provide the user with a collection of information and the means to access that information

Ink-jet printer ► A printer that creates characters and graphics by spraying ink onto paper

In-line spell checker ► A program that shows the user spelling errors, as the user types

In-place multimedia technology ► An Internet multimedia technology that plays a media element as part of a Web page

Input device ► A tool that gathers input and translates it into a form that the computer can process

Insertion point ► A flashing vertical bar that appears on the screen, indicating where the user can begin entering text

Installation process ► In reference to software, the process by which programs and data are copied to the hard disk of a computer system

Instruction cycle ► The process by which a computer executes a single instruction

Instruction pointer ► The location where the RAM address of an instruction is kept

Instruction register ► A location in memory where the control unit puts an instruction retrieved from RAM

Instruction set ► The list of instructions that a CPU carries out

Integrated circuit (IC) ► A thin slice of crystal containing microscopic circuit elements such as transistors, wires, capacitors, and resistors; also called chips and microchips. *See also* microprocessors

Internal bay ► A location inside the system unit case where devices that do not need to be accessed from outside the case can be installed

Internet ► A multinational collection of computer networks and gateways (also called the World Wide Web)

Internet backbone ► The group of major Internet communication links

Internet communications software ► Computer programs that allow a computer to transmit and receive data using the Internet TCP/IP communications protocol

Internet mail address ► An identifier, consisting of a user ID and the user's mail server domain name, required to send e-mail over the Internet

Internet service provider (ISP) ► A company that provides Internet access to businesses, organizations, and individuals

Internetwork or **internet** ► Two or more connected networks

InterNIC (Internet Network Information Center) ► In North America, the organization that processes requests for IP addresses and domain names

IP address ► A unique identifying number assigned to each computer connected to the Internet

Java applets ► Small programs that add processing and interactive capabilities to Web pages

Jaz disk drive ► A high capacity disk drive with removable disks used for backup

Keyboard ► An arrangement of letter, number, and special function keys that acts as the primary input device to the computer

Keyboard shortcut ► A combination of keys that allows the user to activate a program function without clicking a series of menu options

Keyword search engine ► A means of accessing data about a particular subject, by searching for a significant word relevant to that subject

Kilobyte (KB) ► Approximately one thousand bytes

Laser printer ► A printer that uses laser-based technology, similar to that used by photocopiers, to produce text and graphics

LCD projection panel ► A device placed on an overhead projector to produce a large display of information shown on a computer screen

Level 2 cache ► In the Pentium Pro, memory circuitry housed off the processor, on a separate chip

Links ► Underlined areas of text that allow users to jump between hypertext documents

Liquid crystal display (LCD) ► A type of flat panel computer screen, commonly found on notebook computers, in which light passes through a thin layer of liquid crystal cells, to produce an image

Local area network (LAN) ► An interconnected group of computers and peripherals located within a relatively limited area

Local resources ► The peripherals attached to an individual user's workstation on a network

Locked file ► When a locked file is being used by one user, it cannot be accessed by others

Logic bomb ► A computer program that is triggered by the appearance or disappearance of specific data

Logical storage ► A conceptual model of the way data is stored

Macintosh operating system ► A GUI-interface-based operating system developed by Apple Computer, Inc.

Macro virus ► A computer virus that infects documents such as those created with a word processor

Magnetic storage ► The recording of data onto disks or tape by magnetizing particles of an oxide-based surface coating

Magnetic surface ► The oxide-based surface coating of a magnetic storage disk or tape

Mail client software ► The software on a workstation that helps a user read, compose, send, and delete e-mail messages

Mail merge ▶ A software application that automates the process of producing customized documents such as letters and advertising flyers

Mail server software ▶ The software on the network server that controls the flow of e-mail

Mailbox ▶ A term for the area on a host computer or network server where e-mail is stored

Main board ▶ See Motherboard

Mainframes ▶ Large, fast computers generally used by businesses or the government to provide centralized storage processing and management for large amounts of data

Mapping ▶ In network terminology, assigning a drive letter to a network server disk drive

Mean time between failures (MTBF) ▶ A measurement of reliability that is applied to computer components

Megabyte (MB) ▶ Approximately one million bytes

Megahertz (Mhz) ▶ Millions of cycles per second. A measurement of the speed at which a computer can execute an instruction

Memory ▶ The area in a computer that holds data that is waiting to be processed

Menu ▶ A list of commands or options

Menu bar ▶ A list of menu titles

Menu item ▶ A choice listed on a menu (also called a menu option)

Microcomputer ▶ A small computer incorporating a single microprocessor chip (also called a personal computer, or PC)

Microprocessor ▶ The component of a microcomputer motherboard that contains the circuitry that performs arithmetic and logical operations

Microsoft Windows 3.1 ▶ An operating system that provides a GUI interface

MIDI (musical instrument digital interface) sound ▶ Sound encoded by one of two MIDI standards, FM synthesis or wave table synthesis

Millisecond (ms) ▶ A thousandth of a second

Minicomputer ▶ A midrange computer, larger than a microcomputer, that can carry out processing tasks for many simultaneous users

MMX chip ▶ A special multimedia processor that speeds up multimedia features, such as sound and video

Modem ▶ A device that sends and receives data to and from computers, over telephone lines

Modem card ▶ An interface card used to connect a computer to the telephone system, in order to transport data from one computer to another over phone lines

Monitor ▶ A display device that forms an image by converting electrical signals from the computer into points of colored light on the screen

Motherboard ▶ The circuit board in the computer that houses the chips that control the processing functions

Mouse ▶ An input device and pointer that allows the user to manipulate objects on the screen

Multimedia ▶ An integrated collection of computer-based media, including text, graphics, sound, animation, photo images, and video

Multimedia overlay technology ▶ An Internet multimedia technology that adds a separate window in which multimedia elements appear

Multiple-user license ▶ Legal permission for more than one than one person to use a particular software package

Multitasking ▶ Running two or more programs at the same time

Mylar disk ▶ Material used in manufacturing magnetic storage media

Natural language ▶ A language spoken by human beings, as opposed to an artificially constructed language such as machine language

Network ▶ A group of connected computers that allow users to share information

Network administrator ▶ The person responsible for setting up user accounts and maintaining a network (also called network supervisor)

Network client software ▶ Programs that are installed on the local hard drive of each workstation and act as a device driver for the network interface card

Network interface card (NIC) ▶ A small circuit board that sends data from a workstation out over the network, and collects incoming data for the workstation

Network license ▶ Legal permission for the use of a software program by multiple users on a network

Network operating system ▶ Programs designed to control the flow of data, maintain security, and keep track of accounts on a network

Network printer ▶ A printer on a network to which all network users can send output from their own workstations

Network resources ▶ Peripherals and application software available to users through a central server on a network

Network server ▶ A computer connected to a network that "serves," or distributes, resources to the network users

Network server software ▶ Programs installed on a file server that control file access from the server hard drive, manage the print queue, and track user data such as IDs and passwords

Network service provider ▶ A company that maintains a series of nationwide Internet links

Nondedicated file server (peer-to-peer architecture) ▶ A network computer that acts as both a server and a workstation

Notebook computer ▶ A small, lightweight portable computer

Numeric analysis software ▶ Computer programs that simplify the tasks of constructing and analyzing numeric models

Numeric data ▶ Numbers that represent quantities and can be used in arithmetic operations

Numeric keypad ▶ A calculator-style input device for entering numbers and arithmetic symbols

Op code ▶ (short for operation code) A command word designating an operation, such as add, compare, or jump

Operand ▶ The part of an instruction that specifies the data, or the address of the data, on which the operation is to be performed

Operating system ▶ The software that controls the computer's use of its hardware resources, such as memory and disk storage space

Operator error ▶ A mistake made by a computer user

Optical storage ▶ A means of recording data in which the data is burned into the storage medium, using laser beams. See also CD-ROM disks

Option buttons ▶ Buttons that allow the user to select one of two or more options in a dialog box

Outliner ▶ A feature of document production software that helps the user develop a document as a hierarchy of headings and subheadings

Output ▶ The results produced by a computer (for example, reports, graphs, and music). See also input/output (I/O)

Output device ▶ A computer peripheral that displays, prints, or transfers the results of processing from the computer memory

Palm-top computer ▶ See Personal digital assistant

Parallel processing ▶ A technique by which two or more processors in a computer perform processing tasks simultaneously

Passive matrix screen ▶ A display found on older notebook computers

Password ▶ A special set of symbols used to restrict access to a user's computer

Payload ▶ The disruptive instructions delivered by a computer virus

PCMCIA (Personal Computer Memory Card International Association) cards ▶ Credit-card-sized circuit boards that consists of an expansion card and a built-in peripheral device (also called a PC card)

PCMCIA slot ▶ A small external expansion slot, found on notebook computers, into which a PCMCIA card can be inserted

Peer-to-peer architecture ▶ See Nondedicated file server

Pentium ▶ A recent Intel microprocessor in the x86 family

Pentium II ▶ A version of the Pentium Pro chip with added MMX technology

Pentium Pro ▶ An Intel chip that is optimized for the 32-bit instruction set

Pentium with MMX technology ▶ A Pentium chip with additional circuitry designed to speed up the execution of multimedia applications

Peripheral devices ▶ Components that expand the computer's input, output, and storage capabilities

Personal computers ▶ Microcomputers based on the architecture of the first IBM microcomputers

Personal digital assistant (PDA) ▶ A computer that is smaller and more portable than a notebook computer (also called a palm-top computer)

Personal firewall software ▶ Computer programs that protect a computer from harmful Java applets and ActiveX controls

Personal search engine ▶ A term used to distinguish a search engine that runs on an individual user's computer from search engines that are provided at Web sites

Physical storage ▶ The manner in which data is stored on a physical disk

Pipelining ▶ A technology that allows a processor to begin executing an instruction before completing the previous instruction

Pirated software ▶ Software that has been illegally copied, distributed, or modified

Pixels ▶ Small dots of light that compose the images displayed on the computer screen

Plotter ▶ A peripheral device that uses pens to draw an image on paper

Plug-and-Play ▶ A feature of some peripheral devices that allows them to be automatically installed by operating systems such as Windows 95

Point to Point Protocol (PPP) ▶ A version of TCP/IP software designed to handle Internet communications over dial-up connections

Pointer ▶ A symbol on the computer screen, usually shaped like an arrow, whose movement corresponds to the movement of the user's mouse

Pointing device ▶ An instrument such as a mouse, trackball, or light pen, that allows the user to manipulate on-screen objects and select menu options

Polymorphic viruses ▶ Computer viruses that change, in order to avoid detection, after they infect a computer system

Port ▶ A socket on a computer into which a cable from a peripheral device can be plugged

Port replicator ▶ A device that connects to a notebook computer, by means of a bus connector plug, and contains a duplicate of the notebook computer's ports for connecting devices such as an external monitor, mouse, or keyboard

POST ▶ See Power-on self-test

Power failure ▶ A complete loss of power to the computer system

Power spike ▶ A sudden increase of power that lasts less than a millionth of a second

Power surge ▶ A sudden increase of power that lasts a few millionths of a second

Power-on self-test (POST) ▶ A diagnostic process that runs during startup to check components of the computer such as the graphics card, RAM, keyboard, and disk drives

PowerPC microprocessor ▶ A microprocessor used in recent models of Macintosh computers that implements RISC architecture to provide faster performance

Presentation software ▶ Computer programs that combine text, graphics, graphs, animation, and/or sound into electronic displays that can be output as overhead transparencies, paper copies, or 35-millimeter slides

Print job ▶ A file sent to the printer

Print queue ▶ A special holding area on a network server, where files are stored until they are printed

Print server ▶ A server that stores files in a print queue, and sends each queued file to the network printer

Printed tutorial ▶ A book or manual that provides step-by-step lessons about computer hardware and software

Process ▶ A systematic series of actions that a computer performs, in order to manipulate data

Productivity software ▶ Computer programs that help the user work more effectively

Programs ▶ Instructions and associated data, stored in electronic format, that direct the computer to accomplish a task

Prompt ▶ A message displayed on the computer screen that asks for input from the user

Prompted dialog ▶ A simulated conversation between a user and a computer, in which the computer's responses consist of a series of prompts

Public domain software ▶ Software that can be freely used by anyone, either because it has not been copyrighted, or because the author has made it available for public use

Public key encryption ▶ An encryption method that uses a pair of keys, a public key (known to everyone) that encrypts the message, and a private key (known only to the recipient) that decrypts it

Pull technology ▶ An Internet multimedia technology in which a Web browser is used to request Web pages and "pull" them into view on a user's computer screen

Push technology ▶ An Internet multimedia technology in which the user downloads special push plug-in software that allows a Web site to send the user information without a direct request having been received

QIC (quarter-inch cartridge) ▶ A cartridge tape that measures a quarter of an inch wide, and is used by microcomputer tape drives

Query by example (QBE) ▶ A type of database interface in which the user fills in a field with information related to the desired information, in order to initiate a search

Query language ▶ A set of command words that the user uses to direct the computer to create databases, locate information, sort records, and change the data in those records

RAID (redundant array of independent disks) ▶ A hard disk storage format, used by mainframes and microcomputers, in which many disk platters are used to provide data redundancy for faster data access and increased protection from media failure

RAM address ▶ An identifying value associated with each bank of capacitors that holds information in RAM

RAM cache ▶ See Cache

Random access ▶ See Direct access

Random access memory (RAM) ▶ Memory that temporarily holds data that is being processed

Readability formulas ▶ Instructions contained in grammar checkers that help the user to write at a level appropriate for a particular target audience

Read-only ▶ An indication that a computer can retrieve data from a storage medium such as a CD-ROM, but cannot write new data onto it

Read-only memory (ROM) ▶ A set of chips containing permanent, nonchangeable instructions that help a computer prepare for processing tasks

Read-write head ▶ The component of a disk drive that magnetizes particles on the storage disk surface in order to encode data

Real-time clock ▶ In a computer system, a battery-powered clock chip that maintains the current date and time

Redundancy ▶ The storage of duplicate data in more than one location for protection against media failure

Reference manuals ▶ Books or online resources that describe the features of a hardware device or a software package

Register ▶ A region of high-speed memory in an electronic processing device, such as an ALU, used to hold data that is being processed

Remote control software ▶ Computer programs used to establish a connection, via modem, between two machines

Removable hard disks ▶ Hard disk cartridges that contain platters and read-write heads, and that can be removed from the hard drive

Resolution ▶ The number of dots per unit of measurement displayed by a computer monitor; the greater the number of dots, the higher the resolution

RISC (Reduced instruction set computer) ▶ A microprocessor that uses a streamlined instruction set for more rapid and efficient processing

Risk management ► The process of weighing threats to computer data against the expendability of that data and the cost of protecting it
ROM BIOS ► A small set of basic input/output system instructions stored in ROM, which cause the system to load critical operating files when the user turns on the computer
Root directory ► The main directory of a disk
Router ► A computer found at each intersection on the Internet backbone that examines incoming data's IP address and forwards the data towards its destination

---

Saving a file ► The process of storing data
Screen size ► The measurement in inches from one corner of the screen diagonally across to the opposite corner,
Search and replace ► A feature of document production software that allows the user to automatically locate all instances of a particular word or phrase and substitute another word or phrase for it
Search engine ► An information-locating component of file management and database software
Search feature ► A feature of document production software that allows the user to automatically locate all the instances of a particular word or phrase
Sectors ► Subdivisions of the tracks on a computer disk on which information is stored
Sequential access ► A form of data storage in which data is stored and read as a sequence of bytes along the length of a tape
Server ► A computer and software that make data available to other computers
Shareware ► Software marketed under a license that allows users to use the software for a trial period and then send in a registration fee if they wish to continue to use it
Sheet scanner ► A peripheral device than converts a page of text or images into an electronic format
Shrink-wrap license ► A legal agreement printed on computer software packaging, which goes into effect when the package is opened
S-HTTP (Secure HTTP) ► A method of encrypting data transmitted between a computer and a Web server
Signature ► A unique series of bytes that can be used by a virus detection program to identify a known virus
Single-user license ► A legal usage agreement limiting the use of a software program to one user at any given time
Site ► In Internet terminology, a computer with a domain name
Site license ► Legal permission for software to be used on any and all computers at a specific location
SLIP (Serial Line Internet Protocol) ► A version of TCP/IP software designed to handle Internet communications over dial-up connections
Software ► *See* Computer program
Software license ► A legal contract that defines the ways in which a user may use a computer program
Software package ► The disks containing a computer program, and the supporting reference material
Software pirates ► Individuals who illegally copy, distribute, or modify software
Software publishers ► Companies that produce computer software
Sound card ► An interface card that gives the computer the ability to accept audio input from a microphone, play sound files stored on disks, and produce audio output through speakers or headphones
Source files ► Files that contain instructions that the computer must translate into a format that it can directly use, before executing them
Spin boxes ► Graphical user interface objects that let the user increase or decrease a number by clicking arrow buttons
Spreadsheet ► A numerical model or representation of a real situation, presented in the form of a table
Spreadsheet modeling ► Setting up numbers in a worksheet format, to simulate a real-world situation
Spreadsheet software ► Computer programs that perform calculations on the basis of numbers and formulas supplied by the user, and produce output in the form of tables and graphs
SSL (Secure Sockets Layer) ► A security protocol that uses encryption to establish a secure connection between a computer and a Web server
Standalone computer ► A computer that is not connected to a network
Statistical software ► Computer programs that analyze large sets of data to discover patterns and relationships within them
Stealth technology ► Technology used by computer viruses to hide from virus detection programs
Storage ► The area in a computer where data is retained on a permanent basis
Storage capacity ► The maximum amount of data that can be recorded on a storage medium, usually measured in kilobytes, megabytes, or gigabytes
Storage device ► A mechanical apparatus that records data to and retrieves data from a storage medium
Storage media ► The physical materials used for long-term storage (for example, floppy disks)
Storage technology ► A term used to describe a storage device and the media it uses
Store-and-forward ► A technology such as e-mail, in which information is stored on a server and sent to a workstation when requested
Streaming media ► An internet multimedia technology that sends a small segment of a media file to a user's computer and begins to play it while the next segment is being sent
Structured database ► A file of information consisting of records and fields organized in a uniform format (for example, a library card catalogue)
Supercomputer ► The fastest and most expensive type of computer, capable of processing one trillion instructions per second
Support line ► A service offered over the phone by a hardware or software manufacturer, to answer customers' product questions
Surge suppressor ► A device that protects computer equipment from electrical spikes and surges (also called a surge strip or surge protector)
Syntax ► Specifications for the sequence and punctuation of command words, parameters, and switches
Syntax error ► *See* Error message
SYSmark 32 ► A standard benchmark test that measures computer speed for word-processing, graphics, spreadsheet, and database tasks
System clock ► A device in the computer that emits pulses to establish the timing for all system operations
System requirements ► Specifications for the operating system type and minimum hardware configuration necessary for a software product to work correctly
System resource ► Any part of a computer system, such as a disk drive, memory, or printer, that can be used by a computer program
System software ► Computer programs that help the computer carry out its basic operating tasks
System unit ► The case or box that contains the computer's power supply, storage devices, and the main circuit board with the computer's main processor and memory

---

Tape backup ► A copy of data from a computer's hard disk, stored on magnetic tape and used to restore lost data
Tape cartridge ► A removable magnetic tape module, similar to a cassette tape
TCP/IP (Transport Control Protocol/Internet Protocol) ► A standard set of communication rules used by every computer that connects to the Internet
Terabyte ► 1,000,000,000,000 bytes
Terminal ► A device with a keyboard and a screen, used for input and output but not for processing
Terminal emulation software ► Programs that make it possible for a microcomputer to connect to a host computer and behave as if it were a terminal of the host computer
Text ► In spreadsheet terminology, words used for worksheet titles and for labels that identify columns and rows
TFT (thin film transistor) ► *See* Active matrix screen
Time bomb ► A type of computer program that stays in a computer system undetected until it is triggered at a certain date or time
Time-sharing system ► A configuration in which terminals must share the host computer's processing time
Toggle key ► A key that switches a device back and forth between two modes
Top-level domains ► The major categories into which groups of computers on the Internet are divided
Touch pad ► A touch-sensitive device that allows the user to control an on-screen pointer by running over the pad's surface
Tower case ► A vertically-oriented microcomputer case, usually placed on the floor to conserve desk space
Track point ► A small pencil-eraser-shaped device embedded among typing keys, which controls an on-screen pointer when the user pushes the track point up, down, left, or right
Trackball ► A pointing device consisting of a ball that is rotated in a frame, in order to move a pointer around a computer screen
Tracks ► A series of concentric subdivisions created on a storage disk during the formatting process
Trailer label ► An indicator that signals the end of data in a sequential file on magnetic tape
Trap door ► A special set of instructions, often created during development and testing, that allow an individual to bypass the normal security precautions and enter the system
Trojan horse ► A computer program that appears to perform one function while actually doing something else, such as inserting a virus into a computer system
Twisted-pair cable ► Also called UTP. A type of cable in which two separate insulated strands of wire are twisted together.

Uninterruptible power supply (UPS) ► A device containing a battery and other circuitry that provides a continuous supply of power to a computer system in the event of disruptions of power
UNIX operating system ► A multiuser, multitasking operating system developed by AT&T's Bell Laboratories in 1969
Uploading ► The process of sending a copy of a file from a user's computer to a remote computer
URL (Uniform Resource Locator) ► An Internet address used to access a Web page
Usenet server ► A computer that handles the exchange of comments among members of Internet discussion groups
User account ► A means of providing a user with access to network resources
User ID ► A combination of letters and numbers that serves as a user's "call sign" or identification (also called user name)
User interface ► The means by which human beings interact with computers
User rights ► Rules that specify the directories and files that an individual user can access
Utilities ► A subcategory of system software designed to augment the operating system by providing ways for a computer user to control the allocation and use of hardware resources

---

Valid filename ► A filename that adheres to filenaming conventions
Value-added reseller (VAR) ► A company that combines commercially available products with additional hardware, software, and/or services to create a system designed to meet specific needs
Vector graphics ► In graphics software terminology, images composed of lines and filled shapes
Version ► A new or totally redesigned product
Vertical market software ► Computer programs designed to meet the needs of a specific market segment or industry
Video card ► *See* Graphics card
Viewable image size (vis) ► A measurement of the maximum image size that can be displayed on a monitor screen
Virtual memory ► A computer's use of hard disk storage to simulate RAM during processing
Virus ► *See* Computer virus
Virus detection program ► (Also called antivirus program) Software that examines the files stored on a disk to determine if they are infected with a virus and, if necessary, disinfects the disk
vis ► *See* Viewable image size

WAN ► *See* Wide area network
Wave table synthesis ► A MIDI standard that creates music by playing digitized sound samples of actual instruments
Web (World Wide Web) ► *See* Internet
Web browser software ► Computer programs (for example, Netscape Navigator and Microsoft Internet Explorer) that allow the user to view Web pages and that manage the links
Web authoring software ► Computer programs that help the user design and develop customized Web pages that can be published electronically on the Internet
Web server ► A computer that uses special software to transmit Web pages over the Internet
Webcast ► A continually changing stream of information broadcast over the Web by means of push technology
What-if analysis ► The process of setting up a model in a spreadsheet and experimenting to see what happens when different values are entered
Wide area network (WAN) ► An interconnected group of computers and peripherals that covers a large geographical area
Wild card character ► A symbol, such as an asterisk, used to represent a general group of characters
Window ► A visual representation of a work area in a GUI interface
Windows ► GUI-interface-based operating systems produced by Microsoft Corporation
Wireless network ► A network that uses radio or infrared signals (instead of cables) to transmit data from one network device to another
Wizard ► A sequence of screens that direct the user through multi-step tasks
Word size ► The number of bits the CPU can manipulate at one time, which is dependent on the size of the registers in the CPU and on the number of data lines in the bus
Word wrap ► A feature of document production software that automatically moves the cursor to the beginning of the next line of text when it reaches the end of the current line
Word-processing software ► Computer programs that assist the user in producing documents such as reports, letters, papers, and manuscripts
Workflow software ► Programs that automate the process of electronically routing documents from one person to another, in a specified sequence and time frame
Worksheet ► An on-screen spreadsheet. *See also* spreadsheet(s)
Workstation ► A computer connected to a local area network
Workstation installation ► A process in which some, but not all, of the program files from a program installed on a network server are copied to a workstation's local hard drive and the workstation's menu is updated
World Wide Web (WWW, the Web) ► *See* Internet. Web *entries*
Worm ► A software program designed to enter a computer system, usually a network, through security "holes,"
Write-protect window ► A latch in the upper right-hand corner of a floppy disk that, when open, makes the disk read-only

---

x86 family ► A series of Intel microprocessors commonly used in PCs (for example, 386 or 486 chips)

Year 2000 bomb ► A time bomb that was unintentionally created by computer programmers when they wrote programs that use a two-digit, rather than four-digit, field for the year, with the result that computers will read the digits 00 as 1900 rather than as 2000

Zip disk drive ► A high-capacity floppy disk manufactured by Iomega Corporation, frequently used for backups

Index